D0295489

Steve McQueen

Steve McQueen

Malachy McCoy

LONDON

ROBERT HALE & COMPANY

Copyright © 1974 Max Caulfield
First published in Great Britain 1974

ISBN 0 7091 4867 4

Robert Hale & Company
63 Old Brompton Road,
London, S.W.7

Printed in Great Britain by
Lowe & Brydone (Printers) Ltd,
Thetford, Norfolk

Contents

Illustrations

1.

THE MAN

THERE was no obvious reason, in the month of May 1972, why anybody should have been visiting El Paso, Texas, a border town set amid barren desert, plastic-littered tumbleweed, and tacos, unless they were interested in the municipal garbage dump. And the only reason they might have been interested in that was because that was where some curious things were happening.

On a rise above the dump, directing a film camera, lurked a small, crinkled, gray-bearded figure wearing tinted glasses which, like a one-way mirror, allowed the wearer to look out but nobody to look in—a figure that, if subjected to the zoom-in technique, would be revealed as the physical manifestation of that arch-apostle of vicarious violence, director Sam Peckinpah. At the same time, emerging from the dump where they had been tipped by the municipal garbage truck and picking bits of garbage from each other's clothing were actress Ali MacGraw, still elegant enough, despite the experience, to be described by one observer as a ''chic cheetah,'' and Steve McQueen, who, by all accounts, was still in a psychological daze.

1

The trio were filming sequences for *The Getaway*, the tale of a married couple who rob a bank and escape, after a certain measure of violence and mayhem, into Mexico. Chased by enemies, they have been forced to take refuge in a garbage truck; now, in the search for honest realism, they have submitted to immersion in a profoundly real and profoundly evil-smelling garbage dump. It was Steve's twenty-second film within sixteen years, and although he had now almost imperceptibly slipped into middle age, he still gave the appearance of a man very much in his prime. And what a prime! With his blond, curling hair, sun-seared eyebrows, and luminous blue eyes, he could still claim to be the most potent male sex symbol in a business powered by sex appeal.

Against diverse expectations, shooting had proved to be an exceptionally smooth process, although both Steve and Sam had come to the film with the prickliest of reputations. Liz Smith has categorized these reputations with something rather less than delicacy; the two men, she has written, "are supposed to be the biggest studs and meanest bastards in moviedom." In a craft where a conservative lifestyle is unlikely to earn a man anything more than an attic-full of fake antiques, this benison, of course, is like sprinkling their heads with gold dust.

Throughout the filming, in fact, Steve had been as good as a canonized saint. "He is being a pussycat," purred executive producer David Foster. "We're all pussycats," sang out Sam triumphantly. "Come back tomorrow," Steve invited one onlooker, "that's when all us pussycats get shot right through the heart."

Shooting had been unexpectedly blessed in yet another way. At the start of the filming, Steve had been only lately divorced by his wife of fifteen years, Neile Adams, mother of his two children. Ali, now Mrs. McQueen, was still the wife of Robert Evans, production head of Paramount Studios and the man credited with instigating the hugely successful (i.e., it made a lot of money) film *The Godfather*. As filming proceeded, however, the crew observed that the two stars, who had not met previously, were kissing and embracing in the obligatory love passages with a zeal and fervor over and above the call of duty. Ali soon disclosed that she considered herself a "movie widow." Bob, it appeared, had so immersed himself in the making of *The Godfather* that she had seen nothing of him for months on end, and as a consequence, their marriage was very shaky. What it all added up to, in fact, was that Ali was crazy about Steve, and footloose Steve, in turn, seemed all a-tremble about Ali. On the strength of this effusion of chemistry and emotion alone, the publicity men knew that the success of *The Getaway* was assured.

Otherwise Steve had behaved around the set much as he had done around most of his other film sets. In the heat, he slouched about in careless, if calculated, *déshabillé*—jeaned and booted with torso bared, muscled and beautifully tanned, and with a silver chain-link necklace dangling like a pendulum. He chewed double wads of gum or alternately drank canned beer (he had given up smoking after learning about lung cancer and had turned down a $60,000 fee to do a commercial on cigarettes). Near at hand, parked in a truck, was one of his collection of motorcycles—this one "with plenty of poke in her." When not swaggering about the set with what appears to be a put-on masculine air calculated to stir any feminine interest within range, he tended to stage similarly directed spectacles—but carrying with them other complex overtones.

One such spectacle involved a large mound of earth that had been built up by excavating bulldozers on a piece of El Paso wasteland. Having shifted the location from the garbage dump, stars and crew lounged about a gas station where the plastic pennants flying overhead beat a snapping response to the desert wind. Steve was soon seen regarding the mound with slide-rule eyes. After a few moments of consideration, he hefted the bike "with the poke in her" out of the truck, and leaping into the saddle, he shattered the Texan silence with a succession of ear-splitting revs.

The scene that followed had all the appearances of a movie-within-a-movie. As Steve scorched down the street, he was pursued by a running, swearing, cursing Newton ("Newt") Arnold, the assistant director. Foster, making obvious rapid mental calculations as to the financial disaster involved if Steve should fracture his neck, was seen to begin to sweat. "It's OK, OK," he assured the empty air before adding his favorite catch phrase: "He's got great healing processes." He had first trotted this out when, a mere month before shooting began, Steve had come a cropper from a motorcycle and had broken his collarbone—only valiantly to commence rehearsals less than three weeks later.

"He's in great shape, thank God," Foster reassured anyone who would listen. "Works out every day."

Newt, by now, had given up the pursuit and Steve was bombing his way towards the mountain of soft earth. Watched by the crew with looks of apprehension and, as one observer described it, "a kind of embarrassment," he hit the mound and with a tail of dirt squirting out behind him began the climb. The effort looked spectacular, if actually less dangerous than a hill climb up the rain-greasy slopes indulged in by motorcycle sports freaks every weekend. Steve himself was obviously aware that there was little real danger and that even if he and the bike should dissolve partnership, he was fit and athletic enough to roll down the slope without any real damage.

Nonetheless, there it was: the big investment risking limb and perhaps neck in what looked like a pointless caprice. A quarter of the way up, the bike stuck in the yielding soil, and jerking the machine loose, Steve kicked with both feet and started downhill again. He roared back, circling the crew, revving the engine noisily, playing madly to the gallery. There was the usual adulatory chorus of sycophantic grins, signs, and shouts; but beneath the forced merriment it was obvious that the unit was experiencing a mixture of envy, apprehension, and resentment. All were keenly aware: (1) that if Steve hurt himself, their jobs would go, and (2) that his action was a severe breach of discipline—that only an all-powerful star could get away with this kind of behavior.

Yet no one could or should have been surprised; it was, in fact, typical of the kind of thing Steve had been getting away with for years. Some quirk inside the man demanded that when he was not actually filming, he still had to make himself the epicentre of action. He might argue that his stunts were only a method of relieving tedium and boredom, yet apparently he could not help milking his audience, particularly if there were females in it. Ali herself underscored this by admitting, "Steve performs inadvertently at times. He especially performs in front of women. . . . For instance, if there is a street full of drum majorettes, he's on for them. All charm and sex and kind of dirt kicking. But he's different for them than he will be for you today or again tomorrow, or for me talking at dinner, or with his kids, or for the guys of the crew. He responds to everyone differently, and if they don't want to see what he wants them to see, they don't see anything. Young, dumb girls see the best sex symbol in the world. Motorcycle freaks see the best motorcyclist, and so on. A lot of people don't bother to see the real person—but so what. He doesn't need it."

On that particular day, anyway, Steve, whether exhibiting his real or semi-plastic self, having circled the crew and revved his engine, roared away for another go at the mound. This time, with the right run-up and shifting "at full poke," he successfully made the top and vanished down the other side. Then, sweating happily and cloaked in dust but looking every inch the glamor boy, he eased back to the location and, climbing off the bike, drawled to Ali, "I've been looking at that hill all week and I just had to do it. It just suddenly got to me." After a quick embrace, Ali went to fetch a beer for Steve while he sat down and eventually launched into a monologue about how cheap prices were in El Paso. He announced that he could live easily within the amount of money allowed daily to unit members for subsistence. Ali returned with the beer in time to catch a bit of this and with a slight flair of impatience exclaimed, "Oh, dum-dum, you're always bragging about something." Steve's answer was quick and flip, "I said I was cheap, I didn't say I was easy."

On the surface at least it was all easy-come, easy-go, grins, beer, bikes, noise, stunting, some work, stretches of tedium, and some playing up to the girls. In the nature of things, Steve ought to have been happy; at that, it is not possible to sustain the argument that he was *unhappy*.

And yet there remains the fact that Steve had just ended one epoch of his life and was about to embark on another, and like any voyager entering uncharted seas, he not only felt a measure of trepidation about the way ahead but also a certain sense of nostalgia for the comfortable port he had left behind. Only two years earlier he had been able to stand back and look at himself and decide that at long last he had grabbed the brass ring. He had one expensive house situated in three and a half acres within a stone's throw of Beverly Hills and another, more modest establishment at the desert resort of Palm Springs. He had a loyal, loving, relatively docile wife to whom he shone as a modern version of *le Roi Soleil* and who bawled him out far, far less often than he deserved. He had two children—he really liked those kids and had long ago apparently made up his mind to be an excellent father to them; strong, dependable, essentially patriarchal, extracting the right measure of respect and obedience, and being careful not to overindulge them. His career seemed a titanic success, and his own film company, of which he was the major asset, had been successfully floated off as a public company. His classic car-chase film, *Bullitt*, had returned a massive $35,000,000 on a $4,500,000 investment—and the bread was still coming in. That year—or, at least at the start of that year—Steve seemed unable to do wrong.

Since that time, alas, there had been changes. Substantial ones. His first marriage was over—he was about to embark on his second. His vaulting ambition to found a business empire based on his own film production company had foundered. He could insist that he did not want "to rap" Hollywood, "but I'll rap those things I didn't have the sense to avoid—which was to get very involved. I put up with a suite of offices, a lot of secretaries, accountants, lotsa people on the payroll. I was producing my own films. Just terrific. But I wasn't making any money and I was working sixteen hours a day and I was president of three corporations. And I was, uh . . . not very happy." Today he could talk about "not being around acting much longer," of "not spreading yourself further than you're capable of going," of finding out about oneself and "what makes you happy" and then "stick to it." The problem was that he had "had it all; and I find what's really best is nothing. In the simplest form. Jeans and shirt. I can only ride one motorcycle at a time—that's my mentality." He could further insist that he was "just a dirty old man who can't wait to get out of here and go play in the dirt. I like getting out in the dirt—the open land. That's where I'm heading the moment I'm through here. I won't have to work again until later in the year. I owe the government a little bit of money, so I'll have to work a little. But after this one and until the next one, nobody's going to see me."

He returned to these themes more than once while on location. Those who listened to him were aware, of course, that his ex-wife had received a hefty divorce settlement amounting to a million dollars. They were also aware that his epic film about Le Mans, into which he had put not only a large slice of his bankroll but his entire heart and soul, had been considered by a majority of his women fans to be about as fascinating as a clothes dryer.

He protested again, if unconvincingly, "Nobody will believe this, but I'm practically broke." He could even reminisce regretfully about how, before he became a success himself, he had read an article about Tony Curtis. It described how Curtis had so many cars in his garage that he almost drove himself crazy every morning trying to decide which one to use to take him to work; and now he had found himself in the same absurd predicament. He listed some of his indulgences: he had piled up such a large number of motorcycles so that he had one "in every place I might be"; he had bought suits, ties, shirts, and shoes by the dozen. And now he realized he needed very little of this to exist. "I've started cutting everything out. Now I think of Laurence Olivier when he goes to work. He's got a little black bag with a couple of fake noses, his wig or whatever he's got in there. And that's all I need—a pencil, a script, and a briefcase." And apart from that, "a small place to live." When *The Getaway* was finished, he was going to seek the idyllic life again—to "ride out into the desert, hit a couple of motor tracks, and bounce around and ride a lot."

There was a trace of nostalgia in his voice when he spoke like this. The man, however, is entirely unpredictable. When filming was finished, he left, still protesting about his need and desire to hide away, to be alone, to commune, it would seem, with that natural landscape, full of extraordinary mysteries, which, quite genuinely, I believe, he does love.

In fact, he turned up next in Alaska with one of his few actor friends, James Arness, star of the TV Western series, "Gunsmoke." He and Arness were caught driving up and down the main street of Anchorage, Alaska, whooping and hollering from an open convertible. As one of his critics observed: "For a man who wants to be alone and unnoticed, he can create a helluva noise." When stopped by a member of the Alaskan State Highway Patrol, Steve is alleged to have declared, "Hi, I'm Steve McQueen and I'm having a good time in your two-bit town." To which the cop is supposed to have replied, "Hi, I'm a policeman and you're under arrest."

To observers of the Hollywood scene, this episode seemed completely untypical of the modern Steve McQueen. In his youth, he had not been above committing acts that had earned him, among other life-enhancing experiences, a brief stretch in a reform school. In adolescence and early manhood, his style of life had been, to put it mildly, colorful. Yet perhaps the most striking thing about his career as a film star had been how he had "grown"; how he had rubbed away the raw edges, lost much of his anger, hostility, and suspicion of society in general, learned the meaning of the word "responsibility," and done his best, in his own peculiar, if slightly distorted way, to practice it. What, it was asked, had gotten into McQueen?

Nothing, probably, had gotten into McQueen. He had changed his lifestyle more than once and had still not finished "growing." What, he might ask in turn, was wrong with deciding that a bundle of material possessions were only a bundle of material possessions that could not even say "hello" back if you wished them "good morning"? Who, with the slightest bit of poke in him, had never driven up and down a two-bit town somewhere in the world whooping and hollering and announcing to all and sundry that he was enjoying himself? How could a man whose earning power was at least one million dollars a film be taken seriously when he spoke of being "practically broke"? Like down to his last Ferrari?

None of all this, in fact, can be structured to mean anything more than that Steve had probably decided that when a man reached forty-two, going on forty-three, it might be time for a change in his life. Yet there remains a feeling that within a complicated, if seemingly shallow man, perhaps a moment of truth had arrived. Ali MacGraw, who was naturally closer to him at this juncture of his life than anybody else, dropped a veiled clue or two—although one would almost need to be a seer to read the riddle of her rather oracular pronouncements. "I think he's just beginning to find himself," she said in El Paso. "Just beginning to realize that you don't have to physically lay your life on the line of a motorcycle course. Steve now knows you can also risk your life emotionally and it's just as important. One doesn't only have to be a race driver. One can be a painter and risk his life by putting everything secret about himself on the wall." One might interpret this as an allusion to the chilling disappointment he must have felt over the reception given to *Le Mans*. Next to the great silences of the desert or the wide spaces of an Arizona sky, next to acting, he had loved and admired nothing more than racing machines and the men who raced them, either for sport or for a livelihood. He had put all his passion down in the biggest, toughest, most honest film he had ever undertaken, and, like an eager child who had run into the street with his ball to play, none of the other kids had joined him. As Ali put it, alluding again to his life, work and preoccupations, "and then someone comes along and comments that it's a piece of *merde* . . . I mean, after you've put your whole life up there There are certain terribly private things I've seen. . . ."

But there, for the present, our speculations must rest.

2

MISSOURI ROOTS
AND INDIANAPOLIS GANGS

Slater lies in Saline County, Missouri, about one hundred miles northeast of Kansas City, a typical, small Midwestern town. For many years it was known as a railroad town; it had a round-table, extensive rail shops and yards, and was the main repair facility for the old Chicago & Alton railroad on what was known as "the west end." At one time, the railroad was Slater's main employer, but it now has moved out completely, and all that remains to mark the era of steam travel is a brick depot building at the south end of main street.

The second largest employer used to be the garment manufacturing firm of Rice-Stix, but that firm has also left Slater now, although its old building has been rented recently by another garment manufacturing firm. In the northwest corner of town, there is a Town & Country shoe factory that gives employment to many people in the area. During World War II a plant located in Slater made components for the B-29 bomber.

Slater has a city park, a city pool, and a small airport. It has a K-12 school system, and its athletic teams compete enthusiastically with teams from other towns in the area. Today, Slater exists almost entirely to serve a farm community and has several large grain-storage elevators located right in town. Back in the thirties and forties, it had a single film theatre called The Kiva—but this has long since closed. The only chance anybody in Slater has of seeing a Steve McQueen film now is if one of his "oldies" is shown on TV or if they drive a long way out of town.

Most of the farms around Slater are prosperous—even during the Great Depression, the farmers in the region enjoyed a good standard of living, often housing relatives from the great urban areas who were victims of the economic blight. Saline County, in fact, is said to have some of the richest farmland in the world. Most of the farms are diversified; that is, they raise both crops and livestock—feeder cattle, hogs, chickens, corn, wheat, and so on.

About three and a half miles south and slightly east of Slater lies the Thomson farm. The road out to it, which is now blacktop but was merely gravel back in the thirties when Steve knew it, is usually referred to as Thomson Lane. The farm itself extends to 320 acres and has been always one of the most prosperous in the area. The first owners were a Colonel P. M. Thomson (Steve's great-great-grandfather) and his wife, who had moved to Missouri from Fayette County, Kentucky, where their son, John William Thomson, who lived to be seventy-two, had been born in 1844. The Thomsons first settled in Howard County but later moved to Saline County.

As a lad, John William fought with the Confederate Army as a member of Company E, Gordon's Regiment, Shelby's Brigade, and took part in engagements at Independence, Westport, Little Blue, and Fayetteville, Arkansas, marching through to Texas. Here the Army was reorganized, and John William's regiment was cut down and thrown into Company C, Williams' Regiment, Jackson's Brigade. The regiment surrendered at Shreveport, Louisiana, on June 1, 1865.

Four years later, John William Thomson married Julia Frankland Graves, the daughter of Aaron Graves, and settled down to become a familiar figure in and around Slater—indeed, the local newspaper, when printing his obituary, wrote, "No man was better known in the county than Mr. Thomson." The newspaper added, "He was honest, straightforward, square in all his dealings and could always be relied upon." In early life he became a member of the Rehobeth Baptist Church and "was a God-fearing man." In addition, he was a staunch supporter of the Socialist party, writing many articles in different publications on the question of capital and labor. Years later he entered a sanatorium in Chicago to obtain treatment for cancer. He died at Slater in October, 1916, one of the oldest settlers in Saline County.

The farm itself passed to Claude W. Thomson, John William's son, and great-uncle of Steve McQueen. Claude became highly respected in the area for his knowledge of livestock and was considered a shrewd businessman—his primary interest lay in buying, raising, and selling hogs, although he also raised feeder cattle. While still active enough to raise stock, he would drive his hogs on foot into Slater to the railroad loading pens, sometimes helped by a wiry little lad with looks not dissimilar to those of the young Dwight Eisenhower. Often Claude Thomson's hogs made up the entire trainload of stock going off to the St. Louis market. Even when partially retired, Claude Thomson was still energetic enough to keep between thirty and forty milk cows, separating the cream to be sold and using the milk for feeding the hogs. He died in 1957, at the age of eighty-four.

It was to Claude Thomson's farm, shortly after his birth at Beech Grove Hospital, Indianapolis, Indiana, on March 24, 1930, that baby Steve was brought by his mother, Julia Crawford (daughter of Victor L. Crawford and his wife, the former Lillian Thomson, of St. Louis). The child never knew his father, who left him and his mother within six months of Steve's birth. To the best of Steve's knowledge, his father was called William McQueen. He remains a shadowy, blurred character of whom almost nothing is reliably known. Steve has said he believes he was an experienced pilot who had served for a time in the U.S. Navy and who toured America in the barnstorming days of the late twenties with a flying circus as a stuntman.

"I understand he was quite a guy," insists Steve, who etches a portrait of a rolling stone who tried several jobs, all of them vaguely romantic. "He was a flier with Gen. Claire Lee Chennault's Flying Tigers (a special unit formed to fight the Japanese in China), the Merchant Navy, the lot." He was also, at one time, in the gambling business—in fact, Steve (full name: Terrence Stephen McQueen) was named for one of his father's gambling associates, Steve Hall, known as One-Armed Steve. "I never met Steve Hall," says Steve, "but I understand he was real good people."

Steve seldom discusses his early background (although he has never attempted to conceal it), and the precise reason why his father deserted him and his mother remains unknown. He says, "All I know is that they didn't get along—I've never understood the causes of their troubles; the way I figure it is that it was their business." But he once dropped the remark, "I don't blame him for leaving her." It is hard to assess the exact degree of resentment he nurtured over his father's action. He has said, with an understandable tinge of bitterness, "My life was screwed up from the beginning." Certainly when critic Tom Hutchinson talked to him in London in 1969 and asked him what he would do if he could meet his father right then, Steve's instinctive response was, "I'd probably kill him." After a brief reflection, however, he announced, "No, that's the wrong thing to say. I wouldn't kill him—I'd feel sorry for him because he missed out on me, on me growing up, as much as I missed out on him. He was foolish in what he did."

From the remark, one might gather that he believed his father was still alive. However, this would contradict what he has previously said: "I was too young to remember my parents' bust-up, but when I was sixteen and in all sorts of trouble, I started looking for my father. I didn't have much to go on. When I was in the Marines, I tried the Navy files—he was a Navy flier back when flying was a sketchy thing. But I don't know much about him. I did hear he was a full swinger, though, a guy who really had a love for life. Do I resent him leaving us? Well, as I say, that was a personal thing between him and my mother, and I left it that way. I don't really know how I felt about him. I just wanted to meet him, to stand and talk to him, no more, no less. Neile and I spent weeks writing letters and checking records. Finally we traced him to a little town in California. But by the time we caught up with him, it was too late. Three months earlier he had died. You know, although I never met him, I felt a real sense of loss. I talked to some of the people who lived with him. They say he saw me on TV and said I might have been his boy, that I had the McQueen look." This certainly rings a little more authentic than a later remark, "He died on Long Island—with a pretty girl around. A swinger, my old man," which seems merely a flip way of turning aside a really deep hurt. The search rings true also because Steve has been described by his ex-wife as a "goer-backer"; he tends to go back to his roots and to retrace his steps, a prey to nostalgia. Within a year of their marriage, for instance, he had taken Neile to see his folks in Slater and the farm where he was reared.

His mother was only nineteen when Steve was born. She was a tiny figure, no more than 5 feet, 4 inches tall (Steve himself, who weighs less than 170 pounds, is only 5 feet, 7 inches tall and generally wears built-up shoes), and she bequeathed her blonde hair to her son. She briefly stayed in the old wooden farmhouse outside Slater—a crowded enough place at the time as Claude's son, Pike McFall Thomson, and his family were also living there, doubling up because of the Depression. She then went back to Indianapolis, taking the baby with her. Steve was about three when Julia again brought him back to the farm, where his early upbringing was undertaken by his great-uncle. Julia is reported to have gone off to California to try her luck as a salesperson in a Los Angeles store while the thin and wiry little boy settled down to enjoy what he has called "the happiest days of my childhood" and, as he has added with bitterness, "I came to love and understand animals and to feel that in a few ways they are superior to human beings." It was not, at any rate, an environment that ought to have led a boy into delinquency.

Some years ago a reporter whose ego perhaps had been dented by the explosive McQueen (who can be a prima donna when he wants to, which his enemies say is pretty often) wrote of the star that when he was born and the doctor held him up and slapped him to make him breathe, Steve did not cry; he snarled! Yet there are no grounds for supposing that the boy who rambled about the Slater farm in the early thirties was intractable. His relatives do not recall that he gave more trouble than a normal boy. Steve himself retains a deep regard for his great-uncle—a sign that relations were excellent between them: "He was a very good man. Very strong. Very fair. I learned a lot from him." Neile McQueen, who received a hospitable welcome from Claude Thomson and his second wife when Steve brought her to visit the year before Claude's death, found the old wooden house, the farm, and the people in it "pure American Gothic." Steve's great-uncle and aunt were "farm people, older people and very strict. Something was right and something was wrong—there was no in-between." She saw the tiny room up under the eaves Steve had occupied, and when she left the Thomson farm, she felt she "knew where he came from and where some of his principles came from."

There is no hint of recalcitrance during this period, only, perhaps, of a certain shiftlessness. A female relative who recalls dandling Steve on her knee when he was a baby remembers that as a small boy he learned to milk cows, help in the cornfields, and generally make himself useful. He was not deprived of toys; he himself says he got his first taste for speed from riding a tricycle his Uncle Claude gave him. The picture that emerges, therefore, is of a relatively normal, happy childhood with great-uncle Claude substituting for Steve's lost father. There is no evidence, at this stage anyway, that the boy felt any deep resentments—he had not as yet begun to feel any of those "lumps" that were to give him the menacing coloraion of a jungle denizen, the appearance he had when he first arrived in Hollywood.

Clearly he got himself involved in minor mischiefs from time to time, and like any boy, he tried to evade disagreeable chores. One gets an impression, perhaps, of laziness, although he was obviously quick and resourceful enough. As a protection against righteous wrath, for example, he taught cows to lie down. He would then manage to "keep out of sight," as one of his aunts puts it, by stretching out behind the prone cows.

Apart from this tactically shrewd "disappearing act," his life on the farm was probably uneventful. He did, however, once manage to impress Uncle Claude with his skill as a marksman. One day he came into the house carrying two dead pigeons, which he claimed to have shot—not much of a feat, if it had not been that Uncle Claude never allowed him more than a single shell at a time for the rifle. He had knocked off the two birds with one shot, and there could be no argument about it because the birds were newly dead and had undoubtedly been killed with a rifle shell. What had happened, in fact—although Steve always refused to explain it to Uncle Claude—was that he had gone into a large silo and had fired at some nesting pigeons. His shell carried clean through the first, then ricocheting, passed through the second. For years afterwards, Steve used to grin, "Uncle Claude never did really understand how I killed those two pigeons!"

Steve received a rudimentary education at Orearville School in Slater—a white frame, one-room schoolhouse of a type common in the Midwest during the thirties. Steve admits he was a poor student. "I wasn't clever in any academic way. School wasn't a big thing for me; I didn't click too well in it. I tried. But I liked to hang out with the boys." Backwardness at school, of course, is hardly an augury of future potential—Clive of India and Churchill, to name but two, were both duffers when young. In Steve's case, presumably, abstractions had little appeal for him and he might easily have responded with more eagerness to vocational training. Again, the impression is of a general aimlessness of purpose, of a certain apathy and inability to concentrate.

Today, although his lack of a sound formal education is often embarrassing, Steve is regarded by most of his intimates as a shrewd man with an excellent brain—and enormous reserves of energy. He still admits, however, that "in a way I'm rather limited—if you want to analyze it," and therefore finds himself uneasy in the presence of literate men, such as journalists and writers, and excluded from areas of a kind that normally engage the interest of intelligent men. For example, Tom Hutchinson noticed that the reading matter in his London hotel room was cheap fiction, although it is not always possible to draw rigid conclusions from this (film actors often have to wade through a lot of trashy fiction because it is a staple of Hollywood films). Nowhere, however, in the many interviews he has given or in the thousands of words written about him, does one detect even a superficial interest in what is usually considered an intellectual or artistic pursuit. A farm, of course, is not necessarily the best place to inculcate cultural values, and clearly his teachers failed to ignite any intellectual or artistic curiosity in him; yet brains certainly run in his family. John Thomson was obviously a man of considerable intellectual caliber, and one of Steve's cousins, Claude W. Thomson, today teaches in a Kansas City high school.

For all that, it has been said of Steve—and he has never denied the charge—that the only printed matter he ever reads (apart from film scripts) are magazines about cars, motorcycles, and carburetors—in that order. He has confessed, "I wish I were more into readin' and stuff like that. All I really know about are motorcycles and cars." A little aghast that such an obviously intelligent and well-heeled man, then approaching his fortieth year, should have interests usually considered only suitable for a teenager, Liz Smith queried him on these avowed limitations, only to have him repeat that he had never learned much beyond cars, motorcycles, and the outdoors "because I never read anything."

His statements often appear to be contradictory and this is another example. For instance, he has said that when he was in reform school he was "introduced to Shakespeare" and to "other literature." He has also admitted, "We [Neile and he] bought the *Encyclopaedia* [*Britannica*] but not to read it from A to Z. I realize I should read more, but it seems that every time I sit down to 'a book, somebody drops by and we're off and there's a race comin' up or something. I've just never been academic, which doesn't mean I'm not interested in learning. I am. I just figure that if there's something going on in the world and I want to find out about it, I'll get to reading it. Somehow. After all, I know what's happening politically—current news, the world. You get it on radio or TV. And then there's music and I like it very much—classical music and jazz. I have a stereo in my living room and I have a portable stereo I take everywhere I go."

If his conversational repertoire thus tends to sound appallingly bleak, few challenge his mental alertness or abilities. "He's very intelligent," his ex-wife has insisted, "though not the way you find in encyclopedias." Ali MacGraw, who has a good educational background herself, says, "I wasn't prepared for his intelligence." In an effort to nail down the subject, she added, "His is not the kind of intelligence concerned with Proust, but the enormous ability to do subtle things."

Yet even his interest in his own craft is limited. When last in London, he made no attempt to visit the theatre, usually a "must" for visitors. When someone expressed astonishment at this, Steve blandly commented, "I don't like the theater at all." On an earlier visit, he had, in fact, made a point of seeing performances by Sir Laurence Olivier, Peter O'Toole, and Albert Finney; but, in general, the high craft of a Shakespearean performance holds no magic for him. Acting seems to mean no more to him than achieving cinematic techniques satisfactorily, heightened by an overriding, self-interested need to "give a good performance." When he was asked to lecture to students at the Royal Academy of Dramatic Art, he told them, albeit with admirable frankness, "I'm not a good actor, so I never want to do a stage play. Maybe you could teach me a few things about acting." What he really does, he explained later, is "sort of reach down inside myself every time I make a film and that's what comes out on the screen."

He knows little—and cares less—about the work of eminent European film directors, particularly those who have attempted to transform film-making into an art form. "I don't normally go for Continental films," he admits. Bunuel's anarchic comedy *The Discreet Charm of the Bourgeoisie*, for example, is not his kind of film. As he says, "I don't like him [Bunuel] for the message he puts across." This, presumably, refers to the director's radicalism; yet Steve himself, although he has discovered patriotism since he learned that even a poor and deprived lad like himself can reach the heights, is not a political reactionary. He has expressed enormous admiration for John Wayne—as a film actor. "But that doesn't mean I like his politics" (Wayne holds determined right-wing opinions). Still he obviously sees unqualified merit in the American competitive system. "When I was a kid, an old guy told me only the strongest survive. That's somethin' you gotta believe, man. I concluded about myself that insecurity motivates strength. The struggle within me manifested itself into strength. All I had to do was hang on."

He is nothing, however, if not a mass of contradictions and paradoxes. For instance, a few years ago his financial backers bought a script based on a novel by William Faulkner, the Nobel Prize winner, called *The Reivers*. Scripts based on any work by a major writer are usually looked askance at by film men who recognize that they are not geared to the mass market and that the task of translating dense and complex themes into cinematic terms is often not worth the effort in terms of a return on the investment. Steve's business partners wondered if "it could be made commercial." The indications are that they tried to head Steve's interest in another direction. Yet despite not being "into readin'," Steve liked the book well enough to go ahead with the project; although, in the end, he was not happy with the results (he does not like comedy roles). Yet his decision to make the film underlined his obsession with "integrity" and "honesty"— in his terms synonyms for quality.

Steve was nine when Julia returned to Slater and took him back to Indianapolis. Any biographer of Steve McQueen finds the early material imprecise. As he himself has said, "My early life I try not to think about too much," and he has always refused to reveal details. What happened to him certainly proved traumatic, though there is no way of judging cause and effect. All we know is that, taken away from the relatively sheltered and happy life of the farm and the small-town atmosphere of Slater and thrust into the urban conglomerate that is Indianapolis, Steve McQueen, product of a broken home, sank like a stone. It is not even clear whether Julia married again or had begun an association of some sort with another man.

Steve himself has admitted only that one of his earliest memories is of being whipped by his stepfather. However, when asked, "How old were you when your mother remarried?", he replied bitterly, "Which time?" Whether or not the boy's home life was overshadowed at this stage by a callous and domineering stepfather (as it certainly was later), he began running wild on the streets, getting mixed up with gangs and petty thieves, or, as he has described it with a certain euphemism, "doin' a little stealin'." He adds, "It was a bad scene, man."

Steve's attitude towards his mother seems ambivalent. Whatever form her treatment of him took, he is never portrayed as having shown her the usual filial feelings. Even so, when questioned in an attempt to dredge up his past, he refused to go into details. "My mother always has to take the rap in these stories. They come out making it seem that what happened to me was somehow her fault—which is pretty ridiculous." Evidently while still alive, his mother had raised objections to the candor with which he answered questions. "She gets upset," he once said. "I tell her, 'Look, baby, when you go for the brass ring, you may get yourself hurt—it's one of the hazards of the game.' Still, it's hard for her to understand." We know little more. Ready enough in the early stages of his career to be frank, he soon began to apply the soft-pedal with regard to his mother and her role in his upbringing. He once snarled at a persistent reporter that if it were a question of "a good story" or hurting his mother, he knew what his choice was.

Once asked if he blamed his early delinquency on any lack of parental control, Steve dismissed the idea, at the same time striking a blow for those who believe that zealous reformers, however admirable their motives, are unrealistic. "No," he answered, "I think every man has to stand by himself, and I don't believe in this environmental delinquency kick that everybody seems to be on." He had been up all night with two of his business partners when he said this, and although in a mood when reminiscences flow easily, he was obviously a little tired, for he then seemingly contradicted himself: "I feel I was simply in a neighborhood of Indianapolis where one inevitably grew up with gangs." Still his message was clear enough. Whatever a man's boyhood neighborhood, he is responsible for his actions.

Certainly, membership in these Indianapolis gangs appears to have bred delinquency. All Steve's gang friends ended up delinquents to one degree or another. "We would break into bars," he says. "We would break into lock-up shops—that kind of thing. It wasn't that we did this in terms of money—because we were never short of money—but as a relief from boredom." Friends are convinced that much of Steve's present lifestyle, obsessed with speeds and cars, is no more than part of the battle he has always fought against ennui.

This theme of boredom was significantly underlined by Steve when he referred to his indifference regarding the more intellectual European films. The one outstanding exception as far as he was concerned was Fellini's *Il Vitelone*, which is about a group of Italian teenagers who hang around on street corners. "That one," said Steve, referring to his gang days, "seemed to sum up the kind of kids we were at that time. Whistling at girls, you know—playing pool" (pool, at least, remains a passion). Steve's words, with their hint of directionless vacuity, give us a vivid miniature of semi-slum life and his own struggle against the dark vacuum.

In those days his admitted highest aspiration in life was to be the leader of a gang, an eminence that appears to have eluded him. His seemingly often desperate desire to "prove" himself in the essentially masculine fields of speed-fiend and "car handler" may well be a throwback to this boyish aspiration. He still has not lost his admiration for a certain Sam who apparently was his gang leader and boyhood idol.

Steve was less than twelve years old when Julia took him with her and moved back to California, this time to the Silver Lake area. By this time he appears to have been well on the way to becoming a delinquent; although her motives might have beeen dictated by thoughts for his good, it is more likely that she was following, as before, her own inclinations. Whatever the reasons, the change of scene from Indianapolis to Los Angeles was to make little difference to the boy. If anything, indeed, the downward slope on which he had embarked was to become even more slippery.

3

GROWING PAINS

Late in the afternoon of Thursday, October 14, 1965, Mrs. Julia Berrie staggered into the Harbor Emergency Hospital in San Francisco suffering from intense head pains—the beginnings of cerebral hemorrhage. She was quickly transferred to Mount Zion Hospital where diagnosis confirmed that she was dying. Just before midnight she sank into a coma—shortly before her by-now famous son, Steve McQueen, summoned from Hollywood, could reach her bedside.

In the last years of her life she had been living in a four-room, ninety-dollar-a-month apartment not far from Fisherman's Wharf in the North Beach area of San Francisco. Steve had helped to support her, although relations between them had remained relatively distant. The money he sent her was always dispatched through his business manager, and he had not personally written her a line for at least eight months before her admission to Mount Zion. He had not, however, entirely cut her out of his life. At intervals he sent her photographs of her granddaughter, Terri, and her grandson, Chadwick. The envelopes in which the pictures arrived, though, only rarely contained a note from him. The gulf between mother and son formed during the bad years of Steve's childhood was a barrier right to the end. She is said to have attempted a reconciliation with him and to have tried to show her love for him and her pride, but he never seemed able to bring himself to reciprocate her display of warmth.

Neighbors have described her as a neatly dressed, heavyset woman fighting a continual battle against obesity. In her efforts to lose weight, she visited a herb doctor in San Francisco's Chinatown, and after that she lived on pills and a single meal a day (Steve himself is something of a food faddist and is keen on an "organic" diet).

She has also been described as being obsessed by clothes, constantly dieting in order to squeeze into the latest fashions. Others described her as "a creative woman, always laughing, who liked to sew and make 'crazy odd-things' with her hands"; one of the items she left behind on her sewing table on that penultimate day of her life was a dress she had been making for Terri. Her creative instincts found their outlet not only in making dresses and suits but also in the distinctive way she furnished her apartment. At one time she actually owned a dress shop. In the last summer of her life, however, she was drawing Social Security.

She appears to have been far from unhappy—whatever her relations with her son. She was, as might be expected, extremely proud of him and filled her apartment with magazine articles about him. She always saw all his films at least twice. She had plans just prior to her death for going into "the travel business" and told a friend whom she hoped would become her partner that she was sure her son would back them financially. She had no husband at this time and showed little interest in men, but she had many good friends, all of whom considered her "loyal." One or two described her as having "a kooky view of the world."

It appears that the illness which eventually proved fatal had begun to affect her at least a month before her admission to the hospital. In particular, during the fortnight immediately preceding her collapse, she became very irritable and kept telephoning her neighbors to complain about their babies and cats.

Steve's reaction on reaching Mount Zion at midnight was typical of a caring son. He buttonholed doctors and nurses to learn what could

be done to save her. But this was an occasion when neither his considerable fame nor his fortune could achieve a miracle; medical science was
already doing all it could for her. After standing contemplating her
prone body for a little while, Steve could only retire to the room he had
rented in the hospital for the duration of the crisis. Steve and his wife
sat together, scarcely exchanging a word throughout the long hours,
rising only from time to time to listen to the latest bulletin. At times
Steve reached out and clasped his wife's hand reassuringly. At other
times, unable to stay still, he roamed the hospital corridors, a restless,
frustrated figure. At one stage, during the small hours, the doctors
admitted him to the bedside, where he stood staring fixedly at his mother
now and then reaching to touch the machine that was breathing
for her. "I feel so goddamn strong," he whispered to Neile at one
point, "I wish I could give her some of my strength."

Julia lingered until the following afternoon. Once during the ordeal
a fan, despite some hesitancy, approached Steve and asked him for his
autograph. Steve almost exploded; then, controlling his anger and
shaking his head, he said with unusual gentleness, "Sorry, but the
timing isn't good."

More than twelve hours after she sank into a coma, Julia died.
Steve may have been resigned to her death, but he mistakenly had
hoped, against the medical opinion, that she might regain consciousness just long enough for him to indicate by some word or gesture
that he had forgiven her whatever he had to forgive and to beg her
forgiveness, in turn, for whatever pain he had caused her. She died,
however, without knowing anything more.

His behavior following his mother's death reached one of those
extremes that has led his ex-wife to observe, "Steve is crazy";
a reporter to describe him as "one of the biggest nervous wrecks
in the world"; another to characterize him as "lonely, autocratic,
and self-centered"; and a film director who had worked with him to
say, "Steve is all emotional reaction. He's as subjective as a woman."
He was almost fanatic in his insistence that all details of his mother's
death and her funeral be kept secret. He had decided that she should be
buried at Forest Lawn cemetery in Los Angeles and had her close
San Franciscan friends flown down and driven to the graveside in
limousines. A witness said afterward that he seemed "almost out of

control,'' insisting to her friends, ''No interviews about my mother's death. No interviews. No reporter's going to be allowed to know anything.'' The sheer intensity of his determination was almost frightening, and although any man is entitled to some abnormality of behavior on such an occasion, it was yet another revelation that Steve, off the screen, frequently appears to be the very opposite of the person he portrays on the screen, ''a man who [seemingly] knows his own mind, calm and confident.''

In his grief Steve betrayed his bitterness, summoning up the ironies inherent in the event. Some people indicated that they wished to send flowers to the funeral; Steve replied that he would prefer that money be donated instead to the reform school to which his mother had him committed when he was fourteen. He doubtlessly had mixed motives, of course, and laudable ones. There were always the phonies who like to outdo each other in ostentation; it would be as well if they were forced to forego the privilege of display and made to give to a worthy charity. Was it right anyway that people should lavish money on the dead when so many of the living needed help? Whatever his frailties and faults, there is no denying that Steve, if only because of his own unfortunate experiences, has a highly developed social conscience and gives more thought and care to the weak and underprivileged than is usual among Hollywood stars.

The funeral itself was simple and honorable. Six of Steve's closest friends acted as pallbearers, carrying a coffin covered with large, simple daisies. By Steve's orders there was no clergyman present to conduct a service or lead prayers (although Steve himself at the time was ostensibly a Catholic). As the coffin was committed to the earth, Steve, his wife, and two children, along with a knot of friends, stood with clasped hands. Steve, to his credit, was not above shedding tears. The tough, hard-boiled, cynical facade (the ''image'' built up on the illusions of deprived, dispossessed, and despairing youth who see in Steve some kind of mirror-image of their own disastrous personalities) was sloughed off as Steve allowed himself to display genuine emotion. He made no attempt to hide the tears. Then, when the earth had been thrown over the coffin and friends and family had withdrawn, he stood there alone at the graveside for a moment, hands clasped. Upon rejoining his wife he said, almost chokingly, ''I guess she loved me a lot more than I loved her.'' Then he added, ''I wish we had known each other better.''

It could hardly be said that the difficulties had been altogether his fault. A quarter of a century before, in Los Angeles, Julia found herself with a new love—a stepfather who, in the McQueen canon, plays an extremely unsympathetic role. At this stage it is impossible to judge whether Julia's new husband was really a tyrant, a man who justifiably believed he was saddled with an unruly brat, or an insensitive lout incapable of appreciating that he had to *earn* the boy's respect. All we have to go on is Steve's version: ''My stepfather didn't like me and I didn't like him,'' to which he added, ''I was out of the hatch and running when I was fourteen.''

Steve certainly must have emerged from this period of his life as a tough character, hostile, suspicious, and with a hatred of discipline and authority. At any rate he refused to accept the discipline his stepfather sought to impose on him—and he is said to have been treated savagely. It is also claimed that his mother stood by and did nothing, either unwilling or unable to interfere. The truth is not easy to ascertain, for the boy's exploits in Indianapolis, which he carried on in Los Angeles, are evidence that he needed correction. However, there are several ways of bringing unruly and rebellious youngsters under control—although rebel is perhaps too noble a word to be applied to the simple hooliganism and mindless behavior of the juvenile gangs to which Steve belonged. It seems clear that he needed advice and guidance more than coercion.

Today he shows every sign of possessing qualities of pride, arrogance, and vanity to a more than ordinate degree, mixed with extreme sensitivity—a combination which rarely yields to the whip but can be broken by a rational and compassionate approach. Love and understanding might easily have led the incipient hooligan away from the goals at which he was then apparently aiming—which were, at their crudest, simply to be ''big,'' a leader in the eyes of his friends and schoolmates. ''I wanted to be popular with them. I sought recognition by wanting to become a leader of kids of my own age and a bit older.''

He wanted, associates say he still does, to be liked. ''He's scared to death to be anything but appealing to people,'' says a film director, talking of the man who for all his anarchic, blue-jeaned, racing-car, reform-school background is still, in many ways, shy, introverted, and insecure. "Steve," says his business partner, Robert Relyea, "has the greatest wish to be liked of any guy I've ever known—by everyone." It is impossible, of course, to censure a man simply for wanting to be liked, but an intense search for a kind of universal popularity is sure not only to lead to strange twists in behavior but also to introduce severe psychological problems.

On his own admission, Steve received his initiation into the mysteries of sex when he was only thirteen. This romantic interlude does not appear to have diverted his energies or interests from his gang life; it was at this time that he became involved in a series of street "rumbles," during the course of which, in a particularly violent incident, he was nabbed by the police. This may have caused the scene at home when he is said to have struck back at his stepfather when the latter attempted to "correct" him. In any case, the final break came when Steve was again caught by the police, this time for "a little stealin' "; the offense, in fact, was the theft of hubcaps from a car. His stepfather subsequently told the court that Steve was beyond discipline—"I can't cope with him any longer." Both he and Julia signed the necessary papers that would allow the potential hood to be committed to the Junior Boy's Republic at Chino, California, a reform school for problem boys.

Steve always underscores the fact that he entered the school of his own free will, yet he is being a little less than honest by leaving the resulting impression. "They wanted to make me a ward of the court—but they didn't," he says. "It wasn't a commitment—I went of my own free will." He had, in fact, little option; certainly ninety percent of the inmates of Chino are not given an option but are simply sent there (some 50 percent of them are boys, like Steve, from broken homes). Frank Graves, the present principal, remembers Steve as "a quiet kid who stood on his own two feet pretty much. He was active and energetic—you knew he was around all right—but he was not very articulate. He ran away once in the beginning, but later his record was pretty good." Steve's own explanation of the behavior that caused him to be sent to Chino, incidently, is "I was looking for a little love, and there wasn't much around. I guess I was difficult. I ran around with a bad crowd and I hated school [he was an incorrigible truant]—the regimentation and everything.''

He still remembers his number at the Junior Republic and reels it off like a military serial number: 3188. During his first few weeks he must have been miserable at the school, for the boys are encouraged to learn about life and democracy by running things for themselves under the guiding eye of the adult staff. They live in bungalows, are given extra schoolwork (it was at the Republic that Steve finally managed to achieve the 9th grade) and jobs on the farmland next to the school buildings, and are taught certain vocational skills. Steve has shrugged away the experience by insisting, ''I went to school in the mornings and in the afternoon worked in the laundry, and I didn't make that scene at all. So after three months I got bugged and took off.'' The scene has a romantic ring to it—our dashing, rebellious hero throwing off the shackles of authority and making a gallant break for freedom— but it is doubtful that Steve had this impression in mind when he spoke these words. There was—and is—still nothing to stop boys from running away from the Junior Republic if they want to. There are neither walls nor fences. On the other hand, once a boy is sent there, either by court order or with his own consent, he is not *allowed* to run away.

The fuller version of what actually occurred scarcely presents the star in the flatteringly casual light his laconic words imply. In fairness to the man, however, we must not forget the kind of boy he was and the world in which he found himself—gang ''rumbles,'' breaking into shops and stealing, a little sex, hatred for his stepfather and distrust of his mother, an existence devoid of love, affection, or security, and the immature ideas and instincts which were part of both his survival kit and his mindless way of life. Hard work and discipline, particularly mental discipline, involved values beyond his experience or comprehension; if he or his childhood associates thought about them at all, it was perhaps to regard them as suitable only for ''softies,'' a scene wise guys didn't need.

At any rate Steve rejected ''all that jazz'' of keeping clean his section of the bungalow where he slept, of doing his share of the chores. He was an incorrigible goldbrick, which quickly made him unpopular, and more than once he was beaten up. There were other forms of punishment, too, for a boy who refused to play the game. ''The other guys in the bungalow had ways of paying you back for interfering with their well-being," Steve said. "Say the boys had a chance once a month to load into a bus and go into town to see a movie. And they lost out because one guy in the bungalow didn't get his work done right. Well, you can pretty well guess they're gonna have something to say about that. Yeah, I paid my dues with the other fellows quite a few times. I got my lumps, no doubt about it."

It was after one such session that Steve decided the place "bugged him" and "took off." In fact, he need hardly have bothered; he got no farther than a short distance from the school where he "holed up" in a stable and was picked up by the police less than twenty-four hours after his break. He was duly lodged behind bars in the local jail. Eventually one of the school faculty members visited him. He explained that if Steve didn't choose to go back to the school, he would come under the jurisdiction of the court and would remain in jail. Having no real option, he went back with the school official.

As he later explained, he had the impression that he was due to have his backside warmed "by a butter paddle." Although this apparently did not happen, he did not get off scot-free. If he had reason to dislike the Republic before, his distaste was now increased tenfold. The Boys' Council (or committee) which ran the school handed him a few more "lumps." Instead of getting pleasant jobs connected with the farm, Steve was ordered to clean out lavatories, dig ditches, mix cement, and uproot tree stumps. When the other boys climbed into a bus taking them into town for a night out, Steve had to run an assigned number of laps around the school sports field. In spite of his stubborn spirit and angry determination, even his pride and self-confidence seemingly began to buckle. More than ever, he became an outcast and a misfit. His misery and bitterness reached a nadir.

It was at this point that rescue arrived in the shape of the superintendent of the school. "His name was Mr. Panter," Steve recalled once. "Everyone called him that, and I don't think I ever knew his first name." Twenty-five years later he was to remark, "He reminded me very much of Spencer Tracy in *Boys' Town*—without the man's piety."

Panter sought out Steve in his bungalow and put an arm around his shoulder. It was one of the rare occasions when any symbol of authority had ever laid a kindly hand on him; until then authority's hand had always meant a blow.

"Mr. Panter pointed out why I was where I was," says Steve. "He said it all in a quiet and friendly way—not in any sense trying to lecture me. He tried to teach me something of the meaning of a very basic word—kindness. 'Don't keep fighting us and everyone else,' he said, 'it won't get you anywhere.' Why didn't I use my energy for constructive ends? 'You could achieve something. Become somebody.' I thanked him and said I'd think about it. My first reaction was that he was crazy. I just couldn't accept that anyone should be concerned about my future, my welfare.''

As he lay in his cot that night after lights out, Steve must have reconsidered Panter's words. As he analyzed the ideas put forward, he evidently saw sense in them. "When I thought things over more fully," he says, "I decided to go along with Mr. Panter. In the end he made me a member of the boys' committee which ran the place." Far from being a "rebel," then, he found himself suddenly a member of the Establishment—and apparently happy in his role.

Today Steve says of the Republic, "It's damned good for boys. You know, those years from 12 to 18 are pretty crucial in a boy's life. I mean, he really shapes up in that time, or he doesn't. I think it's a good idea for the boys to run the boys. After all, adults are deadly enemies to the young, especially to kids who have been in some kind of trouble. Believe me, a boy learns to toe the line when he's got the force of twenty other boys seeing to it that he behaves."

It could never be said that consistency is one of Steve's virtues, however. He can solemnly declare, "Look, I'm not the kind of guy who lets himself get pulled into that sentiment trap. I'm not on that kick at all. To me, nothing is more important than right now. What's past is long ago, and it can stay there as far as I'm concerned." Yet in fact, he is incorrigibly nostalgic—"a goer-backer." To his credit he is vulnerable, as any decent human being is, to sentiment. He has, in fact, never forgotten the Boy's Republic—a monument not only to his sense of nostalgia but to one of the genuinely admirable sides of his character—his sense of charity and his concern for the less fortunate. He admits, "I go back when I can. I just sit down and talk to the boys; that's the best way I can function with them. Boy, they're smart and bright. They know the scam. But they have a hard time adjusting to school, just as I did. It's different from the streets. You've got to learn to get along. But they make it. Insecurity is a pretty good motivation.''

According to the superintendent, Frank Graves, Steve visits the school ''every four or five months'' even now. He has set up an annual award scholarship for the best student in the ''graduating'' class and does his best to attend to present it. He keeps track of winners after they leave and is available to listen to their problems and give them man-to-man advice. He insists that he is never too busy to help a boy from the school. In November, 1966, when two youngsters, aged fourteen and fifteen, were convicted of breaking and entering and were incarcerated in a prison in Florida because in the judge's opinion there ''was little hope they would be rehabilitated at a boys' school,'' Steve had them transferred to the Republic whose recidivist record is extraordinary— of the 8,000 boys who have been sent there, less than ten percent have gotten into trouble after leaving.

His talks to the boys are usually informal and always off-the-record and ''he mainly chooses ones who are more or less like he was when he was in here,'' says Graves. Steve, who was at one time a food eccentric (for a while he liked to eat a compound tasting of seaweed and fishmeal and often patronized a Hollywood restaurant specializing in ''hamburgers'' made of vegetables and minerals), admits that on occasions he has ''talked health'' to the boys. On one visit he allowed a magazine reporter to accompany him. As they approached the school, he confessed, ''I get kinda nervous when I head back to this place.'' Referring to the occasion when he ''took off,'' he pointed out the actual spot where he had hidden—''over in that stable, then over there in that ditch. Yeah, they got me all right. Get hit? Well, they kinda changed my smile for about three weeks.''

There were some dozen boys waiting to greet Steve on his arrival, most of them looking awkward and shy. One youngster wanted to know if he was ''still racin'.'' Steve nodded, then asked if any boy was ''getting out soon.'' When a boy answered ''Yeah,'' Steve advised him, ''Thing is to find some chicks. Ya get pretty horny here, I remember.'' He pointed out the laundry where he used to work (''Man, it sure got hot in there.'') and then after lunch astonished some of the boys by eating ice cream with a fork—''just like us!'' He likes to play pool and went into the school poolroom to shoot pool with some of the youngsters for two hours. As someone has said, Steve not only wants to be thought of as a "tough guy" (in his case rather as one who has seen it all than as a physically aggressive person) but also as a "good guy," an all-round sport, a regular guy. And certainly, whatever reservations one might have about him, he is, in fact, generously breaking precedence as far as most Hollywood film stars are concerned by becoming so personally involved in trying to help others. Neile says that when she first met him, Steve had "a heart like steel," but that she recognized "a great yearning in him to be tender." His friend Rick Ingersoll, who handled his publicity for several years, says, "When Steve sees someone in trouble, he thinks, 'There but for the grace of God, go I.' There was a time in his life when he could have gone down and he truly appreciates the success he has now."

He sometimes makes a show of a little tightfistedness: "I throw pennies around like man-hole covers"—but all he is doing is serving notice that he is neither an easy nor foolish touch, that he knows and appreciates the value of a dollar. He is never stingy when it comes to deserving causes, with time or money. When he was filming *The Sand Pebbles* in Formosa, he wrote a check for $12,500 to enable Father Edward Wojmak, a missionary priest, to purchase land on which to build a hostel for homeless young girls wandering the streets of Taipei.

He serves on the Advisory Council for Youth Studies at the University of Southern California. Two or three times a year he drives up with Dr. Herman Salk, brother of the discoverer of the polio vaccine, to the Navajo Indian reservation situated where Utah, New Mexico, Arizona, and Colorado meet, bringing clothing and medical supplies to the impoverished Indians. "Of course, it's not entirely unselfish," Neile once explained. "He likes an excuse to run his truck and he loves to get out in the open and sleep outside for a few nights." The journey, however, is long and tough and the weather is not always clement; yet he never shirks the job unless he is filming. The Indians themselves have no idea who he is beyond the fact that he is a friend, a white man who is trying to help them. In fact, there is nothing either in the trip itself or in what he does for the Indians that would, in any sense, boost Steve's ego. He is genuinely interested in the Indians' plight and finds much to admire in their culture. He likes their saying "a land where there is time enough and room enough"—which strikes a responsive chord in him.

Altogether, Steve spent eighteen months in the Boy's Republic. By the time his term was up, his stepfather had died and his mother had moved to New York City. He says, "So after I cut out of school, man, my mother was in New York and she was gonna get married again and she sent me the bread and I went across from Los Angeles to New York and I was really broke." He paints a rather touching picture of his arrival in New York. "When I arrived in New York I felt like Li'l Abner, man, because when I got out of the bus station, I was in my big high shoes and my levis and my levi jacket and a white shirt and a California tan and a square-cut haircut and I was standin' on Thirty-fourth Street and that was a bad-lookin' crowd I was goin' into."

He made another attempt to get along with his mother, but their reunion was brief. "So I was in New York and it was the summer and I didn't have anythin' to do and I met a guy in the Village called Ed Ford who later jumped off the Staten Island ferry and committed suicide. He was a bosun's mate on a tanker, see, but him and another guy named Tinker—he probably has one leg now because the last time I saw him he had an infection in his leg and it smelled so bad you couldn't get close to him—he and Tinker were both on a ship and I fell in with them and was in the Village and there was broads . . . you know, all kinds of scam goin' on.

"So these guys got me an able-bodied seaman's card and I got on their boat which was an early tanker; it was in Yonkers and the damn thing caught fire and damn near sunk, man, but then we took off from Yonkers and we went all the way down to Cuba and we ended up in the Dominion [sic] Republic and I jumped ship there. I lived in a cathouse in a little town for about eight weeks. There was a shortage of blond men around, so the girls liked me, I was a happy kid. . . . And I went back to New York City a little richer and a little wiser." So goes the story, but while the basic facts still stand, he has since amended some of the more raffish implications—particularly the alleged eight-week stay in a cathouse.

Even before he was out of his teens then—and he was later to say

that at seventeen he "felt like an old man inside"—Steve had structured a background for himself that was bound to make him a sympathetic and easily idealized figure for the anti-authoritarian youngsters
of his generation. He had "challenged the system," and even when he
became famous, he still could be seen tilting at windmills. Many
youngsters felt that society had gone wrong. Despising the affluence
and acquisitiveness of society, finding unfair a system which pro-
duces enormous material wealth at the price of an exacting work-rate
that distorts man's true personality and in turn disregards those
qualities which alone have any real value, they saw in him a cult
figure. For his part, Steve never dreamed that the empty, purposeless
part of his life would give him an edge over his competitors, men
who were careless enough not to equip themselves with a checkered
background. At the time, in fact, Steve's mind was no more than a
blank. "I had no ambition—gee, I don't know, there were so many
things goin' on, I sure wanted to see everything so bad, really wanted
to see what was happenin'—but other than that I had no plans."

In any case, despite his reform-school history as well as his other
experiences—and in contrast to those "rebels" who saw and perhaps
still see in him some kind of "soul-mate"—Steve quickly learned to
work within the system and even profit by it. The lessons of the Boy's
Republic, which preached a certain conformity, were not entirely
lost on him. Today he can casually admit that he lacked plans or
ambition at the time, but only because opportunity had not yet presented
itself. When it did, he seized it like any other entrepreneur.

For a few more years, however, he was destined to drift as the
winds blew, living with "itchy feet." He admits, "I was fortunate
not to get into real trouble" and has insisted, more than once, "Man,
if I hadn't made my own scene, I could have wound up a hood."

This is not, one would imagine, background and equipment helpful
in scaling the heights of that pink-egg and cotton candy *soufflé*
called Hollywood.

4.

GETTING THE SCAM
ON THE HUMAN RACE

N<small>ATALIE</small> Wood, the actress who worked opposite Steve in his earliest screen success, *Love with the. Proper Stranger*, once insisted, when someone argued that the modern crop of film actors was "colorless" compared with that of the twenties and thirties, "I don't think that's true—and I think Steve is proof of it. He's an exciting personality on and off the screen . . . and a nice man into the bargain."

There is tenderness, compassion, consideration for others—particularly if they are no threat to him—and probably as much goodness in Steve McQueen as in any of us. Yet "nice" is hardly a word one would apply to him—or one he would particularly thank you for using about him; or one that accords with his history and much of his behavior; or the image he seeks to give of himself.

Writing about him Sheilah Graham, the Hollywood gossip columnist, has made a point of what she calls "his suspiciousness"—his instinctive distrust of people and their motives—possibly well justified in his case. According to her, he even considers "every offer of a film a plot to put him out of business.'' Justified or not, it is behavior unlikely to make him seem charming. She records, too, that Warner Brothers-Seven Arts, which had signed a six-picture contract with him, starting with *Bullitt*, found him so ''dictatorial'' that they decided it was ''better to cancel the contract, this in spite of the actor's top rating and popularity on the screen all over the world.'' She has criticized him as a man who says ''yes'' to your face ''and then takes steps to have the army of people who work for him change everything so that he is still the good guy and they take the brunt of the blame.''

He has, she says, as noted earlier, an almost paranoiac desire to be liked. Combined with an instinctive generosity and a desire to ''do good,'' this can lead to embarrassing situations. As an example, there was Steve's gesture following the completion of *Bullitt*. The mayor of San Francisco had extended every courtesy to the film unit, even closing certain city streets for the sensational car chase. As a result, Steve asked him, ''What can I do for *you*?'' On reflection, the mayor suggested that a poor section of the city ''could use a swimming pool.'' Cost of installation would be $250,000. ''It's yours,'' replied Steve, in a magnificent gesture.

The money, it appeared, was intended to come out of the film's budget and not from Steve's own pocket—although, as producer, it would eat into his share of the profits. The backing company, Warner Brothers-Seven Arts, estimated that Steve's special demands had already added a million dollars to the budget and an unholy row developed between Steve, who insisted that he had publicly given his word and that the money must be paid, and the company, which insisted that it could not afford it. A compromise was reached, and the company handed over $25,000 to the mayor, who was pleased to receive it. Yet an analysis of the situation shows that in the end, the company was *wrong* and Steve was *right*. His extra demands and his ''dictatorial'' attitude, however awkward and annoying at the time, particularly to accountants, was justified by the results: *Bullitt* proved a smash hit at the box office and one of the greatest financial successes of the decade. Nor was his gesture anything to be ashamed about; the cause was a good one, and in the end, the money was peanuts compared with the profits.

Still, if this action can be excused as an instinctive—and rather noble—

gesture suitable to a prince of Hollywood, particularly one carried away by momentary euphoria, some of his other gestures seem rather less amiable, as his relations with the press indicate.

In Hollywood anyone even vaguely connected with the profession of letters has been traditionally regarded as someone to use. From its inception, the Hollywood film industry was largely in the hands of hucksters from poor, illiterate backgrounds who, when they found themselves in the seats of power, took a sadistic delight in humbling those who were artistically creative. Talented writers, lured to the film capital by large checks and engaging promises, found themselves treated worse than office boys by the moguls. Actors and actresses, of course, have always been a caste apart, and even Bernard Shaw had to indulge the foibles of Mrs. Patrick Campbell. Childish, petulant behavior by "theatricals" is a hallmark of the breed.

Relations between the film industry and the press, on the other hand, have been based on a wary recognition that both benefit from each other's existence. Cold-bloodedly both exploit and manipulate the other. Newspaper and magazine men see film stars and their activities as the light relief leavening more weighty matters. Editors in the past have seized on such "scandals" as Ingrid Bergman's desertion of her husband for Rossellini or Elizabeth Taylor's heady romance with Richard Burton as "talking points" or "gossip points" that, however insignificant in their own right, balance the normal diet of grim news.

On the other hand, press publicity, while not *totally* essential to the film machine—if totally embarrassing when a scandal does break—is easily the cheapest and best method by which a filmmaker can sell his wares to the public. Gossip about a film, from its inception to the moment when it is finally projected on the screen, is the most certain way of arousing public interest. As a corollary, gossip about individual actors makes the public more aware of them, not only increasing the actor's self-esteem, but also making him a more valuable "property" and placing him in a position to command a higher salary. On the whole, therefore, actors and press get along fairly well together. The exception tends to occur when an actor feels himself sufficiently well established to ignore the press—Frank Sinatra, for instance, often betrays a hostility and arrogance towards reporters for which there is little genuine warrant. Press photographers, of course, frequently make unnecessary pests of themselves; yet the yawning cultural and educational gulf between an editorial writer and a photographer is rarely appreciated. Nor is the fine distinction generally understood between a staff photographer, bound by the ethics and responsibilities of his newspaper, and the hordes of amateurs who masquerade as freelancers.

It is sometimes said nowadays that Steve "gives no interviews," a phrase generally construed by the press to mean that an actor feels he has reached the stage where he no longer needs publicity and can slam the door on men who have helped him reach his goal. In Steve's case, the charge is not easily substantiated. He seemingly dislikes interviews, and he has never been entirely at ease with journalists; yet I personally have twice interviewed him in recent years and he has put himself out to give special interviews even when it meant facing up to searching questions following a night without sleep. If he appears less than eager to talk to reporters, this is because he probably feels that he has largely said everything of significance he has to say; it is even more substantially because he has become so deaf in *both* ears that talking to the press—or even ordinary socializing—is now an ordeal. When in a room with only a few people, Steve cups his hand behind his left ear. When trapped in a larger gathering—say a press conference, for example—he wears a kind of hunted look as he makes the enormous effort of concentration necessary to pick up the questions flung at him.

On one occasion, Steve's deafness produced an absurd scene. David Lewin, then staff show-business writer for the London *Daily Mail*, and Victor Davis of the London *Daily Express* decided to interview him on location. Steve was kept busy filming all morning, and the two newspapermen grew impatient. Finally, during the lunch break, they spotted Steve alone at a table and, without waiting for the assistance of the small army of publicity people hanging around, charged across to where Steve was sitting. To their astonishment, Steve blandly ignored their questions and went on eating lunch. This was too much for the veteran Lewin who had been writing film gossip for years and was a confidant of many famous stars. A man capable of a temper tantrum himself, Lewin rose from the table and stalked angrily towards the publicity people, indicating his disgust in tones that boded lack of goodwill towards Steve in the British press. The misunderstanding was soon sorted out and a publicity aide carefully placed Lewin at the side of Steve's good ear. The star himself was astounded to find that he had, quite by accident, upstaged two of the most powerful newspapers in Britain.

Yet not all his behavior can be so easily excused. During the making of *The Thomas Crown Affair*, Steve behaved in what many people consider a shabby manner toward a New York reporter who had made a special trip to Hollywood to do an in-depth report on him. Steve had agreed beforehand to give as much of his time as was required, and initially he extended every cooperation. On the last day of the scheduled talks, however, he abruptly announced that he was off to visit some Navajo Indians. The reporter understood the importance of this mission to Steve but pleaded that he needed only two more hours at the most to complete his work. Steve remained adamant. The fact that by doing so he was jeopardizing the reporter's work carried no weight with him. Although Steve could rightly argue that he put his responsibilities to the Indians above his publicity chores, it was a tactless and apparently needless discourtesy, earning him a reputation for arrogance.

A solitary example of inconsiderate behavior is scarcely evidence of a man's general attitudes, and at that, Steve is as much entitled as anyone else to be thoughtless or rude whenever circumstances or inclination dictates. He makes no claim to be a paragon. Rather more maddening, however, and more indicative of his general character is what Sheilah Graham describes as his ''quality of indecision.'' This is a tendency to dither and fuss and change his mind or demand continual reassurance where none is really needed that has led people other than his former wife to describe him as ''crazy.'' Robert Relyea, his partner, long ago took to leaving his telephone off the hook at night in order to avoid having to smooth away Steve's nocturnal anxieties. As reporter Betty Rollin puts it, ''The thing about crazy people is that they drive everybody else around them crazy.'' She has recorded the bizarre preliminaries to her first meeting with Steve. First, his secretary rang to announce that he would be calling her ''in one minute.'' Steve, who has described unpunctuality as one of his pet hates, telephoned exactly on the dot and then began ''tearing through

his words like a shredded fandango.'' She listened while the bundle
of nerves and anxieties at the other end explained that he was taking
part in a car race that night (the publicity people had already made all
the arrangements for her and her photographer to cover the event); he
was, however, practicing that afternoon and perhaps she should also
cover that. He then asked her, if she came along, to pretend to be merely
a friend and not a reporter, ''as otherwise the mechanics might be upset.'' Then he changed his mind again and suggested it might be better
to forget the practice altogether and just attend the race in the evening.
He would arrange to leave press passes at the gate (the press agents
had already done this); then, finally, still in a tremulous state, he
asked to know what kind of car she intended turning up in—it wouldn't
be a limousine or anything like that? It appeared that the sight of a
reporter turning up in a limousine would cause him a disastrous loss
of face among his hard-bitten buddies.

Much of his behavior off-screen seems in direct contradiction
to his screen *persona*. The public Steve gives the impression of
having great reservoirs of will and an even clarity of purpose. Yet,
on at least one occasion, he had given his publicity people stern
instructions that no interviews or photographs were to be permitted
in connection with a visit to the set by his children and then proceeded
to encourage both when they turned up—only to kick up the devil's own
fuss in an attempt to prevent publication when it was too late to halt
publication. Such behavior, of course, might simply arise out of
tedium and boredom or possibly because he feels that it is necessary,
every now and then, to demonstrate his power and emphasize his position.
No one but Steve himself, however, knows the answer to this.

The impression he sometimes gives of indecision and insecurity
might, of course, be partly a pose—he is, after all, a fine actor and often
has unlimited time at his disposal. Great men such as Churchill and
his crony Lord Beaverbrook, the newspaper magnate and member of
the British War Cabinet, were both notorious for calling aides or
colleagues in the middle of the night, often on some spurious excuse,
simply because *they* were bored. Steve's actions possibly are caused
by a mixture of anxiety *and* boredom. Generally he seems pleased
and happy when he finally makes up his mind to accept a new role,
for example. The euphoria induced by the thought of exciting work

ahead and relief from the need to make a decision lasts until just
before shooting begins. Then he displays—or affects to display—signs
of nervousness and insecurity more suitable to a stand-in forced to
take the stage for the first time on the opening night of an important
play. He has been known, immediately prior to shooting, to telephone
a director at midnight and pour out his anxieties in an apparent search
for a reassurance he is unable to find within himself.

Yet a suspicion remains that beneath much of this apparent insecurity,
indecision, anxiety and the steps he takes to remedy them, lies a
need to exercise his power. He is a man who knows all about power
and the psychology of exercising it. "Power," he once said, "is
forcing someone to give in to you." When he first arrived in Hollywood and became known on television, for example, he gave the
impression of taking an almost perverse delight in forcing people to
accept him as he was; and he may have felt a sense of growing power—
and the pleasant feeling *that* can bring—when he realized that not
only were people accepting him on his own terms, they were actually
beginning to *copy* him. He arrived on the scene, for instance, with a
vocabulary so unintelligible that few people even pretended to understand him. Richard Crenna, who starred with him in *The Sand Pebbles*,
says, "When I first knew him, his jargon was so odd it was like talking
to a Zulu warrior." Steve would inquire, "Who's the head honcho?"
or remark, "Let's get down to the nitty-gritty"—a phrase which appears
to have spread from him to the popular media and thence into the
common parlance. He went around "hondling" for things—that is,
bargaining or negotiating for articles (it may be a symptom of ingrained
habit that even today, when he is wealthy, he still "hondles" for trifles
such as spare tires or bits of machinery, doing his best to get them
for nothing). He was one of the first persons in Hollywood to use words
like "dig" for understand or "bread" for money. One of his early
favorites was "scam"—which appears to have a subtle meaning
lying somewhere between a confidence trick and knowing the score.
For example, "Life's just a scam" is a piece of homespun philosophy
indicating that the whole of existence is a dirty confidence trick; yet
he will remark of the kids at the Junior Republic, "They're smart—they
know the scam." When talking about how he keeps fit and remains
looking superbly lithe, he says casually, "So I work out in the gym.

When you work out, the way I see it, you're puttin' your neuroses back in your body. See—you're scammin' them!'' Yet for all his seeming efforts to provide a credible alternative to Dr. Johnson's Dictionary, gradually he has polished his manners, and communication with him has become much less difficult. He still addresses everyone, regardless of age, sex, or color as ''man'' and all cars and motor-cycles as ''her.'' He once accosted the nubile Tuesday Weld as she bounced past his dressing room during the making of *The Cincinnati Kid* by asking, ''Where are you going, man?''

His early use of hipster/carnival-show talk was sometimes in-terpreted as his way of ''scamming'' people, of covering up a basic shyness natural to a normally inarticulate man with nothing very significant to say. His lack of gregariousness is certainly often painfully apparent; he is about the last person I personally would approach in a crowded room if I were searching for wit or sparkling conversation. Obviously women would be attracted by his looks, not to mention his status, but many people find him a trifle withdrawn. When he first went to Hollywood, he was described as ''a loner,'' meaning one who is self-sufficient and prefers it that way. He has rejected this description, insisting that he was forced into the life of a ''loner'' rather than having chosen it. He says he prefers to be considered an ''oblique'' person (an ''oblique'' person in his terms means ''a Negro, Jew, long-hair, someone different''), and the word does sum him up better.

Personally, I think that it is Steve's deafness, rather than his lack of formal education or natural lack of gregariousness that is responsible for much of the way he appears to stand back. There are few greater barriers to a full life than to be hard of hearing, and it is his misfortune that the problem is getting worse.

His strange vocabulary is a relic of his colorful youth, especially perhaps his early working experiences. When he first went to live in Greenwich Village, for instance, he worked at such jobs as bartender or truck driver. Then, having surveyed the New York scene as it appeared shortly after World War II, he decided to ship out and dis-cover what else the world had to offer. ''I scrounged around for the next couple of years trying to get the scam on the human race and just where the hell I fitted in—I discovered there were no openings.''

A sea trip seemed one solution, and Ed Ford and Tinker helped him get some seaman's papers by adding a couple of years to his age, and he shipped out, as already related, from Yonkers, on the S.S. *Alpha*. Steve has always remained laconic and imprecise about this period of his life, although it obviously contains nothing discreditable. At worst, his behavior might be classified as feckless or irresponsible or impulsive. Certainly it seems absurd to attribute to it some spurious philosophy such as "rebelliousness" or "dislike of regimentation," or to give it any kind of special quality, or even to describe it as colorful. Which of us is not rebellious and does like regimentation, anyway? And his experiences do not markedly diverge from those of thousands of youngsters who, in any country, coming from humble homes and lacking both education and defined objectives, tend to drift aimlessly about from one job to another.

The authorized version, as Steve has filtered the story out, is that when the S.S. *Alpha* reached the Dominican Republic, Steve, disliking the hard and certainly boring work aboard ship and deciding that wherever his future lay, it did not lie at sea, decided to jump ship. He survived in Dominica by getting a job as a carpenter's assistant. His looks and sex appeal appear to have made him a hit in Dominica, although it is not all that easy to disentangle fact and myth in Steve's case. There is his tough-sounding talk to the boys at the Junior Republic about getting themselves a chick when they got out; and there is his own claim to have experienced sex for the first time when he was thirteen; and yet there is a report that he was "still scared of women" when he was in Dominica. The one thing that seems beyond dispute is that by the time he left the Dominican Republic, he felt more confident of his own abilities and more certain of his talent for survival.

His Caribbean spell enabled him to save enough money to pay his passage back to the United States. Landing at Port Arthur, Texas, he got a job euphemistically described as "waiter" in what was apparently, at best, a tenth-rate hotel. His brief stay in Port Arthur has given rise to one of the more colorful myths surrounding him—that as a blond *enfant terrible* he worked as a waiter in a brothel. The source of this story appears to be his own recorded words about living "in a cathouse in a little town for about eight weeks," but he has since modified the myth and the exact truth is difficult to pin down. He has said that, apparently as part of his duties as a waiter in the hotel, he used to "deliver groceries" to a brothel in the port. Subsequently, even this version has been further modified, and the official story now is that he delivered groceries only *once* to a brothel. No doubt, whether it was on only one occasion or more often, the ladies of the house, confronted with a blond youngster with his obvious sex appeal, would have made a fuss over him.

From Port Arthur it is only a short distance to the oilfields in Waco, Texas, and there Steve got a laboring job. After this, he may or may not have stayed briefly with Uncle Claude on the Slater farm—he certainly went back for a visit sometime during these years—but his next major stop was Canada, where he got a seasonal job as a "hijacker" in an Ontario lumber camp—work which entailed climbing high trees and lopping off excess branches. Then he returned to the United States and "bummed around" doing odd jobs. One job was with a traveling circus. He worked in a booth selling cheap ballpoint pen-and-pencil sets and he spent most of his time "scammin' " his boss, i.e., cheating him. "Man," he explains, "they were, like, sixteen cents apiece—and I was selling them for a buck. It was a full scam. The boss was scammin' from the public and I was scammin' from him. Anyhow I gave it up. Why? Well, my conscience got the best of me. You don't believe it? Well, that's not exactly right, either. You see, the guy got on to me, so I left."

He finished up at Myrtle Beach, South Carolina, by now pretty "beat and broke." He recalls, "It was all very pleasant just lying in the sun and watching the girls go by, but one day I suddenly felt bored with hanging around and went and joined the Marines." He joined the Corps in April, 1947, less than a month after his seventeenth birthday.

He entered the Marines as an ordinary private and came out with exactly the same rank. "I guess the only way I could have made corporal," he recalls wryly, "was if all the other privates in the Marines had either dropped dead or refused promotion." The highest honor he achieved was to be posted as part of the Honor Guard protecting President Harry S. Truman's yacht. His induction, however, proved not entirely unprofitable. Daily exercise drills meant that he came out of the Corps much fitter than he went in, and he has never entirely forgotten the lessons of physical fitness learned in the Marines. He found the stint necessary, too, "for basic disciplines—but not the kind you'd let society jack down your throat." He became a tank driver with the Second Marine Division of the Fleet Marine Force, and it was by working with mechanical things here that his interest in cars, bikes and, indeed, any kind of machinery was first stimulated.

He was not, as might be expected of a boy with his background, an entirely model Marine. He was sentenced to forty-one days in the brig (the first twenty-one on bread and water) for allowing a weekend pass to drag into two weeks and then, or so the legend goes, fighting with the shore patrol when picked up. When his outfit sailed for coldwater amphibious exercises off Labrador, he became so "browned off" with K rations that one night he and his closest buddies, a pair of twins, scrounged a few tins from the officers' mess under the impression that they contained fruit salad, chicken, and tongue—only to find that they were tins of lard. Steve and his co-conspirators had to scrub decks for the rest of the voyage.

Normally he seems to have enjoyed Marine Corps food and usually had a healthy appetite; today his manager says a typical McQueen meal is "some meat, two orders of mashed potatoes and gravy, some candied sweet potatoes, a double thick milk shake, hot tea and lots of bread, butter, and jelly!" The Labrador trip with its K rations proved a gastronomic ordeal, and despite the incident of the tins of lard, Steve tried another dodge. "They were starvin' me to death on those funky rations" ("funky" is a word describing a city slicker's contempt for a village hick), he insists. He got his chance again when an officer ordered him to help unload rations for the officers' mess from a landing craft—Steve at this time was driving a caterpillar tractor. "I jumped· into that mother (meaning thing), and I drove down to the boat and heisted as much food as I thought I could get away with and hid it in the tractor. They were mostly cans of beans—which was fine with me, man, I love beans. But they were ice cold." Steve's solution was to ask the crew chief to rev up the tractor's engine while he held a can of beans over the exhaust to warm it. "But I'd forgotten to open the can and suddenly there was this tremendous explosion. It blew beans over everything— tents, jeeps, radar equipment, everything!" For days afterwards, so his story goes, every time he raised his arm to salute an officer, a bean would fly out and the officer would "have a bean stuck on his helmet." Disciplinary action is said to have included cancellation of leave.

He redeemed himself, however, heroically and in the very best traditions of the cinema when a transport struck a sandbank and flung a number of tanks and their crews into the Arctic water. Some Marines drowned immediately, unable to get out of their tanks. Others either managed to swim clear or clung precariously to the turrets which projected just above the surface. Steve was among those who volunteered to help in the rescue—a tricky business in water where immersion for more than a few seconds meant death. The seas were too rough for boats, and Steve and the others had to make the attempt in amphibious craft. He personally assisted in the rescue of five Marines, who were almost frozen to death.

In April, 1950, having signed on for a three year term only, he was honorably discharged from the Marine Corps at Camp Lejeune, North Carolina. He spent the next few weeks—and most of his accumulated pay—at his favorite resort, Myrtle Beach. His main reason for returning was a romance. "I'd been going with a girl there so I stayed at the Beach and ran around with her crowd, nineteen-year-olds, college kids, you know." It was a style of life he found himself suddenly aspiring to: "I thought it was wonderful, going over to people's houses for dinner, getting dressed up, going to dances and everybody liked you and you were saying 'hello' to people. I mean, I never had this before." He picked up something more than an ability to mix with well-to-do people, or a new aspiration—he picked up a pouty-lipped Southern accent, or at least the ability to mimic it, which he turned to excellent account when he got his first big chance some years later in television.

He soon, unfortunately, again had to face the bitter realities of life. He was without money, and he had no job. He has never hinted that he felt envious of the youngsters with whom he was running around, products of stable homes with fathers who were comfortably well off. We can only presume that yet another scar appeared on his tough hide as he mentally compared the privileged life they led with his own bleak future. There were compensating factors, of course.

His was not the kind of mentality that dwelt too long on future difficulties—sufficient unto the day and all that. He had, too, already
crowded a fair degree of experience into his short life and had learned
that if you did not demand too much, you could always survive on
surprisingly little. What was life, anyway, but a "scam." He would
get by. Over and above all else, too, he was only twenty and had all
of youth's optimism.

5.

EVOLUTION OF A
NEW BREED ACTOR

I N 1958, far from being the golden figure in the entertainment industry that he is today, Steve, if he had come a long, long way, was still not much more than a small-time TV hero. Yet he ought to have considered himself lucky beyond his wildest dreams. He had well-paid steady employment (salary plus share of profits); his face was known throughout America; and his career was on the rise. It was a truly remarkable change of fortune for a man who, by his own admission, could easily have sunk into a criminal career. Film and TV producers and directors liked his work, and a few were sufficiently acute to realize that there was a public ground swell, particularly among the young, that could easily lift him to the status of superstar.

But shortly after his twenty-eighth birthday, Steve McQueen guessed almost cataclysmically wrong. Possibly heady with recent achievements and at last pretty sure of where he was going, he found himself once more at odds with authority. As a result, the word was soon racing around Hollywood that he was about to be blackballed. The "rebel" figure in the hipster jeans, talking that strange lingo that seemed the prerogative of youth, whose disordinate personality was seen by some as both a symbol and a symptom of the anarchy of the times, was on his way out. And all this before it could be said that he was really in!

Suddenly and startlingly, however, Steve announced that he did not like acting, that he was ready to sacrifice all he had struggled for. When the smoke cleared a little, however, it was clear that Steve's disillusionment was not with his new-found profession. Rather, it was simply that he did not like having to do as he was told to in his role as Josh Randall, bounty hunter hero of the CBS Western series, "Wanted—Dead or Alive," produced by Dick Powell's Four Star Company. It had been an open secret for some time, of course, that Steve had an uneasy truce with those who considered they had a right to put a halter on him, and now it had ended in a tempestuous flare-up and walk-out. He was even said to be planning to fly off to Australia with an idea of becoming a sheep farmer in the outback.

The news was gossiped about in TV and film circles with startled incredulity. Steve, certainly, was known far and wide as a tough, itchy, utterly unpredictable egg, a "wild man." Yet for him to throw up his career just when he appeared on the verge of a major breakthrough was one for the psychiatrist's notebook. That is, if it were the unvarnished truth   a quality always at a hefty premium in Hollywood.

What, in fact, *had* happened?

Steve's disenchantment had part of its roots in the deadly scheduling that accompanies all TV series. If not exactly work for amateurs, it makes extraordinary physical and mental demands on leading actors. Normally, for instance, it took no more than ten days to churn out an episode of "Wanted—Dead or Alive." Steve found himself on a treadmill that made life in the Marines seem cozy. He rose around dawn each day in order to start work about seven in the morning. He got home, if he was lucky, around eight or nine in the evening to wife Neile and their tiny house. This kind of dedication, of course, is a natural prerequisite to success, and now that he had finally found his niche in life, Steve was the last man on earth to shirk work. Still, to someone so assured of his talents and capabilities, the assembly-line technique had its disadvantages. An honest fellow might get the feeling, for instance, that he was simply working for money— and then swing round to the rather *outre* idea that if he had to sweat merely for that, he would prefer the weekly check to be more substantial.

He was largely encouraged in his impatience—although his TV program enjoyed a high rating—by the fact that he had one stunning full-length feature credit under his belt. This was his cheeky, scene-stealing role in director John Sturges's *Never So Few*, which had starred Frank Sinatra and had been Hollywood's first vehicle for the gorgeous Italian, Gina Lollobrigida. Cast as a perky Army master scrounger who drives a jeep with manic obsession, Steve had delivered his lines with Cagney-like precision. Compared with the almost morose, monosyllabic, allegedly menacing figure that is his screen persona today, this was a deft performance by a master light comedian and points up the scope of Steve's acting ability. Sinatra, never an easy fellow to be around, showed considerable forbearance, even generosity, in not demanding his dismissal, for Steve's performance was sheer larceny. Sinatra, of course, was probably reminded how he himself, when at the nadir of his career, had made an extraordinary comeback by out-acting everyone in *From Here to Eternity*. Anyway, when shooting had finished, Sinatra generously turned to Steve and said, "It's a good movie, kid—and it's all yours."

It was not exactly, alas, the kind of encouragement likely to transform Steve into an angelic figure around the Four Star lot. His baby blue eyes were dazzled by more film contracts and, he recognized, to employ his own extraordinary version of the English language, that this was "the big brass ring." He soon began making it clear that he wanted out of TV and into the clover of full-length screen films. He became *spiky*. It was all, of course, strictly in the interests of better business—or, at least, Steve's better business.

To be fair, his behavior was not entirely dictated by a desire for self-aggrandizement. He was never a man satisfied to voice the lines someone else had written for him, stand where the director told him to stand, grab his wages at the end of the week, become a regular guy and all-round lovable figure, and then go home at night and use up a bottle or two. There was too much stubborn integrity in his makeup for him not to want to extract the best values he could from anything he did. He did not, apparently, like the casual

way films and TV often got things *wrong* when it was as easy to get
them right, nor the way certain producers were content to pour out
any old fodder on the assumption that the public lacked discrimination.
Years later, the climax to this kind of thinking would be seen when
he made *Le Mans*, as painstakingly accurate a record of a big car
race as, if in a larger and more complex way, Ernest Hemingway's
Death in the Afternoon was a written account of the minutiae and
atmosphere of a bullfight.

One way or another, then, he was seemingly looking for a bust-up
that would get him out of his TV contract. Everybody knew that a fuse
had been lit and that it was only a question of time before the bomb
went off. Then it happened. As Steve explains it, "I fell out with the
company over the interpretation of Randall. One row was over my
cowboy hat. They thought that all cowboys had shiny new saddles and
that their hats were never crumpled—I ask you? Anyway, I quit and
stormed out." Anyway, that was an explanation—and if not exactly
the whole truth, a part of it.

The situation leading up to the crisis had been simmering for about
seven weeks, and the man who had borne the brunt of it was Ed Adamson who, besides writing many of the scripts, normally produced the
show. Adamson and the other writers on the series saw Randall in
more idealized terms than Steve apparently envisaged. The public,
as they saw it, wanted gloss; it demanded fantasy heroes. This was
the premise that had made Hollywood great. Who wanted *reality*?
If the figures on film screens or TV sets were no better than average
Joes, who would watch? Steve demurred. Seemingly, he wanted a
Josh Randall who would look and behave as near to a real bounty
hunter as possible. He probably felt, too, with some justification,
that the Randall figure that appealed to the public was as much his
conception as that of the producers or writers; he had lived the part
so long, had thought his way so deeply inside the role, that he had
become Josh Randall.

So first there was a row about the saddle and then about the hat.
This was followed by another when the script called for Steve to knock
out three toughs who had told him to leave town. If life had taught
Steve anything—and no one disputed his "lumps"—it was that nobody
who was not a total fool tried to take on three guys *at the same time*.

"Listen," he is reported to have told the producer at rehearsal, "where I come from if three guys told me to leave town—I'd leave. If I wanted to beat them up, I'd sneak back one night and sort them out separately." The producer was not prepared to indulge quibbles. "Just keep to the script," he told Steve. That out of the way, Steve apparently started looking around for something else to niggle at. He found it in his horse. He said he thought the part demanded a young, spirited mount; instead, they had saddled him with an old, placid hack. The game continued until one day Steve "allowed" his temper to get the better of him and "chucking his shooter" to the producer, declared, "You take over the part," and walked off the set. Contrived trantrum or not, the balloon had gone up.

Steve's agent was on the telephone at once warning him, "If you go on with this, you'll never work in Hollywood again." Steve reportedly stormed: "If I've got to give a phony performance, I'd sooner quit." Later he explained, "I knew if I left I'd be blackballed. But I couldn't take that kind of thing; my values were at stake." It was a good line, anyway, whether anybody actually believed him or not; yet in retrospect, it looks to have been a crazy risk, and there seems little doubt that for a time, when the producer refused to back down, Steve must have felt he had lost the hand. It is clear, too, that at one stage he supposedly toyed with the idea of going back and producing such dire performances that Four Star would have had no alternative but to cancel his contract. However, John Sturges, his close friend and the man who believed he had an immense future, gave him some brutally direct advice in words to this effect: either do the series as well as you can, or don't do it at all; either try to get released from your contract, or if you can't, then do your best. He had one other option: if those ideas won't work, then take up some other kind of work.

Steve, in fact, actually reached the point of telling his wife that if the blackball stuck and he was unable to get another part in Hollywood, he intended to sell out and try his luck somewhere else—and, as Sturges had advised, do something else. As days went by and he faced an impasse, he actually called up the local airline and booked tickets for himself and wife to, of all places, Australia. "I didn't really know what I was going to do," he says. "I was going to be a sheep farmer or something. I just knew I wanted to quit acting."

Before they could vanish into the outback, however—and the subject of lighting out for Australia is a recurring theme in Steve's life; it even crept into the script of *Junior Bonner* years later—the late Dick Powell, president of Four Star, the production company making the series for CBS, telephoned Steve and suggested urgently that they talk. At this time, Steve and Neile lived in a small and unpretentious house in one of the more modest areas of Hollywood. Powell, a star since the mid-thirties, was both wealthy and influential. However, despite the gulf in status, Powell and his wife, the actress June Allyson, called on the McQueens and as soon as they sat down, Powell said he wanted to hear Steve's side. Steve may have been almost ready for a compromise, but kept his sights high. He told Powell that difficulties had arisen not only because he felt that his integrity was at stake but also because the success of the series itself was at stake. To hammer home his point and rid Powell's mind of the suspicion that he was just making trouble in order to get out of his contract, Steve produced a notebook in which, from the start of the series, he had jotted down all his ideas for improving it. Powell, for his part, desperately wanted to end the impasse, and finally an agreement was reached that was to keep Steve, albeit reluctantly, with Four Star for another three years, enabling him to chalk up 117 installments altogether. In return for his word that he would put no more obstacles in the way of production and would go back to work immediately, Powell undertook to see that Steve's ideas regarding the show were adopted.

It was the first time that Steve had flexed his muscles, the first feeling of the sense of power that star status can bestow on an actor. If the arrangement forced him to soldier on for another few years, it was, at least, under conditions better suited to his temperament. From then on, in short, he became king and front charger around the lot of "Wanted—Dead or Alive." It was a "cool" situation, if still far from the "big brass ring" he saw lying just out of his reach.

Arriving in New York in 1950, following his discharge from the Marines and a stint as a taxi-mechanic in Washington, D.C., Steve had once again made for Greenwich Village, where he rented a cold-water apartment at nineteen dollars a month. He made no attempt

to contact his mother. For six years, apart from the brief interval
when he saw her after his discharge from the Junior Republic, he had
lived his own life without any assistance or interference from her.
In that time, of course, he had picked up many of the "lumps"
which were to mould his paradoxical and ambiguous character—which
means, among other things, a man whose triumph over adversity
constantly feeds a hefty egotism while simultaneously allowing him
to channel his natural energies into a sense of responsibility. When
Steve uses the word "responsibility," which he does often, he is
talking about several things. First, he is saying that he understands
that many people depend on him, that he is an industry in himself;
second, that the Hollywood entertainment business has been good
to him and he would like to show his gratitude; third, that his fame and
wealth now allow him to care about underdogs and the underprivileged
and that he must express this concern in actions and not only in words;
fourth, that he remains a symbol to a large number of people and particularly to young people who have come from backgrounds not so dissimilar from his own. He evidently does not, however, see himself
as a "symbol" in the glib, cynical sense in which the word has been
used by his various publicity agents, but as something objective,
simple, profound, realistic. "Somewhere, right now, there are kids
going through what I went through. Maybe if they know I survived,
they may find hope. I can't promise that they'll ever forget what's
happened to them. But if they hold out, they'll get through okay and
learn to live with bad memories—still learn to love."

Steve returned to a Greenwich Village, which, despite its seamy
nature and its poseurs and phonies, still had much to teach him.
Here he met aspiring novelists, musicians, painters, and philosophers.
"For the first time in my life I was exposed to music, culture, a little
kindness, a little sensitivity. It was a way of life where people talked
out their problems instead of punching you." Well, that could only be
an improvement. This time around, too, he appears to have been
determined to do something more constructive with his life. The first
time, to hear him tell it, he had simply "bummed" around, aimlessly
doing just enough odd jobs to pay for his food and hiring a bed for a
quarter per night unless he could find a girl willing to give him bed
space. He had tried being a bartender, making sandals in a crafts-

man's shop, working as a bag loader in the post office, working in the pottery department of a large store (where he lasted only one day), recapping car tires, and working as a dockhand in the New York docks. It had been tough going. At one stage, "I fell in with some bad guys, some hard people—and I even rolled drunks."

Once again, however, as with the first time around, life pressed its harsh realities against him, and he was soon back peddling his services anywhere they were acceptable. He tried being a truck driver's helper. Then he made artificial flowers in "a smelly little dark cellar" of a shop on Third Avenue, "but I couldn't make that scene at all." He resorted to that almost last resort, selling encyclopedias, door to door. "I felt like a shark going into those poor family houses and talking them into encyclopedias."

It was rough, and then it got a great deal rougher. At one point, when jobless, hungry and penniless, for example, he wandered into a drugstore in the Village and idly picked up a shower nozzle. He had it in his hand, he says, when the clerk came across and inquired if he had brought it back. Steve, without really thinking, said "yes" and, as he recalls, got $5.30 for it. "And I ate for two days on that. It happened by mistake, but I used the idea after that."

His pattern of life, it would seem, was not all that different from the "scene" still current in large urban centers where young people play about with their lives in a desperate effort to adjust circumstances to their needs and constantly find the two incompatible. They demand, perhaps with justification, a right to the pleasures and enjoyments of this world, yet they make it a condition of this demand that they should earn them "doing their own thing," which means refusing to work in factories or offices, primary sources of wealth in cities. In Steve's case, he seems to have found a partial solution in sharing with a group of friends; those who had money or work helped out those who temporarily had neither. Reminiscing about those days, Steve has said, "I've always been drawn to people I can trust and the kind of people I can trust are blood people—racers, seamen, poets, artists, fighters. Men who, when it gets down to the short strike, give blood. It's important to be able to trust a man. What often happens in Hollywood is that men come up to you, shake your hand, and smile, and you can't trust it. You can't read them; they're trying to get next to you for one reason or another; they're trying to sell their soul or yours. I beat down on that. Trust is different when you're broke. You're on the other end then, and the common commodity is sharing with other guys. We all shared a lot in the old days in New York.''

It is when he talks about such qualities as ''trust'' that Steve sometimes allows us an intimate glimpse of the kind of life he led in the early fifties when, as he says himself, he could so easily have wound up ''a hood.'' Trust, for instance, meant an Italian cook at ''Louis' restaurant, a guy named Sal, who kept putting me in for dinner.'' Steve laughs, ''I don't know why. If ever there was a guy nailed loser on his forehead, it was me.'' He would, from time to time, go into Louis' and tell Sal that he ''didn't have a dime but how about some veal and I'll pay you back the first job I get.'' Sal would exclaim, ''Ah, *desperado*!'' and would not only dish up the veal but spaghetti and French bread as well. Sal repeated the order daily until Steve finally managed to land a job somewhere, perhaps a few days driving a truck; then he would pay back the twenty dollars he owed. What impressed Steve then, as it still does, is how Sal trusted him. Years later, Steve brought Frank Sinatra and Peter Lawford into Louis' to taste Sal's ''great veal parmesan.'' Sal, ignoring the other two, then much better known than Steve, greeted him with a yell of delight, ''Ah, *desperado*!''

It was, of course, a desperate enough life; yet he was young enough and resilient enough and sharp enough to survive. In between jobs, he and some of his friends took ''holidays'' in Miami where they picked up pleasant, if inadequately paid, jobs as lifeguards or beach boys at a posh hotel. Back in the Village, he found another way of surviving—playing poker. Sometimes he managed to scoop up between $150-$200 a week, which eventually enabled him to get ''a pad'' of his own. Then, ''Man, I had the chicks comin' out of the woodwork, really flyin' in from all areas.''

All this time, as he says himself, he was still ''trying to get the scam on the human race,'' trying to find ''just where the hell'' he fitted in. He had changed though. If his life seemed aimless and purposeless it was no longer because he didn't care. ''I discovered there were no openings; then I decided to make one for myself. But that wasn't easy.'' He had brains, quick wits, great energy—

and whatever his experiences, whatever his environment, whatever kind of crowd he "bummed" around with—he says he had made up his mind about one thing: "I didn't want to be standing on a street corner when I was fifty without any money."

All easier said than done, of course. Under a congressional Bill of Rights for ex-members of the U.S. Armed Forces, however, he was eligible for a grant if he chose a career. "One career which crossed my mind was tile laying," he says. "I wasn't all that hooked on the idea but I heard these guys could earn as much as $3.50 an hour." However, he never quite got around to tile laying. Fortuitously, one of the "chicks" he was "shackin' up" with at the time was a drama student. She suggested that he become an actor; she could introduce him to Sanford Meisner who ran the Neighborhood Playhouse, an acting school.

"I didn't rush into things," says Steve. As Neile remarked some years later, "He was not exactly a pretty boy, and nobody believed he would ever become a successful actor. He was a far-out guy from Endsville," or, as he himself has said, "I sure don't get goose pimples when I look in the mirror. If my face were my fortune, I'd still be scammin' for nickels and dimes in Greenwich Village." His hesitancy was understandable. These were the years before Hollywood discovered the new cult of the anti-hero—the ugly, ordinary guy who played in lifelike dramas. It was still the era of pretty boys and schmaltzy romances. "I made a few inquiries," Steve explained, "and I learned that the Playhouse wasn't easy to get into and that the fees were high—it was full of students from wealthy families. I was figuring that that counted me out when I remembered that maybe the Bill of Rights could help me. Then I took stock of myself. I'd drifted around so much that I knew I'd have to start on the ground floor of any career I took up, so why not with acting? Anyway, one day I telephoned Meisner, mentioning the name of this chick. He gave me an appointment and I remember walking towards his office, telling myself it was a hundred to one against me having the talent to break through. But I also figured that here was my chance, and I had plenty of energy and ambition. A secretary showed me into Meisner's office. He shook hands and said, 'Mr. McQueen, pleased to meet you.' "

Meisner says that there was something about the young man that impressed him at once. "He was an ordinary personality. Like Marilyn Monroe, he was both tough and childlike, as if he'd been through everything but still preserving a certain innocence." If Meisner was perceptive enough to give him an audition and to accept him, few of his fellow students were particularly impressed. Steve, indeed, had to face a hard road, and it was a long while before his acting aspirations were taken seriously, even though Meisner felt that he had an instinctive feeling for the craft. Steve himself says, "I realized I had finally discovered somethin' that was easy for me."

Since his Marine days, Steve's behavior, if not his character and personality, had been changing. He had learned the lesson of "the basic disciplines." Now he began almost dramatically to develop that dynamic drive that was to lift him to the heights, that has led a friend to comment, "Steve always seems in a hurry." Years later, Steve recalled this as a period of his life when, since he had made up his mind where he was going, the dynamic side of his nature took over and he found himself hurrying to reach his goals. He "hurried" to get onto the stage; "hurried" to get married; "hurried" to become a success. Gone was any hint of shiftlessness or aimlessness. His bandwagon had begun to roll, and he had decided he was going to drive it as though it were a racing car.

He claims that Meisner was the first man in his life to make sense. Meisner assured him that if he stuck to a schedule of hard work, he would succeed as an actor: "If you'll stay with it, McQueen, you can make it." A fellow student remembers that Steve worked twice as hard as anyone else at the school. "When we had to do, say, five improvisations as a class assignment, Steve would come in with ten."

In retrospect, it was one of the happiest and most satisfying periods of Steve's life. The GI grant, of course, was inadequate to fully support him, but he found ways of supplementing his income. He had gotten into motorcycles by now, and partly supported himself by motorcycle racing. He says there was a "drag-strip on Long Island" where the winner's prize ranged from $25, through $50, to $100 a win. The cycles did more for him than that, of course; they gave him a release from the regimentation that work and the need to earn one's living imposed on him and from the claustrophobic atmosphere of life in the concrete jungle of New York. "All the room I needed for my freedom was the room for my hands on those little handlebars, and every once in a while a bug goes splash on yer forehead, know what I mean?"

He supplemented his income in other ways, too. The list of jobs he worked at makes one marvel at the ingenuity of a man who could find so many ways of "scammin' " a living. Yet it remained, apart from the grinding stint of trying to learn his craft as an actor, a relatively easy-come, easy-go sort of life, roaring around the Village on his bike, a blonde chick riding behind. In late 1952, for example, he was one of the regulars in the back room of the White Horse Tavern. This was usually a noisy, animated scene with Korean veterans hobnobbing with the vaguely artsy-craftsy people who gave the Village much of its ambience. Steve probably liked the company of the military men because he had been one himself. "They were a great bunch of guys," he says. "They knew how to live and wanted to make up for lost time." A Village resident who recalls those days says, "Everyone had a closeness and a camaraderie sprung up. Everybody got along well." Steve was one of the "swinging leaders" and "appeared to have a different chick hanging on to his waist every day as he roared around the Village on his motorcycle.

One night an old buddy from his Marine days, identified only as "Red," came through the Village and bumped into Steve in the back room of The White Horse. When in the Marines, Steve and "Red," a big, bluff guy, had apparently done a lot of skin diving together, and "Red" asked if Steve would like to have another go at it. Steve was always ready to move at an instant's notice and agreed. So the two men took off south for sunny Florida. In Miami, they hired a deep-sea fishing boat and skin-diving equipment and headed out into the Atlantic swell. "They figured on having the time of their lives," said one of Steve's Village friends.

It has been said of Steve that the one aspect of his character that sets him apart from all other Hollywood stars is his total honesty. He coolly defies most of the traditional conventions that have guided the conduct of stars. He hates lying or polishing the truth. He refuses to compromise, even refuses to cooperate if it does not suit him.

He refuses, it is said, with an almost frightening display of energy and fanaticism to be what he calls "a phony." When he first became prominent as Josh Randall, he almost drove the publicity men to hysteria by disregarding the "glamorous" image they sought to construct for him. He told a reporter at the time, "I'm a little embarrassed by my success. Most actors are a little troubled in the head. I'm not eager to be a member of that group, and I don't have enough vanity to imagine that I'm an exception. So I'll just play it by ear, and that's no joke because I can't hear out of one of them." The reporter was astounded and the publicity men aghast that Steve should admit to a physical defect that might easily undermine his appeal for women. "You just don't confess those things to the public," fumed one of his associates. "Sorry," Steve reportedly replied, "talk into my other ear. I can't hear you with this one." By the early 1970's, Steve's plight had become so serious that it was causing deep concern to his friends and associates. One ear was more or less useless and the other was also failing. Just how long he could stave off a real crisis no one but his medical advisers could say. Yet he has stubbornly refused to hide his affliction or to accept the medical options. Crinkling his face, he once snapped, "I ain't gonna wear a deaf aid for anyone." Then again, "It would take an Act of Congress to make me go under the knife."

Why a person should go deaf is a matter even medical science finds hard to establish. Many of Steve's friends believe his love of racing bikes and cars, with their ear-splitting din, is largely responsible—if not for the initial damage itself, at least for the worsening of his condition. However, great racing drivers I have known personally, such as Stirling Moss, the late Jim Clark, and Graham Hill, former world champion, had no perceptible difficulty with their hearing. Many of Steve's friends believe that it was the skin-diving trip to Miami that started the trouble, which was then aggravated by his noisy vehicles. Steve and Red, it seems, had a marvelous holiday. They went into the ocean looking for stingrays and any other interesting fish they could find. Steve, on his return to the Village, said that the colors were the most beautiful he had seen anywhere, that the coral formations and swarms of multicolored fish were magnificent. Occasionally they saw sharks but managed to keep away from them. They were equipped with spear guns but did not want to use them unless it became necessary; if they wounded a shark, a shoal of them would be on the spot within seconds, tearing and fighting at their wounded, bleeding fellow. Steve and Red made several dives and each time went deeper, with Steve eagerly chasing the fish down into the depths. Eventually, he went too far down for the equipment then available, and the water pressure and the pressure inside his body failed to equalize. As a result, he punctured his left eardrum, which subsequently has become almost totally useless. "Steve is such a hard, gritty guy that he didn't let it upset him at the time," says his old Village friend. "He told us later that he was just happy he didn't get the bends coming up from those depths."

Steve evidently made up his mind not to let the handicap affect either his career or his life—a decision for which he deserves full credit. Hollywood divides sharply over Steve. There are those who say simply, "He's the greatest"; and there are those who add, "the greatest bastard." Nobody so determined and uncompromising, of course, could fail to make enemies, and his extraordinary success alone would ensure him a large army of the envious. Yet it simply cannot be denied that he has fought and overcome handicaps that on any rational basis of expectation would appear insurmountable. His hearing became a handicap as early in his career as 1958, when he was playing Josh Randall; it was then he first discovered that *both* his ears had been affected. "For a long time it didn't slow him down at all," says a friend. "He's such a tough guy that he doesn't let physical barriers prevent him from doing what he wants."

His guts, determination, and tenacity were very much in evidence while he was still studying with Meisner. Although his fellow students were prepared to bet any odds that he was rapidly going nowhere, Steve took the air out of their tires by winning a scholarship to the Uta Hagen-Herbert Berghof Dramatic School in Manhattan. By this time he had already made his stage debut; he earned his first money as an actor when Meisner got him a part in a long-forgotten Yiddish play on Second Avenue. He had to deliver a single line a night, for which he earned forty dollars a week. As he admitted later, possibly with tongue in cheek, acting seemed an easy way to make money. "I thought it was a racket—no forty-hour week for me.

But now I'm working seventy-two hours a week—so there you go.''

He joined the Hagen-Berghof school in 1952 and studied there for two years. It was in the summer of that year that he made his real professional debut. This was at Fayetteville, New York, where a man called Paul Crabtree had established a loosely organized theater company to encourage new talent. Steve's part was a small one in *Peg O' My Heart*, starring Margaret O'Brien. He was anything but a sensation. Says Steve, ''I remember one of the other actors coming to me after the performance and saying, 'Steve, I want you to know that your performance was just embarrassing'.''

He managed, however, to gradually improve his technique and was certain he was on the right road when he auditioned for The Actor's Studio, run by Lee Strasberg, developer of The Method school of acting, and won a scholarship. It was a notable achievement, for out of 5,000 entries only five aspirants were chosen. Soon he would realize that he was on his way and had become known in theatrical circles on Broadway. ''I'd go to an audition and I'd find that they'd put me on the stage right away because so many other actors had talked about me,'' says Steve. One thing even his tuition at The Actor's Studio was unable to spoil—Steve's ability to be himself. He never picked up the sloppy diction and expressionless ''emoting'' that is an integral part of Method acting. ''Whatever he learned there, it doesn't show on him,'' said Jackie Gleason, who had found it difficult to work on *The Hustler* with Paul Newman, another graduate of the Method school. It was only a matter of time before Steve found himself in the national road company of *Time Out For Ginger*, starring the great light comedian of pre-war days, Melvyn Douglas; and then he was on Broadway, appearing first with Gary Merrill and Sam Jaffe in *The Gap*, before replacing the young Jewish actor, Ben Gazzara, in *A Hatful Of Rain*. His next role was with the Rochester Repertory Company in *Member of the Wedding*, which starred Ethel Waters. By 1954, he had established a solid background of credits on stage and TV, some of his roles involving portrayals of juvenile delinquents. His fourth TV role was a star part in the Studio One production of *The Shrivington Raiders*. Incredibly and against the longest of odds, he was on the road to success.

6.

NEILE ADAMS
TO STAGE CENTER

Neile Adams, the ex-Mrs. Steve McQueen, is a small, (5 feet, 2 inch) doe-eyed, dark-skinned girl born in the Philippines of an English father and a Spanish mother who, by an extraordinary coincidence, never knew her father, as Steve had never known his. Her parents were divorced while she was still only a baby, and she was reared by her mother. If Steve's upbringing was unfortunate, hers had an even more inauspicious beginning. As the Second World War swept over the Philippines, her father was killed and her earliest memories are of life in a Japanese internment camp. She said later that the lessons in survival she learned there helped her to cope with "the wild man I suddenly found in my life." The phrase sounds less mawkish when spoken, but at least it indicates the impact made when two persons from very different backgrounds, and with very different temperaments, are suddenly brought together.

She was brought up in what she has called "a conventional" manner— a portmanteau word clearly meaning that there was nothing abnormal about her upbringing; at least, after she had been released by the

63

Japanese. She did not go to reform school nor become a juvenile delinquent—did nothing that could be hailed as "colorful." Instead she attended a succession of convent schools: first, St. Alex School in the Philippines, then St. Joseph's in Hong Kong, and finally a convent in Greenwich, Connecticut. At the age of eighteen she saw the Broadway version of a musical comedy *The King and I* and decided she *had* to become a stage star. She went to a school run by the black dancer Katherine Dunham and within a year had progressed sufficiently to land a part in the musical *Kismet*. Her career prospered, to such good effect that within two years of her debut, she landed a part in another musical—*Pajama Game*. She enjoyed the sensation of being feted on Broadway and was invited to go to Hollywood to make a film. When every allowance is made for the hyperbole inherent in all show business chatter, it is clear that Miss Adams, solo, was doing very nicely, thank you. The last thought in her mind, she insists, was marriage. "All I was interested in was in getting out of the chorus and becoming a star—on Broadway and, if possible, Hollywood."

One night in June, 1956, escorted by Mark Rydell, a Broadway director, she entered Downey's, a theatrical restaurant. "As I walked past this table, I was aware of this character with the butch haircut, T-shirt, and jeans looking at me as though boring holes through me." Steve was eating spaghetti at the time with Ben Gazzara and another friend, and when he saw this chick in the tight toreador pants and knit sweater, quite instinctively, he got up from his seat, determined to join Rydell, whom he knew well, and the gorgeous lady. The gesture might have been more adroitly timed, for spaghetti and sauce tumbled into his lap. With an inconsequential air, Steve ignored the mess on his trousers and approached Rydell's table. Following a loquacious interchange with Rydell—which appears to have consisted of the one word "Hiya!"—Steve introduced himself to the lady. "If any other man had done this," says Neile, "I would have been annoyed. But I thought he was cute." The admiration was mutual, and Steve quickly invited the couple to join him at the table he shared with Gazzara. They agreed. At some stage during the subsequent proceedings, and before Neile and Rydell left the restaurant, Steve asked her for a date and she replied, "Why not?"

Steve McQueen as he appeared in *Bullitt* (1968) and (right) as he appeared early in his career.

Steve and Aneta Corseaut in *The Blob* (1958). Although critics faulted this science fiction film, they found Steve's performance both natural and dignified.

Never So Few (1959), the story of an epic World War II battle, won for Steve the admiration of Frank Sinatra. After the filming, Sinatra declared, "It's a good movie, kid, and it's all yours."

After seeing *The Magnificent Seven* (1960), one reporter hailed Steve as "the logical successor to Jimmy Dean."

Steve with his first wife, Neile Adams.

All that night and the early part of the following day, she waited for Steve to phone her. "But I should have known that such a crusty character as Steve would never telephone a girl for a date." That evening, however, as she walked up an alley towards the stage door, she heard a whistle. "It wasn't the kind that means 'Wow,' " she explained. "It was a look-around whistle." She turned and saw Steve. "Hi, baby," he said.

She invited him to join her in the dressing room while she made up for the show. When her call came he remarked, "I'll pick you up after the show," and "blew out."

He was waiting at the stage exit when the performance finished, goggles on his forehead and a BSA motorcycle parked at the curb. She dutifully climbed up behind him although she had never been on a motorcycle before and was more than a little scared. "Put your arms around me and hold tight!" She did as she was told, and then he kicked the starter, and with a tremendous *varoom* the bike sped away. Seconds later, they were in the middle of the Broadway traffic, weaving in and out and, as she puts it, "having a thrill a second."

Although director Robert Wise, who met Steve shortly after this episode, described him as "a kook with a beanie cap," he was by this time a proficient motorcyclist. He was a veteran of drag races on Long Island and other dirt tracks on the city outskirts; he had even raced the leather-jacketed youngsters who were his friends—and competitors—along the highways and streets of New York. He still recalls the machine he had in those days. "It was a beautiful bike, real trim and swift and handled very well. You could lay it all the way down." Like anyone who has driven a car or motorcycle, he had narrow escapes. "[One day] I was racin' this guy along the main highway [New York's West Side Highway] and we'd agreed to a course which took us down an exit ramp connecting with a minor road. I was in the lead and doing over a hundred. As I turned off, I looked around to see how far ahead I was of the other guy. When I looked in front again, I saw that for some reason there was a traffic jam at the bottom of the ramp. There was no use getting scared. I threw my weight on the bike and hit the brakes as hard as hell. I saw the back of a big stationary truck looming right ahead. I skidded up to it with the tires screeching and just tapped the back bumper. If I'd reacted a split second slower, I'd have been playin' a harp.''

To Neile, however, it would seem that characters who fling motor-cycles or cars around in an abandoned fashion (she had never been to Paris, Rome or even London, naturally) were wild and unimaginably crazy people. ''Do you always race around town like this?'' she once asked him.

By the end of the ride Neile ''realized that from out of nowhere there was now a wild man in my life and there was nothing I could do about it. I'm glad I didn't.'' Steve continued to call for her at night after each performance and also took her out on afternoons and Sundays. ''He introduced me to a new style of life,'' she says. Apart from sheer chemistry, they appeared to have very little in common; indeed, their lifestyles and experiences were poles apart. ''I'd never been exposed to this type of man. I'd been brought up in convents.'' Steve says, ''I showed her a way of life she never knew—the Village, parties, not getting dressed up, no makeup, and going on long rides on the bike up into the hills. Man, it was real romantic.''

Initially, though, she was not all that taken with him—natural enough considering her rather gentle and devout upbringing contrasted to his tough, street-smart background. She liked him all right, but ''at first I resented his attitude. I don't know why, but I couldn't take his point of view. To him, there was only one purpose in life—conquest. It didn't matter whether the object was a pinball machine or a girl. In some ways he was right.'' ''Nobody trusts anyone,'' he used to say. ''or why do they put *tilt* on a pinball machine?''

He was, as she says, a ''rough kook,'' and she still laughs when she recalls the first time she introduced him to her mother. He had been playing baseball and Neile had been rehearsing at the theater. Her mother was there. Steve, dressed in ''jeans, sneakers, and T-shirt,'' dropped by. Although her mother knew of Steve's existence, she had no idea of the kind of rough diamond he really was. ''She was so shocked, so disillusioned, it was funny. I felt for her. Steve came from a different world.''

Neile herself found it difficult continually adjusting to the unpre-dictable, almost savage, moods of her new boyfriend. It took her a little time to grasp that he was ''inwardly an insecure young man still smarting from the hurts of his childhood.'' She first began to understand him one warm and sunny spring afternoon while they were walking in Central Park. Steve ''was glaring around at everybody as usual, fully expecting a perfect stranger to turn on us suddenly.''

She asked him, ''Don't you like spring? Don't you like the trees coming out, the air warm and gentle, the sun high in the sky? Doesn't it make you feel good? Doesn't it make you feel that life has some promise of love and hope for you, for me—for everyone?''

''Nah,'' replied Steve shortly, ''that jazz is for women and children.''

She looked incredulous, and Steve reconsidered. ''What do you mean, 'love and hope'? I don't get you.''

Neile claims that this remark brought tears to her eyes. ''I guess it was at that instant that I really understood what made Steve the way he is. Because for the first time I saw innocence in his eyes and heard it in his voice. You see, he didn't really know what love was. And hope was something he dismissed as a trick by others to soften him up. He was so tough, so ready to tear the world apart at the slightest provocation, so sure that life was one long dogfight. Yet for all the ugliness that smeared his life, he was an innocent man. He had never known the meaning of love and hope. It's what I saw at that instant that made me cry. He didn't know about love and hope because no one had ever loved him. No one had ever given him hope.''

The affair began as a loose relationship without any idea that it might end in marriage. ''My goal in life at that time was to become a big star,'' say Neile. ''He wanted to become a star, too, although his chances didn't look too bright then. We decided not to marry but to go steady. Even so, my mother tried to convince me that I ought to go out with other young men.'' Steve says he embarked on the affair on the clear understanding that he was not the marrying kind. ''All I wanted to do was make it with her, you know'' he said much later. ''That's the way it had always been with other dolls, and the way I was thinking then, I couldn't see any other reason for a guy and a dame to get together.''

His contempt for concepts such as love and marriage was such, indeed, that one day Neile bolted from him in tears and refused to speak to him again for three days. Steve says he ''suffered'' and they made it up again. Despite his intransigence, Neile found that he ''made me feel good. He was honest, moral, and very protective. And gentle. Always gentle, except when we had fights, and we had marvelous fights—oh, always about little things.'' Marriage, of course, *had* crossed her mind, if not Steve's. ''Actually we had nothing in common personality-wise.'' Yet there it was; he seemed special.

Emotionally, of course, they were closer than either imagined. She, too, as already observed, had never known a father. At one stage in her life, her mother had sent her away from the Far East to boarding school in the United States, ''where I, too, felt left out.'' She showed Steve the long scar on her left leg where a piece of Japanese shrapnel had ripped it and he had murmured, ''poor kid,'' and called her ''spunky.'' She felt that both ''he and I hungered for the same thing— someone to love and be loved by, and never to feel left out again.'' Nonetheless, everybody thought she was ''crazy'' even to contemplate tying up her future with his. She had few illusions, actually, having heard him expound his philosophy: ''I live for myself and I answer to nobody and I'm not trying to sound pompous or anything like that, but I live for myself and I feel that I have no obligation to answer to anybody for anything.''

The truth was that neither was in a position to contemplate marriage, even without the complicating factors. Her star was in the ascendant and it was now time to press ahead, not to get involved in marriage. She recognized, of course, that Steve had a special, if somewhat indeterminate, talent (particularly after watching him in a charity performance of *A Hatful of Rain*), and that his ambitions were not all that far-fetched. ''He wasn't right for the part, actually, that of a dope addict; he was too young for it. But he *had* something. No doubt about it.'' Still, as yet, he was no more than a struggling actor.

The crunch, as they say, came when Robert Wise, who later directed Steve in his first epic, *The Sand Pebbles*, offered Neile a screen test and she decided to quit *Pajama Game* and fly to Hollywood. Steve's play closed on October 13, 1956, just as she was ready to leave. He was off on a brief trip to Cuba—going along with ''a coupla buddies'' and the faithful motorcycle—and he would like her to come along too. ''No thank you,'' she replied. The idea of an impromptu trip to Cuba, just slipping on a pair of jeans and taking off without even a suitcase, was not her style.

"She didn't know me very well," explains Steve. "She didn't exactly understand the sudden urge to do something. She got a little hacked at me for that."

Neile eventually returned from her Hollywood test to find a cable from Cuba. Steve was in a fix having run out of money. Could she send some? She cabled back saying no and telling him to come home. He was back in New York within a few days, having sold most of the special equipment on his bike to pay his fare. He was scarcely back when she received a cable from Hollywood telling her that her test had been OK and that Robert Wise had cast her in *This Could Be the Night*.

She was staying in a small motel just across the road from the MGM studios when, three days after her arrival in Hollywood, the telephone rang. When she answered it, it was Steve, asking her to marry him. In a condition halfway between surprise and shock, she said yes, adding jokingly, "I just can't turn anybody down." She has explained, "Perhaps if we'd been older we wouldn't have rushed it so quickly. But we loved each other, and if we hadn't got together at that point, it could all have petered out. Our careers were taking us in opposite directions, and we didn't want to lose each other." Steve's comment was, "The last thing I wanted to do was fall in love with any broad, but one morning I woke up and found out that without Neile nothing at all seemed worth a damn." His impetuosity was typical of his new, driving personality—the man in a hurry that was to become so familiar to all his new friends and associates. There was a furious dynamo within him, and it would be years before he learned to control its tempo.

Neile herself had not only second, but apparent third and fourth thoughts about the whole idea before Steve finally arrived in Los Angeles in November, 1956. On her way to the airport she even rehearsed a little speech to herself. The tenor was: "Steve, I do love you and it's been a great three months, but let's keep it the way it is." She knew him too well now. Was it really conceivable that this rough diamond of a man could settle down to the shackles and responsibilities of marriage? She thought not. Then as the New York plane rolled into its parking bay and the cabin door opened, she caught sight of him standing in the doorway, a lithe figure in jeans and T-shirt, carrying a duffelbag. He came running across the runway, grabbed her and kissed her before jabbing an engagement ring on her finger.

"Baby, we're getting married at San Juan Capistrano, the Mission, you know, the swallows and all." Neile's little speech died on her lips; she realized she was being swept off her feet by Steve in one of his most dynamic, irresistible moods. Protest, she realized, would be useless—even if she could have gotten the words out. That evening, after she had finished at the studio, they left Hollywood together in a rented car. Steve, as usual, "drove like crazy." They halted for a bite to eat, then drove on down the California coast. Whether it was because of pre-wedding nerves or the sheer frightening energy and ruthlessness of purpose that she could now descry in Steve, she was "so nervous I didn't want to sit next to him. I stayed way over, next to the door. I kept looking at him as if he were a stranger. I was terrified. Did I even know him, this wild, moody man?"

Eventually they reached Capistrano Mission—only to be told by the nun in charge that a church wedding there was impossible. Even if they were Catholics—Steve had been baptized a Christian and probably was prepared to embrace Zen Buddhism if it would help him get married—they had to have letters from their own parish priests guaranteeing that there were no impediments to the marriage, and banns would also have to be published. Steve's reaction scarcely does him credit. A man who had now conditioned himself to crash through any barrier to get his own way and who had always hated rules and authority anyway, he gave full vent to his frustrations. He broke into what the uncharitable might call a tantrum. "Steve was just wild," said Neile, "ranting and storming around and then threatening to 'live in sin.' " The little nun, who had probably never had to face such a tornado of a man in such a mood "was really shook up" and pleaded anxiously, "Oh, don't do that." Yet she was unable to help. In an apparent attempt to get rid of the problem, however, she suggested they try San Clemente, a little farther on, an odd suggestion in its way as Catholic practice would be no different there. Steve's behavior had been so dreadful that when they got back into the car, Neile says she tried to sit even farther away from him. One has to guess at her feelings as she curled herself into the corner of her seat and Steve, the speedometer reaching 80—85 miles per hour, went "honkin' " through villages, working out his anger and frustration in speed and the sound of the horn. As daylight waned he continued to drive furiously. Inevitably, something had to give, and it gave suddenly in the shape of two motorcycle cops. Then Steve had the most extraordinary slice of luck. "Look, we only want to get married," he told the cops. To his astonishment this touched some romantic chord (obviously the cops had seen too many grade B movies). One cop was actually from San Clemente and on hearing the tale, telephoned the Lutheran pastor there and explained the position. The Lutheran ministry being rather more flexible in such matters than the Catholic, the minister opened his door to the couple at midnight and married them with the two state troopers as witnesses. The scene had all the makings of one of those thirties film scripts starring Claudette Colbert.

The ceremony produced an astonishing change in both of them. Steve's anger and frustration at once vanished to be replaced by an apparent awareness that he had given up the rootless, hobo-like "scam" of an existence that was all he had known since he was fourteen. He even glanced at Neile as though seeing her for the first time. Then he showed signs of the traditional nervousness. Neile, for her part, once they had climbed back into the car, reminded herself "this is my husband," and forsaking her spot by the door, snuggled close to him. Neither appears to have really relaxed until they reached the Mexican border where it occurred to Steve that he ought to celebrate the occasion. So he pulled up at the first Mexican village they came to and bought firecrackers. Then, while the car was being filled up with gas, he went round the back of the filling station and let off the fireworks, throwing a few of them over a high wall. This was at one o'clock in the morning, and although to both Steve and Neile it seemed very funny, it was obviously not so comical to a man who came dashing from his house, clad only in pajamas, who complained that a firecracker had landed in his bedroom. Steve apologized, explaining that they were just married; then he drove away until they came to a lonely beach where it was safe to let off the rest of the fireworks.

He was a man of oscillating moods, of a totally unpredictable temperament, however, and years later Neile could recall that his first words to her the following morning were, "Don't talk to me until after breakfast." Right up to the collapse of their marriage in 1972, she frequently had to treat and humor him almost like a child. He remained changeable and moody; at one moment apparently savagely frustrated or impatient, the next gentle, protective, loving; then again displaying a wild streak that could be only assuaged by physical action.

Marriage, in a sense, was to prove more beneficial to Steve than to Neile; for her part it would bring sacrifices, in particular the temporary cessation of her career. Among other sacrifices, she gave up a chance to play the lead in the Broadway production of *West Side Story*. For Steve it was a coming of age; one can date his growing up from that November evening when he and Neile exchanged vows that were to last for fifteen years—an eternity by Hollywood standards. He has said himself, "There's a funny feeling a guy gets when it's time to marry, and I felt this very strongly. I felt a terrible drive to succeed. I learned a great responsibility towards myself. I think my wife was responsible for that. It wasn't something I had basically. It was something that happened because I had somebody to take care of. She really shaped me up good. I was a kind of taker—and she a full giver."

They remained in Hollywood until Neile had finished her picture. Steve himself landed a small part (so small his name does not appear in any lists of credits) in a picture called *Somebody Up There Likes Me*, starring Paul Newman and directed by Robert Wise who later became one of his best friends. Then they drove back across country to New York where Neile made a TV appearance. On their first weekend back in Manhattan, Steve suddenly announced, "OK, this is Sunday. We're going on a picnic." It sounded delightful, but she should have known better. They climbed aboard the faithful BSA and after crossing the Washington Bridge into New Jersey, headed for the hills, finally halting beside a river. There they had their picnic, but with a whole bunch of Steve's motorcycling buddies. Worse was to follow. As they rode back towards New York, Steve's buddies opened up their throttles, and soon the whole crowd was roaring breakneck down the hillsides and along the highways. It never seems to

have occurred to Steve—then or during all the years of their marriage—
that many women are terrified by speed.

The marriage, in fact, got off to a bad start, although it was neither's
fault. Neile, prior to marriage, had signed a contract to appear at
the Tropicana, a Las Vegas nightclub. Even had Steve been earning
enough to keep them both—which he was not—she would still have had
to fulfill it. "It was the one and only terrible period of our marriage,"
Neile has said. "Steve used to fly in from New York every other
weekend. And when he did get there, I was working. Then he'd be
gone again and we'd talk by phone and fight constantly." It was two
more years before Steve's career had begun to run sufficiently
smoothly for her to give up work. It was a miserable time. "We
were so far apart, and Steve just didn't feel secure. At that time
he was probably making about five thousand dollars a year, and I
was earning over thirty-five thousand. It didn't bother me. I knew
he would eventually take over, no question about that. And I never
cared about money, anyhow. I never saved any and we were just
sharing. But it didn't set well with him. He's not the type; he just
can't let a wife support him. And he didn't want me alone in Las
Vegas without him. And his career hadn't yet begun to move into
high gear."

The smallest incident was enough to make him "fit to be tied."
One weekend he bought a second-hand car and taught Neile to drive.
When he went back to New York, she took the car out at nights and
drove around the back streets of Las Vegas, practicing. When confident enough, she took a driving test. Fortunately for her, the ex-
aminer had seen her show at the Tropicana and although "I did absolutely everything wrong," he gave her a license. Delightedly, she
took the car out and drove up the Strip at speeds between 70-80 miles
per hour—"just like Steve." One night, however, as she drove up a
back street toward the Tropicana, she took a turn too fast and skidded. The car shot right into a second-hand car lot. "I took two Lincolns with me, skidded, spun, and slammed into a pole." The accident
occurred forty minutes before she was due on stage, and she was
in a state of shock throughout the performance; some of the shock,
she admitted, was due to the thought of having to tell Steve what
had happened when he called after the show.

"I had a little accident with the car. I bumped a fender," she told him over the telephone.

The passionate lover of cars and all things mechanical at the other end barked furiously, "What do you *mean*—bumped a fender?"

"Well, I nicked two Lincolns." According to Neile, "he was screaming."

She admits that at this period, she was genuinely frightened that the marriage could never succeed. She said she tried to tell herself that there was nothing either of them could do about it. She was making more money than he; that was clearly at the root of the problem. Yet what was the answer?

It cost $1,200 to fix the car, and Steve was so angry that for two whole weeks he did not telephone her. Then he broke silence. Not with a phone call, but with a letter—an unusual thing for him because he hates writing anything. He covered two sides of a sheet of paper with handwriting—how much she meant to him, how much the marriage meant to him, how "groovin' " it was going to be. "I like you, baby," he wrote. "Love is one thing, but I like you very much. You're part lover, part friend, part mother, part sister, above all, we're pals." If not exactly Hemingway, it was at least explicit and sincere.

By 1958, the McQueens' marriage and lifestyle had settled down to an even tempo. Neile quit the Tropicana in February that year, and she and Steve rented a small house in North Hollywood where she started cooking. "He won't let anyone cook for him but me, which is flattering but sometimes an awful bore, although he likes simple food," she once explained. She did one show with crooner Eddie Fisher, ex-husband of Elizabeth Taylor, and played opposite that great craftsman of the pre-war Hollywood era, Paul Muni, in a production called *Grand Hotel*. She turned down, as already mentioned, an offer to play in *West Side Story* on Broadway. Looking back on that decision, she has said, "I had something better—my husband, the most exciting man I know." And while the marriage lasted, she never admitted to any regrets, although she may well entertain them today. However, she had probably decided that if the marriage were ever to succeed she had no choice but to play the traditional wifely role—attend to the needs of her husband and, when they came along, to her children.

Steve showed her the many other facets of his nature. The man who, for all his trendy image and his harsh insistence that he lived only for today, could not—and apparently did not want to—escape his past. She found him a man who wanted to look back over his shoulder and see it the way it had been. In the first year of their marriage, he brought her to the farm at Slater, from which she came away convinced that he was basically "a very religious man, period" and that there was even something Puritan in him. Later on, back in Los Angeles, they searched around the Silver Lake area until an elated Steve finally found the house he had lived in as a youngster. This particular quest ended in a comic anticlimax, though. Steve knocked on the door and when it was opened, told the man, "I used to live here." He got the reply, "So what?"

He was still a comparative unknown, of course, although his career was gaining momentum. In 1957, under the name Steven McQueen, he played a leading role in a rubbishy film melodrama called *Never Love a Stranger* based on a story by that master of epic balderdash, Harold Robbins. The star was John Drew Barrymore, son of the Great Profile of silent days, John Barrymore. The story hardly bears thinking about; young Barrymore, cast as Frankie Kane, is brought up in a Catholic orphanage and befriends Martin Cabell, played by Steve, a Jewish law student whose sister Julie becomes Frankie's sweetheart. At sixteen, Frankie learns that he is himself Jewish and therefore has to be moved to a Jewish home. That prospect proves so awful that he runs away—and goes bad. Years later, he returns to the district and gets involved with a crime syndicate that his old pal Martin, now assistant district attorney, has pledged to clean up. Frankie, however, bumps into Julie again and, finding he still loves her, decides to help the straight-shooting Steve smash the syndicate. The climax arrives when Frankie sacrifices his own life to save a Jewish gangster who has been put on the spot. The story ends in a sea of bathos with Julie asking a Catholic orphanage to take in herself and the baby son she has had by Frankie.

The critics, with remarkable self-control, dismissed this effusion as "confused and episodic," a melodrama with "a dash of everything—crime, anti-Semitism, religion, sentimentality, beatings-up, sex, pseudo-psychology and mixed-up youth.'' It was a rare feast that Steve, for one, would be happy to excise from the records.

While Neile was still working in Las Vegas, Steve was on location in St. Louis, the city from which one of his grandfathers had come. This time, he had a part in an amateurish, low-budget film called *The Great St. Louis Bank Robbery,* a documentary-type reconstruction of an actual bank robbery that had once taken place in the city. Steve played the part of a weak youth, a former college football player, who agrees to drive the getaway car but who is forced to surrender after a teller sounds the alarm and the raiders are trapped by police armed with teargas. Despite the small budget, the critics found it a patchily brilliant film and Steve gained good notices, one writer relievedly noting, ''He played with a distinction owing nothing to Method mannerisms.'' Steve, even at this early date, was clearly his own man, confident enough to project himself and his own ideas and refusing to be inhibited by anything he might have picked up at the Actors' Studio.

That same year, still under the name Steven McQueen, he played a leading role in a sci-fi effort called *The Blob,* another movie he would be happy to forget. In this he played a teenager called Steve who, with a girl called Jane, attempts to persuade a community that it is threatened by a Blob of gelatinous mass that consumes people. The Blob can squeeze under doors, indeed, go anywhere water can flow. In one instance, it attaches itself to an old man's hand, spreads up his arm, and finally eats him. Eventually it storms a whole cinema and creates panic before flopping down on top of a restaurant inside which Steve and Jane find themselves trapped. By chance Steve finds that the Blob hates cold, so the police turn every available carbon dioxide fire extinguisher on the Blob, finally incapacitating it, though not killing it. It is then dumped in the Arctic wastes, from whence, presumably, if we ever suffer a climatic change, it will return again to menace us all. Critics found the special effects ''splendidly contrived'' but found the Blob's efforts to swallow an entire restaurant ''beyond conviction.'' Steve's performance was hailed as both natural and dignified, and although the film had its ludicrous side, his participation did his career no harm.

Unknown to him, however, even as he worked in these essentially grade B movie roles, events in another part of Hollywood were taking place that were to raise him from relative obscurity to national fame. Televiewers would shortly be tuning in regularly to a pouty-lipped blond young man, equipped with a southern drawl, called Josh Randall, bounty hunter.

7

A Star's Beginnings

THE two men primarily responsible for the upswing in Steve's fortunes were TV producer Vincent Fennelly and an agent, Abe Lastfogel, head of the giant William Morris agency. Abe had signed up Steve when he first turned up in Hollywood. Shrewd though Abe was—and people claimed he was the shrewdest in the business— it only gradually dawned on him that he had unearthed a gold mine in Steve McQueen. Steve's career is remarkable in several respects, none more so than the fact that he was never subjected to the big build-up, the thunderous clashing of the publicity drums. His success was achieved by the purest of soft-sells. Indeed, he can justifiably claim that he did it basically all by himself.

He was probably very lucky. Had his future depended on the old Hollywood establishment where a handful of mogul-like figures, sitting behind enormous desks, controlled the destinies of the great studios, his personality might easily have escaped the net; pretty boys were what pulled in the public, according to the text handed down by L.B. Mayer, Cecil B. deMille, and the rest; and ex-hoboes and other bums were not allowed in through the studio gates, on principle. Television, however, had brought the seemingly monolithic structure of the studio system crashing down. And it was TV that made Steve.

Fennelly, an executive producer of a TV series called *Trackdown*, began around 1957 toying with ideas to replace it. In his quest for a successor, he decided to build one episode around a bounty hunter—a man who, in the Old West, was paid a reward for every outlaw he captured or killed. Fennelly's idea was to make this a "pilot." Abe heard about Fennelly's plans and persuaded him to test Steve for the part. Steve himself was said to be at first only mildly interested in the idea, for he had his sights apparently set mainly on feature films where the big money lay. Fennelly, however, sent along a script and Steve spotted the potential. "The character wasn't really developed much, and the inner stuff wasn't showing yet," he said, yet he knew it could click. He therefore tested for the role and got it. "I picked him because he was a little guy," explained Fennelly. "You know, a bounty hunter is a sort of underdog. Everyone's against him except the audience. And McQueen was an offbeat guy. He wasn't the best-looking guy in the world, but he had a nice kind of animal instinct. He could be nice but with some hint of menace underneath." The pilot was accepted and the series, sold to CBS as "Wanted—Dead or Alive," soon proved among the most popular programs on American television.

On the surface, it seems an unlikely position from which to project oneself to star status. A bounty hunter is an unsympathetic character, a man who hunts down and kills a criminal simply for money. Steve succeeded, however, in the words of one critic, in making Randall "both believable and sympathetic without resorting either to spurious sentiment or showy heroics." What viewers saw was a man doing a sordid, unglamorized job as best he could and without fuss, in order to survive himself. It had the smack of reality.

Yet if Josh Randall performed his mean function without fuss, it was soon apparent around the Four Star set following Steve's *rapprochement* with Powell that there was nearly always a fuss when Steve was around. One of the show's directors tactfully explained, "He's an itchy guy. Things have to be done his way." Hilliard Elkins, Steve's personal manager, tried to explain away what many considered

Steve's arrogance by announcing, ''Steve has a chip on his shoulder. He's been pushed around so much in his life that it's instinctive with him to push back, sometimes when nobody's even pushed him yet.''

Following his pact with Powell, Steve could wallow in a supreme new luxury—the exercise of power. If he were not titular boss around the Four Star set, he now knew he was the effective boss; when the occasion arose, he was prepared to prove the point. By normal standards, perhaps, his behavior *was* objectionable. Surging ambition, drive and determination, a certain selfishness, a measure of arrogance and vanity—all qualities most of us possess but generally manage to keep under control—suddenly surfaced in Steve's personality. Viewed for themselves, such qualities are never likeable, even if they are the instruments that normally make men successful. But nice guys don't win ball games. And Steve, visions of a bright future already opening before him, seemed determined to win the ball game.

Having taken John Sturges's advice, he set about interpreting the Josh Randall character with a dedication worthy of a nobler cause. Seen in context, he was right. Churning out episodes of a TV Western may appear a trivial, even pointless, project to many people—if one ignores the fact that they make money and provide harmless entertainment. It is not the end product itself, however, that matters. Steve's job might not bear comparison with that of a Muslim craftsman laying tiles on the roof of the Taj Mahal, yet he brought to his work a similar all-consuming dedication; he was doing ''the best he could.'' He had, in fact, come to feel a personal responsibility for the series far beyond that usually assumed by actors who remain, by and large, puppets in the hands of writers, producers and directors. He was prepared to argue points with colleagues—the men who were, in fact, responsible for creating the story itself, as well as the scenes and dialogue which he was being merely asked to transform into visual terms. As a critic acidly remarked, this ''did not always endear him to those gentlemen.'' Steve's answer to the charges was brusque but honest, ''I'm not out to win any popularity contest. I'm out to get a job done. I don't care whether Four Star burns down, but as long as I'm with the show, I'll do the best I know how.''

Even those who could scarcely conceal their dislike of him had to admit that his enthusiasm for the job ameliorated the worst aspects of his behavior. Steve could say, "Everybody is catching this enthusiasm, and that's what I want"—which meant tearing pages from the script and having them rewritten on the spot. It also meant allowing a cameraman to butt in with a suggestion about a different camera angle or someone else to come up with the bright idea, "Hey, let's change those lines." Improvisation—or as Steve would say, "improvement"—and enthusiasm became the keynotes. Steve himself often usurped the director's function and shouted at a fellow actor, "Hey, play it this way, man." He had to admit: "A mistake I have made is sometimes to forget the dignity of my directors." He had often noted "a funny look" on a director's face when he did it, "So I'll go over and say I'm sorry. I mean, I wouldn't like it done to me." Apologies or not, however, life with Steve was merry hell.

Ed Adamson, scriptwriter and one of the producers on the show, was perhaps the person who suffered most. They clashed frequently and bitterly, although Adamson tactfully dismissed the rows: "Steve isn't argumentative arbitrarily. Nobody would know more about Josh Randall than Steve. He knows exactly what Randall would do and what he wouldn't do. That doesn't mean I like it any better, but I do have respect for Steve. And when I look at the finished product, I love him. Many times I think he's wonderful, and that's hard for me to say some days."

Josh Randall and the TV series in which he appeared have long since disappeared into the rubbish bin of old programs, and even a cursory examination of them is valid only insofar as it demonstrates how Steve's mind must have worked in carrying out his job, in successfully creating a credible character. While still engaged on the series, he explained, "I try to think what Randall would do in a situation and I also try to put in some of my own ingredients—what I would do." Even at this relatively early stage of his career, he seemed obsessed with realism, credibility, integrity. He knew a bounty hunter could never hope to live long if he disregarded the odds against him. "If three guys came down the street," Steve said, and told Josh to get out of town, "then he would git." A bounty hunter, also, would be constantly on the move, a loner, and would be responsible to no one but himself. He would also enjoy danger. "He'd be a little thrill-happy."

Consciously or not, Steve was probably talking about himself, not the fictional character he was portraying; for in real life, as he admitted, "I'm not going to fight a guy who's eight feet tall or shoot it out with Billy the Kid or John Dillinger. I'd say, 'Look, let's talk this over.'" On the other hand, "If somebody pushes me so far that I don't have anywhere to go, I'm going to fight with him, and I'm going to get him anyway I can. If I rip his ear off or put his eye out, that's the ball game. I don't play around. I want to win."

There is every reason to suppose that Steve, who picked up much of his philosophy from street gangs, has always meant exactly what he says. To prove his point in regard to this particular claim, for example, he mentioned an incident from his days in the Marines. "I remember once there were these two guys who always stuck together. One kept provoking me, and one day we had a real argument; but his friend was standing there, so I bowed out. But I got him alone the next day. I waited for him in the toilet, and I said, 'Hey you,' and he turned around, and I punched him and kicked hell out of him. And the other guy never bothered me. I made my point." He could also get under the skin of the Randall character perhaps better than anyone else because "I'm essentially a loner myself. I was always alone, man. I mean, I dug being alone." Yet he insisted that despite the tough and rugged image of himself that he was projecting, he was a pacifist. "I don't like fighting. I try to talk my way out of it if I can."

Still, for a man who protested his pacifist nature so loudly, Steve had an uncanny knack of arousing hackles with consummate ease. He tried to explain his competitiveness: "I love my craft. I swing with what I'm doing, and I'm still learning. Any actor who works on a TV show and just takes home the money every week is crazy. I mean, this is a great opportunity to learn your craft. Emotionally it's important to me to be a good actor. I don't want to be second best." The truth is he had learned that the prizes went to the best competitors, and from his street days, he no doubt knew exactly what was involved in surviving. If it meant trampling on toes, it meant trampling on toes—provided, of course, they were always someone else's.

John Sturges is a very large man with the build of a prime heavyweight and is, by and large, one of the supreme practitioners of the craft of film directing. He is also a man with a robust lust for life who can enjoy a night out as well as anyone and, in his own right, once established an interesting reputation as "a hell-raiser." From the beginning, he and Steve found they had an affinity for each other. For a while, if Steve had a bosom chum of any kind within the film industry, it was John Sturges. Sturges, for his part, had his eye on the blond, bullet-headed young man from the first moment he saw him in an early episode of "Wanted—Dead or Alive." Yet Steve's big chance came about totally by chance—Sturges did not plan it.

Sinatra, then at the peak of his popularity, had been signed by Sturges to play in *Never So Few*, a story of an epic fight between 600 Burmese Kachin guerillas and 40,000 Japanese during World War II—a story based on a novel by Tom Chamales. This, of course, was the heyday of the little group of actors in Hollywood known as The Clan, all close personal friends of Sinatra: Dean Martin, Peter Lawford, and Sammy Davis, Jr. Initially, both Lawford and Davis had supporting roles; but before the film could go into production, there was a rift in The Clan, and Davis was out. A replacement had to be found, and Sturges picked Steve.

Critics found that Millard Kaufman's script did scant justice to Chamales' central theme—the effects of responsibility of command in a guerilla campaign where there are no rules. In particular, the ramifications of Sinatra's decision (as an American leader of the guerrilla band who finds that some of his putative Allies, the soldiers of Chiang Kai-shek, had massacred a whole American convoy simply for loot) to conduct a reprisal raid into China, which involves the execution of all Chinese prisoners, is never properly explored. Yet there were good things in the film. Gina Lollobrigida's glowing beauty overcame the obstacle of the traditional Hollywood glamorization process. Sturges included some magnificent frames of the Himalayas and other beautiful scenes. Sinatra gave a creditable performance although the old pro, Brian Donlevy, stole most of his thunder in the second half of the film. Nor was Kaufman's script all bad. He produced some dialogue on which Steve, as Bill Ringa, erected a cameo performance that relieved much of the overall tedium of the film. Seen in retrospect, the film did nothing to improve Sinatra's standing; it showed Lollobrigida, for all her beauty, failing to make the transition from Rome to Burma; and Lawford as competent, if colorless. Kaufman, by and large, laid an egg; Sturges did nothing a lesser director could not have accomplished; and only Donlevy could boast that he had risen above the general level of mediocrity. Donlevy, that is, and Steve.

Steve knew all about Sinatra's reputation—that he was a "difficult hombre" and as vain and temperamental as they come in Hollywood. "But when I first met Frank, we sort of found ourselves on the same wavelength—we dug one another. We're like minds; we're both children emotionally." He had, in fact, accepted Sturges's invitation with some misgivings simply because Sinatra was the star. Steve probably foresaw a tremendous collision. As a friend of his once put it, "A lifetime largely spent in single-handed combat against a hostile world has taught him to expect thorns even in the rosiest prospects—and he's been rarely surprised."

This time the surprise was, at least, pleasant. Steve, apparently determined to seize his chance, had decided to take no risks. One morning, he sat down in the canvas chair provided, determined to run over his script and soak himself in his part while waiting for the cameras to be set up. While he was deep in concentration, Sinatra and Lawford "sneaked up behind me and put a lighted firecracker in one of the loops of my gun belt, and the thing blew up and shot me about three feet in the air." Well, it was a good joke and everybody enjoyed it, with the possible exception of Steve. It was, in an immature way, a character test, and Steve had two options. He could grin sheepishly and gracefully accept the role of fall-guy. Or he could do something about it, something that would set him up as a joker himself. Yet Sinatra was Sinatra—and heap big medicine in the world of show-biz. He might be grinning all over his bashed-up Vesuvius of a face just at the moment; yet any retaliation might be considered *lèse majesté*. Steve seemingly did not weigh the odds too much. "I went and got one of the tommy guns we used in the picture and a full clip of blank cartridges. As Frank and Peter Lawford and the others were walking away, I called out 'Frank!', and they turned around, and I went 'Wa-a-a-a' with the whole clip. At close range the wads and flash from blank cartridges can be both shocking and painful and that set went just dead still for about ten seconds."

It was not only one of the tensest but most critical ten seconds in Steve's life. If Sinatra had given the thumbs down then, Steve might have had to think again of the Australian outback. But suddenly Sinatra laughed, "and at that I knew everything was OK." From then on the two men spent most of their time tossing firecrackers at each other. "We had about six hundred cherry bombs on the back lot at Metro," says Steve, "and everybody had a ball." It was the good life. "What a way to live! You know, just organized chaos."

Every now and then, Hollywood manages to rise above itself and create a cinematic landmark—it does so, one suspects, more by accident than design. Certainly compared with European filmmaking, the bulk of the Hollywood product has been suitable only for the garbage can. In Europe, filmmaking is generally regarded as an extension of the literary and theatrical arts, and the result, by and large, has been a generous body of masterpieces. On the other hand, American filmmakers, incomparable in a purely technical sense, have been forced to work within the severe framework of the box office. American films are products, like washing machines or plastic bottle tops, and they are just as expendable. Typical of Hollywood's hollow standards was *Gone With The Wind*, the sort of epic distillable from serials in women's magazines. Now and then, nevertheless, Hollywood has managed to rise above its mediocre self, and it is to its credit that it produced *Citizen Kane*.

It is typical of Hollywood's basic poverty of thought, however, that one of the outstanding Westerns of the post-war years, *The Magnificent Seven*, owed its inception not to some measure of brilliance or originality within the Californian film community itself but to the Japanese. Akira Kurosawa's *The Seven Samurai*, which followed an earlier Japanese masterpiece, *Rashomon*, onto Western screens, proved to be a stirring film, albeit tinctured with subtleties, of how seven samurai, or professional warriors in medieval Japan, were induced to rescue a village threatened by bandits. Although its battle scenes were brutal, they never seemed arbitrarily interposed for effect; they underscored the reality of life and death and man's eternal need to stand up for himself against both nature and the forces of evil. The role of the professional warrior, bound by his code of ethics and at the service of the community against the forces of disorder, was given an aura of nobility that perhaps it deserves. In any list of the greatest films ever made, *The Seven Samurai* ranks high.

It could be dismissed, of course, by anybody insensitive to true artistry, as a Japanese "Western." And it was, perhaps, inevitable that someone in Hollywood should see it as such and decide it should be transposed to an American setting. The man who did so was Walter Mirisch. Having purchased the rights, he appointed John Sturges to direct and decided to set the whole thing in Mexico. Locations were just outside Cuernavaca.

It is an extraordinary thought that although this film was made as late as 1960, Steve McQueen was not then a full-fledged star. Sturges, of course, had no doubts about his future; but even he was unaware of the ground swell, particularly among the young, that already existed. In inviting Steve to be one of the film's seven badmen, Sturges was paying him a big compliment, for his practice is to cast players more for their ability to project strong individual personalities than simply to fill character parts. Alongside Steve, for instance, were such distinctive players as James Coburn, Charles Bronson, and Robert Vaughn. The star was Yul Brynner.

Like most successful stars, Brynner had a sense of humor. On-screen he had shown himself a likeable light comedian while off-screen he was a good raconteur. There seemed no valid reason why he and Steve should not hit it off together. Brynner might have an actor's vanity, but his ego, though well nourished, could scarcely outmatch Sinatra's. Steve began the film with much less foreboding than he had with *Never So Few*. In the event, the collision between Brynner and Steve, in the context of what they were about, was thunderous.

Steve's explanation is: "I think I represented a threat to him. He doesn't ride very well, and he doesn't know anything about quick draws and that stuff. I know horses. I know guns. I was in my element and he wasn't."

The news of a "feud" between the two men was not long finding public expression in a newspaper column. Yul read it and, newspaper in hand, walked up to Steve, face and body tensed. "He came up behind me," explains Steve, "and grabbed me by the shoulder—you know: 'I want to talk to you.' Well, I don't dig that stuff. He said, 'There's an item going around that we're having a feud, see? And I'm an established star, and you're an up-and-coming star, and we're not having a feud, and I want you to send a letter to these people saying it isn't true.' And I said, 'Well, sure, I'll see you Friday, baby. Just stand back on the thirty (30-yard line in football) and punt, you know.' '' Whatever that might mean in English, Yul got the message.

Steve later elaborated, ''I don't like people pawin' me.'' When Brynner laid a hand on his shoulder, Steve bawled ''Take your hands off me!'' He added, ''What had I got to lose? I've got a busted nose and teeth missing and stitches in my lips and I'm deaf in the right ear. What could I lose from a little fight? No, we didn't get along. Brynner knew I was a fast gun. He wanted me to use a rifle in the film so that I couldn't outdraw him, but I wouldn't have that. We were shootin' the first battle sequences. I got three shots out before he even had his gun out of the holster. Two shots in 2,700th of a second is my average.''

John Sturges admitted that Yul and Steve never became firm friends and that there was some ''friction'' between them, but he discounted the suggestion that it ever amounted to a ''feud.'' ''There was no feud, really. Naturally, there were some clashes. They're dissimilar characters; Yul is like a rock while Steve is volatile. Steve probably figured that Yul was being a big star and that he wasn't willing for anybody else to catch flies (meaning drawing an audience's attention away from the main business). Yul probably thought Steve was being an undisciplined smart aleck, always trying to catch a fly. He got sore because Steve was always fiddling with his hat or something. I had to tell Steve not to busy it up all the time: 'don't do something; just stand there!' ''

It is to everyone's credit that none of this spoiled the film. Brynner emerged as the masterful leader of the Seven, and as it happened, Steve's performance enhanced rather than diminished the star's performance. Audiences rarely draw the clear-cut distinctions between various actors that the participants appear to think they do. They respond to a film as a whole, and if one player does well or the director photographs something particularly nicely or the story is so good that nobody can actually make a hash of it, then everyone on the screen emerges with credit. Throughout the thirties, for instance, Hollywood films invariably had flair because the subsidiary roles were so beautifully played. Without such characterizations as the immortal Ned Sparkes and his famous line, "Leave it lay," or James Gleason and others, a legion of indifferent offerings would have been disasters. In *The Magnificent Seven,* Steve added that extra touch that not only confirmed him as a star in his own right but also brought real distinction to the film. From the audience's viewpoint, they had two stars for the price of one.

With its brassy music by Elmer Bernstein and its spectacular Panavision photography by Charles Lang, Jr., *The Magnificent Seven* earns a place among the best half-dozen Westerns ever made. That is not to say it ever aspired to or achieved the greatness of the Japanese original. It was a loud, noisy Western, impressive and hugely enjoyable, but there its merits ended. To many cinema buffs at the time, it seemed odd that although Kurosawa owed much to John Ford and his great series of Hollywood Westerns, it proved so difficult to transpose the Japanese plot back into Western terms. William Roberts' screenplay had its ingenious moments, but he appeared to be hampered by the Hollywood tradition. Kurosawa had apparently pondered deeply on the background and motivations of the Samurai, and there was a deeply expressed irony in their decision to defend the beleaguered village. None of this, for some reason, showed up in the American version. The gunmen turned up from nowhere and had no particular reason for embarking on their adventure. They appeared to become noble simply on impulse rather than for solid reasons, and their self-sacrifice, in the face of the villagers' lack of appreciation, bordered on the incredible.

If the story line never quite worked out and many of the scenes seemed stagey and unrealistic, the film nevertheless overcame the bulk of its drawbacks. It certainly succeeded in doing one thing magnificently—projecting Steve. He was at once deft and deadly, coldly menacing and wryly comic. He came over as a real cool character, relaxed and easy-going on the surface but inside a charge of dynamite waiting to be detonated. There is no argument, either, that during the historic shotgun ride on the hearse with Brynner, he completely overshadowed the latter and emerged as a great star.

Throughout its history Hollywood has invariably had to create its stars—put them through the process known as The Great Build-up.

Steve, however, is one of the few in the history of the American cinema to become a success without the help of the publicity machine. Lee Strasberg had once remarked to him while Steve was still studying at the Actors' Studio, "With that face, you've got to be something in acting," an ambiguous statement that took into account a Hollywood capable of accommodating every kind of mug from the pretty features of Robert Taylor to the craggy, bomb-blasted physiognomy of Humphrey Bogart. On the other hand, whatever his success with the "chicks" in Greenwich Village, Steve did not have the facial contours likely to convince Hollywood executives that he had magnetic sex appeal. It has been argued, in fact, that he was lucky to have appeared on the scene when he did; that is, when the studio system was collapsing and independents were moving in to make the kind of films *they* liked, with the kind of stars they wanted to use. Far from being manipulated to stardom in the old-fashioned way, Steve in fact, faced a gauntlet of prejudice. When John Sturges, on one occasion, notified the backing company that he had hired him, a top man declared, "We're not having that bum in this film," whereupon Sturges snapped back, "In that case, you won't have me directing it." In the old monopolistic days, even Sturges would not have dared to talk back like that.

When the publicity machine eventually did begin to roll, it was soon discovered that Steve needed no build-up; he already had a public. One reporter described it all as a matter of fate; Steve was simply around at the right time: "He's the logical successor to Jimmy Dean. The clique that worshipped Dean's flounderings and self-searchings and hostility sublimations, the crowd that identified so rabidly with all that nonsense, has a new messiah in McQueen. Luckily he is living longer than Dean did, so the cult will have a long, long time to thrive." Another reporter wrote: "His outlandish antics, aided and abetted by his hippie and beach-bum pals, made Hollywood seem like Cheltenham Spa by comparison, with the old-style wildmen cast as bath-chair colonels. Spencer Tracy asked, 'What is this guy trying to do—make us look like the Dolly Sisters?' "

Steve began by breaking quite a few of the rules. A caste system formerly operated in films and TV—stars chatted with stars, extras hung about with extras, the crew mooched about among themselves.

Steve crashed right through all this by joining the gaffers, juicers, grips, and others outside the sound stage, ripping off his shirt to get the sun and talking with the technicians as an equal. He insisted that these men were "family" and that he saw himself as no more than a member of the team. In fact, he showed a natural rapport with men who had a skilled job to do and did it conscientiously and without flattery or sycophancy; more so than with his fellow actors. Consciously or unconsciously, he seemed to regard his place as being with the "underdogs" and against the "overlords"—actors. "I do work hard," he said at the time, "and if someone else doesn't—and I do mean actors—I lean on 'em."

Off-screen, his behavior aroused more antagonisms. Aggressiveness and pushy determination to get to the top apart, he seemed deliberately to be thumbing his nose at the Establishment. While still working for Four Star and subsequent to his appearance in *The Magnificent Seven*, he was described as "riding a battered motor scooter around the studio as if his only speeds were Full and Stop." One of his favorite tricks was to rear the front end of the scooter up and squirt the machine along on its rear wheel. A photograph taken at the time shows him sitting on the scooter, clowning with stunt girl Valley Keene, his tongue stuck out. At first glance, it all looks a bit childish, and it is difficult to believe that Steve was then in his thirtieth year.

It was a time, of course, when the old Hollywood rigidities and conventions—always something of an absurdity, anyway, in what was essentially the capital of schmaltz—were due to be handed over to the demolition contractors. Hollywood's efforts to achieve "dignity" had always seemed at odds with the sheer razzmatazz of the undertaking, and Steve and his antics were really little more than a throwback to the old silent days when stars were *expected* to be different. Steve's favorite mode of dress around the studio, for instance, was sneakers and very short shorts, often worn with the top button undone. His speech remained a high-speed mumble, larded with hipster slang and Marine Corps epithets. Like Marlon Brando, he was a public scratcher, a habit he managed to discard as his career boomed. "All this ratchin' and scratchin' jazz," he once said when somebody mentioned Brando. "I don't think Mr. Brando is really like that; I think he uses it as an actor, which is great. But I come from a world of ratchin' and scratchin', and I'm trying to get away from it. I don't want people staring at me in a room like I'm some long lost bird from Ethiopia." When he speaks like this, of course, Steve instantly disarms all criticism.

Yet the facts were that he was difficult, temperamental, hard to control, and seemingly irresponsible—name a vice and he appeared to have it. A decade later when Tom Hutchinson reminded him that he had been once considered a "hell-raiser," Steve did not try to deny it. "Those days are over," he insisted. Yes, he had done a lot of "boozing and got into lots of scrapes. [But] I've grown up a lot in my years of film-acting. I used to say some pretty silly things early on. I lost my cool very, very easily. All right, I used to get into fights quite a bit. I have the handle of being a tough actor, so guys out with their girl friends would probably try to do the impressing bit and try and pick a quarrel. My scuffling days are over, however; I try to talk my way out of those situations. I have a little bit of an edge over opponents, anyway—I studied with this Chinese cat for three years. That was some judo I learned." Ten years, in fact, had changed him almost beyond recognition. "Like I said, I've grown up a bit. My prime purpose now is to pay off the responsibility I feel to California and Hollywood. Because if it hadn't been for Hollywood, I'd have been selling bathroom tiles today—or dead in an alley." He was now concerned more with both his own dignity and that of his craft. "I have to keep Hollywood's dignity as well as my own, because every actor lives in a glass house. In my country actors are still looked down on. Not in Britain . . . because there you have the background of theatrical dignity. Many times I have paid the dues for some actor who has handled himself badly. An actor has to believe in his own dignity. And to do that he has to carry himself well. I'm not Peter Perfect—my God I'm not. I've done many bad things in my life. But I have this responsibility, and I feel this deeply. The kind of films I make, the kind of person I am—they all contribute to the impression I make."

If his manners had changed, his basic personality seemingly had not. "I have to like the directors I work with," he said, speaking with a clarity and precision that would have astonished his friends ten years earlier. And how did he get to know or like a director? "Well, the only way to get to know a director is to go and get drunk with him, and this I always try to do. With John [Sturges] one is usually drunk all the time'' (delivered with a half-grin, indicating that the remark was not to be taken literally). Indeed, whatever his past misdeeds with alcohol, and some of the anecdotes are clearly apocryphal, Steve drinks nothing but beer nowadays. He had to like a director ''because then I have to take orders, and I don't like taking orders''; at least the years had not brought any change there. On the other hand, he made allowances for a director's status, and he could distinguish between a genuine order and mere pomposity. ''If I like the director or not, if I think what he says is important, then I'll try and fit into the mold of what he wants done.''

The thoughtfulness, the dignity, the responsibility—these were qualities that he had managed to graft onto himself as he grew older. Even in those days when he squirted around the Four Star lot, clowning it up like a fifteen-year-old kid, he had already begun to hone himself down a little. Rapidly, he showed every sign of being a less tense person, a little less aggressive and ruthless, although there was no sign that he had lost his competitive edge. He took life a little easier, though. ''After all, what's the point of being successful if you can't goof off a little? A guy bucks for sergeant so he can goof off, not because he is so gung-ho about being a sergeant. And so now I am taking a little advantage of my position. I can leave a little earlier at night from the series. I can come in a little later in the morning. I get a nicer dressing room. I get a little more respect from the producer than I did before and from the directors.''

Once he could consider himself a relative success and realize that he had a future, he had no difficulty sloughing off some of the prickly hostility and suspicions that had made him such a testy character. He was apparently ready to appreciate that he did not live in the world all by himself, nor did the world turn simply on his account. As both a star and a married man with a family, he had to take into account the existence of other people. ''It's one thing to be irresponsible and be dangerous and hack around, to start racing (he had taken up sports-car racing in 1959) and stick your neck out, face death and all kinds of tricky situations. But it's another to be a father and a husband and a provider. So I say to myself, 'Well, let's grow up a little, Steve-o-reno.' " He had even begun to lay plans, solid plans, for the future. He was earning some $100,000 a year from his TV series and, following *The Magnificent Seven*, could command $75,000 a film. "Every bit of money I make I am investing in things that will make my family and wife secure." Among these early investments was an interest in a Christmas stocking factory and he had plans—which never materialized—for a health food bar and a sports-car garage. He had also formed his own production company, Condor, to buy scripts for film and TV production. It was all an extraordinary and rapid metamorphosis. He was evidently even prepared—and this would have drawn horselaughs only a year or two earlier—to express a sense of gratitude.

"I worked hard at my acting, long before I ever made a film," he explained. "I think a lot of people have got the wrong idea about how I got my breaks. I'm sure a lot of folks think I just tough-guyed my way up to a studio boss and bullied myself into a part. They don't know what I went through. You get used to going in and coming out of offices without a job, you know. Now, I've tried to use what power I've been given by my luck and God and what talent I've got to achieve the things that are good for TV, because I love my craft."

As he changed, or "grew," or "shaped up," as he put it—so he seemingly sought a different image. One has the impression that although he was very likely prepared to fight his corner right from the moment he set foot in Hollywood, it may never have occurred to him that he might be projecting a tough image. He was simply what he was. And as he worked away at the rough edges, honing and refining himself, it probably never occurred to him either that he might be destroying an asset. Even when it was pointed out to him, he could not help scoffing at the idea and even spoofing it. One anecdote has it that one day a producer insisted, "You're an Angry Young Man." "Look, I'm not," protested Steve. "I'm very glad to be out here, man, and I'm like eager to make all this bread."

"No!" The producer shook his head, "You're angry!"

"All right," said Steve, "have it your way, man. I'm like angry." He immediately went away and hung a sign on one of his two motorcycles—he had a Honda and a Triumph by this time—bearing the legend "The Mild One" and drove about the studio and the back lot with it prominently on display.

Yet for all his protestations, he had not changed sufficiently to give up his beloved motorcycles—nor change his behavioral patterns. He continued to keep at least one motorcycle around the set. Then, when shooting finished each day, "The Mild One" disappeared in a shattering roar, careening over cables and steering among the lights and cameras, and scattering his colleagues in all directions—a noisy demonstration that had the producer and director in fits, but apparently fazed him not at all. He was, as ever, living with his paradoxical—some might say paranoid—self; a man apparently fighting to grow up and yet a prey to immature impulses. Nonetheless, he probably could not see why his desire to shatter convention, to let rip a little merry hell, to simply experience the exhilaration of being alive should earn him the label "angry." He insisted, "I'm not angry—I'm happy. I come from a world where people will step all over you and kick your teeth out. And if you get out of that, you're not angry. What do I have to be bugged about?"

Scorching away from the studio like that, revs blasting the roof of the sound stage, probably seemed to him no more than adding a touch of badly needed comedy and horseplay to the day. He needed, and still needs, a channel to release his sense of humor, for he is not noted for his wit, although he has a sardonic way of enunciating things that on occasion bring a laugh. Although he has played two notable comedy roles, in *Never So Few* and *The Honeymoon Machine*, he seems to recognize that he is not properly suited to comedy, on or off the screen. "After the life of the party goes," he says, "I'll crack a joke and maybe get a laugh—but that's about it."

What sense of humor he does possess tends towards the homespun. One example is the story he used to tell about the horse he rode in "Wanted—Dead or Alive." "I must tell you about this horse," he said. "When I first started, they gave me this real old horse they put on roller skates and pushed in on the sound stage, so I went to see Dick Powell, whom I liked very much. I said, 'Listen, let me pick out my own horse. We're gonna be in this series for a while. I'd kind of like to have a horse I got something going with, you know.' He understood and said, 'OK, go out and get yourself a horse.' So I went to a friend of mine, a cowboy I know, and I asked him if he had any good quarter horses. He said, 'Yeah,' and we looked at a sorrel and a dapple-grey, and they had a white palomino, and they had this black horse that the cowboy was working. I said, 'This one,' and I pointed to the black horse. He'd just been broken, and he had a very tender mouth, and he was shaking all the time, almost like a thoroughbred, very nervous. I got on him, and he bucked me right away, and it took quite a while to subdue him. So this decided me in his favor, I wouldn't have any other horse. We got him onto the sound stage, and that's where we made a mistake. Because you can't take a horse and put him on a sound stage with all those strong lights and deep shadows. A horse walks from the lights to the shadows and he can't see. And then he bumps into something, and then he hears strange noises and gets even more nervous. And he starts kicking. So, the first week we were shooting, the horse kicks out four or five lights, bites other horses, broke my big toe stamping up and down and bit me in the back about four times. That was the beginning and it went on for all of three years. That horse and I fought for three years. Both of us went on winning. He would step on me—on purpose. Just reach over and go———right on my foot. Again and again. And I'd punch him each time for stepping on me, but he would do it again. We never did compromise. The sonofabitch, no matter how much he was paid back in kind, he stood his place. He was black with white stocking feet, and his name was Ringo, and we really loved each other. But he never surrendered and this is how he taught me a lesson. He proved better than me, and smarter—and he beat me.''

To Steve, of course, this was—and is—more than a comic story. He told it as an example of relentless struggle against the odds and a refusal to give in; what he really liked about it, what had significance for him was that, as he would phrase it, it was his own story and his own philosophy ''all down the line.''

8.

THE GREAT ESCAPE

THE motorcycle chase scenes in *The Great Escape* are perhaps the most memorable parts of one of the most popular post-war films, although it is perhaps typical of all filmmaking that it was technical wizardry which, in the end, gained for Steve kudos he scarcely deserves. Ironically, his real contribution—important suggestions that improved the actual story line—still largely remains unknown.

The film itself was based on a book by Paul Brickhill and tells the true story of how seventy-six Allied prisoners-of-war tunnelled their way to freedom from Stalag Luft North—the greatest escape project of World War II. More than five million Germans were actually involved in the real search; the Nazis were so exasperated by it all that, contrary to the Geneva Convention, they shot fifty prisoners on recapture. Producer-director was John Sturges. The cast, besides Steve, included Richard Attenborough, James Garner, Charles Bronson, and James Coburn. Steve settled the details of his participation in the film without a conference, a contractual agreement, or even an agent—even without seeing a script. ''I settled

it on the spot—with a handshake. Why wouldn't I trust John? He gave
me the breaks in *Never So Few* and *The Magnificent Seven*." Never,
if Steve means us to take his story literally, has trust been so well
placed.

The public found it a gripping film. Stalag Luft North was a sort
of mini-Colditz, a POW camp for hardened escapees. On the arrival
in camp of Bartlett (Richard Attenborough), three escape tunnels are
started, named "Tom," "Dick," and "Harry," as part of a breathtak-
ing plan for the escape of 250 men. The actual tunneling, manufacture of
special equipment, and forging of documents, and so on moves over
ground made familiar by earlier films, and while competently handled,
proves little advance on such films as *The Wooden Horse*. Three completely fictional incidents are inserted into the more-or-less authentic
story; and paradoxically, these prove to be the most successful parts
of the film. One is a fantastic booze-up on synthetic whiskey, organized
by the American contingent; the second is the discovery of the "Tom"
tunnel; and the third is the tremendous motorcycle escape attempt by
Virgil Hilts, nicknamed The Cooler Kid, played by Steve. Steve's role
was completely in character. He plays a rebellious youngster who
finally learns the hard way that the task of escaping is a team effort;
that success on the grand scale is not a one-man show. "The part
seemed sort of ready-made for me," admitted Steve. He earns his
screen nickname because he keeps trying to escape on his own and
keeps getting recaptured and chucked in the cooler.

In the book, once the seventy-six men have tunneled to freedom,
most of them head for the local railway station to get away by train.
In the film, however, Steve snares a German Army motorcyclist by
fixing a trip wire across the road and then, taking the machine, zooms
away across the magnificent Bavarian countryside. Location scenes
were shot at Geiselgasteig, outside Munich; the sheer beauty of the
Alpine foothill countryside plays no small role in the film's success.
Steve's ride was equally spectacular. "Riding that bike up and down the
hills, through streams, over and under barricades, skidding, swooping
up and down, meant a lot to me because it's only when I'm going fast,
in a racing car or bike, that I really relax." If you put one of Steve's
statements alongside another, however, you often find that they do not
quite match; they may suffer because they have been pulled out of con-

text. For example, we find him declaring that he settled his participation in the film, ''with a handshake.'' Then he is on the record as saying, ''Well, you know me and motorcycles. So my little deal with John was this: I'd do the picture, sight unseen, if he'd agree to let me do my own motorbike riding, without benefit of a double. He almost agreed. But as it turned out, I did all my riding across country with a friend of mine doing the actual pile-up at the finish, something I couldn't actually attempt and still finish the movie if things had gone wrong.'' None of this is incompatible, of course; what is at variance, however, is yet another version, which squares with what we know of the original story and of the eventual screen version. According to this version, Steve was supposed to get on a train with the others, but at a story conference in Hollywood presided over by John Sturges, ''I found myself suggesting I escape, not by train but on a motorcycle. John said he'd like me to give a demonstration, which I later did. He fell in with this idea— despite the possible trouble with the insurance people.''

Certainly we know the motorcycle escape was not in the original story, and we also know that Steve's passion for racing bikes and cars was hardly a secret. So it is not surprising that the motorcycle chase was inserted and, incidentally, produced a climax to the film that makes the intended climax, the massacre of the fifty recaptured prisoners, something of an anti-climax, earning Steve the accolade from one critic: ''Steve McQueen gives the one arresting performance in the film.''

As the film was finally edited, the attempts by the Germans to cut off and recapture Steve on his motorcycle are both novel and gripping. Steve ends his dash over rolling countryside with a hair-raising attempted leap across a barbed wire barrier between the Reich and Switzerland. He has been forced into a corner by his pursuers and is almost ready to surrender when he spies this rise in the ground ahead, he revs up the cycle, hurtles up the hill, and sails right over the wire. Then he piles up and is recaptured. That leap, in particular, won him a host of new admirers for everyone knew that in real life he was a daredevil motorcyclist, and it was generally accepted that Steve had done the stunt himself.

Stars, of course, are to some extent the prisoners of their own publicity, and Steve was not well served when publicity men insisted that he "does all his own stunts." On a different occasion and in connection with another film, a publicity man told a Hollywood reporter exactly the same story, although the reporter had actually seen Steve's stuntman and double hanging around the studio. In fact, Steve's escapades in *The Great Escape* were restricted to those sequences which show him doing some relatively hazardless riding, well within the scope of anyone who has learned not to fall off. The leap over the barbed wire, Steve eventually admitted, had been beyond his capabilities. He had made one attempt and fallen "on my melon" (head), and the actual stunt was performed by Jeff Smith, a British "scrambler." And although John Sturges loyally insisted that Steve did all the rest of the riding, rumors have persisted ever since that Jeff Smith also helped out in one or two of the other rough spots.

What is beyond doubt, however, is that Steve, as a result of this film, established himself as a major figure; the kid from the street gangs and the reform school who had "scammed" all his life and finally arrived. Thereafter, his career became largely a matter of superlatives. In due course, he would win a nomination for an Academy Award; be named top box-office star; hailed "star of the year" for 1969. It was typical of Steve, however, that he apparently set about winning these accolades in a way nobody else would ever have thought of; he rode a motorcycle.

John Sturges declared, "Steve is like nobody else in films today; only once in a long while does an actor like him come along," and explained, "He brings a fresh, inquisitive mind to his work." Richard Attenborough (a superb actor and an intelligent and literate man capable of tackling any job in films and who directed, years later, the magnificent *Oh, What a Lovely War*) said that Steve "makes acting easy, and that needs great skill." In due course, producer Robert Wise enthused, "Steve just has to stand there to command attention," which, while true, seems to put down Steve's talent. He has been called "a natural." He says himself, "I'm just me—that's all I can be." Yet that would hardly explain, or not entirely explain, the ease with which he has played a considerable range of characters and succeeded in making them all credible. When pressed, he admits, "I believe in lots of preparation. I want to look the part of the character I'm playing.

It takes time. It takes study. It takes a deep understanding of the character involved.''

Yet this is also true for every other actor and cannot be the complete answer. Tom Hutchinson, the critic, has a different theory. "It is true that when Steve is on the screen you can't take your eyes off him. One can argue that this is just a matter of camera work. One remembers how Josef von Sternberg used to linger interminably on the face of Marlene Dietrich. Yet all the fancy camera work and fancy angles can't help someone like Barbra Streisand, for example. Despite all the money lavished on her, she doesn't command attention. It *is* a simple question of possession of a certain type of personality, which has nothing to do with acting at all. In fact, in my opinion, it amounts almost to a personality defect. Think of Marilyn Monroe, coming from the same kind of broken, deprived background. It is almost as though people like her and Steve are adoring the camera, hoping that the camera will adore them back—and it does. Your more stable people don't need the camera, which is why I think stable people don't usually become stars. They don't need this peculiar little eye, gazing at them intently. The others *give* to the camera. They love it. Of course, I'm not ignoring the overriding thing—the fact that both Steve and Monroe exerted this strong sexual attraction. But other men and women, if just as attractive in real life, have not this talent for wooing the camera—and through it the audience.''

Steve's own reaction to his success in the film was typically tangential. "I feel my riding has given a boost to motorcycling. Till then the public image of motorcyclists was leather-jacketed types with long sideburns and little regard for the public. But Hilts (the character he played in the film) was a clean-cut type you'd be happy to have as a friend.'' Well, we all cherish our illusions.

Steve's passion for machinery appears to have developed while he was in the Marine Corps. From it stems his love of fast machines and speed—and thus to what has been described as his second career, motorcycle and sports-car racing. He says, "I love machinery. I'd walk a hundred miles to see a piece of good machinery. Why, I even love washing machines!'' When still living in Greenwich Village, he learned to strip down and rebuild a motorcycle. When he became an actor and could afford two bikes, stripping down and rebuilding them became a hobby for him the way playing bridge is for other people. Then, when the money began rolling in, he "got into cars." His first purchases were a conventional American sedan that Neile partly wrecked when she skidded into a used car lot, and then a small popular European sedan. His next investments were a Porsche 908 and a Jaguar. With the acquisition of all this machinery, he took to speeding along the California highways with that same apparent contempt for the regulations that had distinguished his leather-jacketed days in New York. In 1958, he was booked twice for speeding and in January, 1959, avoided losing his licence only by lying to a policeman. With Neile, then six months pregnant, he was driving the Porsche to Phoenix, Arizona, for some location shooting. "I'd lost my license twice [he had been fined twice], and if I got another ticket it would be all over. I'd be driving pogo sticks. We were on this long stretch of highway, a nice flat road, safe, no bumps, and I was going 100 miles per hour in the Porsche when all of a sudden this cop came up in back of us out of nowhere, and I asked Neile if we were still in California. She said 'Yeah,' and I said, 'Well, it's all over, baby.' " Steve pulled over and then, brain whirring rapidly, got out and rushed up to the policeman and explained that his wife was expecting a baby. He carefully omitted to point out that it would not be born for another three months. The policeman, full of compassion and sense of duty, escorted them to the nearest hospital, siren wailing to clear the way. Steve waited until the policeman left the room, then told the bewildered nurse that his wife "had been taken faint" and that the baby was not expected immediately. "Forget it, she's cool," he told the girl.

Someone once remarked about Steve and his passion for speed that "at least he contributed a new activity to the conventional off-duty pastimes of booze and broads in Hollywood." Steve himself once said, "Speed rivals making love," and if his experience is anything to go by, one sounds as dangerous as the other. Over the years he has twice had plastic surgery on his face; he has broken two fingers and both wrists, and also smashed his kneecap. From time to time people have tried to find out why, with all his money and fame, he insists on risking his neck. Talking about his motorcycling, he explains: "It drains me. It cleans me out. I ride off all the anger that's in my gut at the phonies

I have to meet and work with. If I didn't, we'd be mixing buttonholes the next day on the studio lot. I don't mind a man doing what he has to do. I don't care if he collects garbage—it's a smelly job but it has to be done and he's worth something. But phonies, no-good operators? Man, they bug me. So I burn it out on the road and keep cool on the set. I must be a peace-loving man to go to so much trouble to stay out of trouble.'' And sports cars? ''There's nothing like comin' to a nice tight curve in the road at about a hundred per to tune your reflexes. It clears your brain and purges your heart. Danger is seductive.'' Well, what, if anything did he *think* about when he was racing? ''The only thing I'm thinking of is making that next tight curve and coming out of it in one piece.''

In Europe, where most men drive their family sedans flat out at speeds of 80-90 miles per hour on suburban roads (often where the speed limit is 30), Steve's passion is understandable. What, by and large, sets him apart from the herd is his bank account. He can afford good cars, and he has the requisite leisure to indulge his hobby. By 1965, his earning power had risen to $300,000 a film, plus a share of the profits. He could afford to buy an ornate Spanish-style stucco villa in three-and-a-half acres on a hilltop at Brentwood for a reputed $220,000 and had amassed a collection of fast, if not particularly distinguished, cars and motorcycles. He had a green Jaguar Excalibur SS with black fenders and chromium exhaust pipes; a burgundy Ferrari convertible; a red Chevrolet; an under-slung Jaguar XK-SS, which he christened ''the old green rat,'' a collector's item (one of only five in existence) whose combustion chamber he rebuilt himself. He also had six fast motorcycles—two ''straight'' and four ''dirt''— plus two pickup trucks, one green and the other brown. Earlier, he had had a Lotus Le Mans.

His first car race was a novice affair at Santa Barbara where, driving his Porsche, easily the fastest and best car competing, he won. ''The trouble,'' he explains, ''is that I won. The bug then hit me deeply. I found car racing both frightening and beautiful.'' He later admitted, however, ''It's a beautiful sport, but every time I used to get into my car, I used to get scared. I remember my first time out, I said to myself, 'What the hell am I doing here?' I was out there skidding in between cars and going into the turns as deep as I could before I hit the brakes and dicing for position and everything—you know, really on the ragged edge all the time. And I finally thought to myself, 'Man, you can get *killed* doing this!' But I like the idea of having to overcome fright, you know. It's quite a feeling, a real pure feeling.''

Entering that novice race cost him "a small bundle to get the car ready." This was just a week before his first child, his daughter Terri, was born—on June 6, 1959. "Neile was unhappy because I had blown the baby money that weekend. Things were kind of tight for us at the time." At first, Neile did not object to him racing. "When he began, I just couldn't understand it," she admitted. "I knew there was danger, but I didn't know how much." She was soon to regret her complacency.

Between 1959 and 1960, Steve took part in six races, each time putting in a creditable performance for a beginner. A slightly closer examination of his performances, however, detracts a little from the impressive sounding nature of the record. A photograph of him competing at Riverdale, California, for instance, shows that many of the other cars in the event were U.S. sedan cars and unlikely to be a match for his European sports model.

Fatherhood itself was more than welcome to Steve who longed, like the product of many broken homes, for his *own* family; nevertheless, it created certain dichotomies for him. Seemingly, he desperately wanted to race sports cars and fully open the throttle of his motorcycle, if only because of the feeling of freedom speed gave him. Yet, as the quieter joys of domesticity and a recognition of his responsibilities became borne in on him, he must have felt himself being tugged apart. One bit of him apparently desperately desired all the freedoms of a bachelor, the other no doubt reached out for all the comforts of home. So he compromised. He continued to race, insisting to himself that with all the pressures that were increasingly falling on him, it was his only "way to stay free." It was a compromise that Neile refused to agree to. And the final nail in his plans was Four Star's insistence on a no-racing clause in his contract. "The elements," he declared, "seemed against it. I'm married. I've got a kid I love very much [this was before his son Chad was born]. I've got a house. I'm very happy here. Everything's going OK. I don't want to kill myself right now." So at the end of 1961, he pro-

mised Neile and his business associates that he would quit racing.
He even went so far as to sell the Lotus, which had ensured that
only twice in all his races did he finish worse than third in his class.
Neile gave a sigh of relief and took him at his word. And, for quite
a few months, it really seemed as though he were prepared to keep
it.

We are principally indebted to Neile for much of the portrait we
have of Steve in his private and personal life during those years
when he was just beginning his ascent up the ladder.

She had recognized that he was "really wild" when they first
married; she had her doubts, she says, about the kind of father
he would make. "It took me two-and-a-half years to get pregnant,
and I couldn't believe it when it happened. But at the time I wasn't
too ecstatic."

The reason for her uncertainty was Steve's attitude. "He wanted
a boy for the first child. When he found out he had a girl, he was
stunned, speechless. He hadn't even *thought* it might be a girl. I
was praying our second child would be a son; otherwise, I'd have had
to get pregnent again as soon as possible. When I *had* a son, I'll never
forget Steve's face. I've never seen him look so happy before. It was
beautiful when they told him. He came in beaming. 'I have a son,'
although he added, 'He looks like Al Capone'."

Then rather typically, he "proceeded to ignore the boy for a year.
When I asked him why, he said, 'I have to wait till he talks or does
something. What can he do? He can't do a damn thing.' " No, Steve
wasn't "at all domesticated, I'm afraid; he would never change the
baby's diapers or anything like that. He's never washed a dish."

One of the many paradoxes associated with Steve McQueen is that,
even though he once seemed to be a symbol of the ideas of hippies, drop-
outs, and leather-jacketed motorcycle fiends, he still has so many old-
fashioned attitudes and ideas. Once, for example, queried about Women's
Lib, he said, "I've read a lot of spiel about just what is women's position
in this so-called twentieth-century society. I've known a lot of women
in my time because I began young—I was thirteen the first time. All
I can say is that so far as I'm concerned, a woman should be a woman.
By day she should be busy making and keeping up a home for the man

she loves. At night she should be sleeping with him.'' Told that this
last might be considered a little indelicate by some of his fans, he
laughed, ''You've got to be kiddin'. How else can a man prove his
love for a woman than by choosing to live with her, to be the father
of her sons and daughters?'' An impeccably old-fashioned view—as
old-fashioned as the image Neile inevitably sought to construct of
him. ''Family means more to Steve than most men,'' she said. According to her, she and Steve would have liked more than two children,
but her pregnancies were so difficult that they toyed with the idea of
adoption instead. They had thought of adopting a child from one of
the underdeveloped countries. ''Steve knows what it's like to be un-
wanted, which is why, particularly, his heart goes out to those deprived babies.''

One sees a McQueen steadily growing (''I've got to keep growing,''
he insisted), maturing, discarding much of his hipster language and
some of his wilder attitudes, growing more sophisticated, yet still
driven by demons. Like many a man who as a youngster was aimless
and drifting, squandering energies in destructive purposes, he had, under
the stimulation of a goal in life, become a ruthless, dynamic machine
hell-bent on achieving his new visions. He became a restless young
man, itchy and temperamental as a thoroughbred, and in a hurry to
get where he was going. He admitted himself, ''I did everything in a
hurry—I joined the Acting School in a hurry; I got married in a hurry;
and I've spent every free moment from films hurrying around race
tracks both in the U.S. and abroad, on motorcycles and then the fastest
cars I could find. I have a million plans—movies to make, movies
to direct and produce with my own company. I want to go places
and I want to go fast. I've hurried all my life. It's a way of life with
me.''

Some of the breakneck speed at which he tried to live his life
had to do with ambition, that is certain. Yet there was also a catch.
''He's deeply concerned about being poor again,'' confessed Neile.
''He's got the brass ring now, but he's afraid it might be snatched
away. When things are going too well, he worries. For instance,
we'll be talking or having dinner, and he'll suddenly get a very an-
guished look on his face. He'll get up and walk around saying nothing.
But I know what's bothering him. It's the fear of being poor and

lonely again, of everything good vanishing. I leave him alone or tell him to take a ride in the car. If he wants me to go with him, I go along; if not, he goes alone. I don't press him—I must let him do what he wants to get over this feeling.''

He had his own private phobias. Always, until he met Neile, he had been lonely—through circumstances rather than choice. When a man grows up like this, he finds it difficult to adjust, and besides, there was his deafness. "I hate nightclubs, premieres, parties, and receptions. It's not that I'm really antisocial, but I hate being in crowds. I suffer from claustrophobia. Besides I hate having to dress up in a tux and black tie. I'm more myself in a T-shirt and jeans.'' He seemingly wanted the easy, informal life to which he was accustomed, not the *bother* of formal functions. He probably did not want, either, that uncomfortable feeling of being fawned upon by sycophants and phonies and people who thought they might extract something from him—either a job, or money, or the vicarious success that comes from rubbing shoulders with the successful. He could explain the loner bit: "There used to be a lot of hate in me, but I'm beginning to realize that I was suspicious of every person I met. I felt everyone was out to get me, no matter what I did, no matter how I behaved— that's one of the reasons I've been a loner all my life.''

Neile explained that though he hated parties or social gatherings, he nonetheless appreciated fame and success. Yet he "couldn't get used to the idea of people staring at him.'' He himself says, "When I became a success, I stopped living. I liked to watch people. Now they're watching me.'' Still he was pleased, she said, that people liked him and he took care not to be rude to fans, unless they crowded him when he felt hemmed in. Neile had only once seem him lose his temper with a fan. This occurred when they were in a department store, and she was pregnant with Chad. She had fainted—a tendency during both her pregnancies. An anxious Steve had picked her up and carried her to a chair. Then a voice had broken in, "I know it's an odd time, but while your wife's out, can I have your autograph?'' Coldly furious, Steve snarled, "Get out of here!''

Concerning his house, he admitted: "It's the kind of place I've always dreamed about. I'm my own guy and have my own house where I want it. Our area is called Brentwood, *not* Hollywood. Up there, it's very quiet, and there are no cars around, no telephone wires, no smog, no traffic, no people with Chinese lanterns or bells or parties." Among the things he loved best, he had once listed returning to this home.

No, he was not really antisocial, Neile said. It was, she repeated, just that he was against the conventional type of social life; a life where people crowd together because they work in the same company, or have similar business interests, or—as in the case of Hollywood—because it had become the convention for celebrities to hobnob with other celebrities. "He likes people for what they are, not who they are." One of his close friends was James Garner, the actor who had starred with him in *The Great Escape,* but he only liked Garner "because he's an interesting guy, not because he's an actor." Most of his friends, in fact, were neither rich nor famous. What mattered to Steve was the measure of a man.

Steve confirmed this. He says, "I'm quite an ordinary guy, you know. The people I'm concerned about are ordinary guys, and I don't care what a guy does for a living, whether he's a farmer or a statesman—as long as there's something going on inside him." His best friend was still Bud Ekins, a motorcycle man by profession, and most of his other friends were "motorcycle or car racers or poets or artists." Some of his friends were film stars, "but a lot are guys who don't have any money." What he liked was that his friends "treat me no differently than they treat anybody else. As far as how important I am, that doesn't mean a bean to them—or to me."

There is no reason to doubt the genuineness of this. Steve has never showed any aspiration to be a social climber. Fabulous wealth and fame when they arrived basically changed little in his life. They did no more than provide Neile and himself with more comforts, more possessions, more seclusion, and an opportunity to ensure a good life for their children. Steve still sought the company of people with whom he could feel rapport or sympathy; they could be emotionally disturbed, people with a problem, or simply losers. He was, according to Neile, constantly bringing strangers to the house just because he happened to bump into them, found they had some sort of problem, and felt compelled to try and settle it for them. Once he ran into a despondent young man somewhere along the Strip whom he invited home to dinner—"and then they sat yakking in the den until 3:00 A.M."

It sounds like a simple, relaxed, easy, unpretentious way of life. Steve apparently liked staying at home in the evenings because he could dress as he liked—"it's like putting him behind bars to make him put on a shirt." If he disliked parties, she indicated that did not mean he objected to having people about the house; on the contrary, he obviously enjoyed the company of his friends. Neile and he often "sat up all night, yakking with Steve's racing pals," particularly Bud Ekins. Instead of dining out at an elegant restaurant, they usually ate dinner at home, cooked by Neile. "So it was far from elegant, like as not." Then they walked to the nearby hills in the dusk and fired at tin cans.

Steve apparently was torn between a desire to let her be a personality in her own right and yet fulfill the role of an old-fashioned, stay-at-home, cook-my-meals wife (although Mildred, their cook, prepared marvelous meals, Steve liked Neile to cook for him as often as possible). On one occasion, he permitted Neile to take part in a theatre-in-the-round production of *Pajama Game* at Corvina; but whereas the rest of the cast stayed in hotels or other lodgings in Corvina for the run of the show, Steve insisted that Neile drive the whole way back to Brentwood every night. So far as possible, too, he wanted her company on all of his location trips. To both of them, aware of the snares inherent in living apart, however briefly, particularly in the film industry, it seemed a sensible precaution if their marriage were to last. As a token, she gave him a Saint Christopher medal, which he carried about everywhere and which, on the rare occasions when they were parted, reminded him of her. It was inscribed, "To part is to die a little."

During 1961 and 1962, Steve made three films: *The Honeymoon Machine* for MGM; *Hell is for Heroes* for Paramount; and *The War Lover* for British Lion/Columbia, which was shot in Britain. In none of them did Steve do less than justice to his talent and personality, yet in none of them did he quite explode. Not until *The Great Escape* did the raw animal magnetism, which women, in particular, were to find irresistible, come bouncing off the screen. After that film, Abe Lastfogel found himself at the center of a storm, inundated with offers for Steve's services. It was a sign, for those who could read the omens, of Steve's new status in the industry, that Abe, head of the largest theatrical agency in the world, began taking a truly paternal interest in Steve. "Abe," declared one of his junior aides in ringing tones, "doesn't regard Steve as an investment. He thinks of him more as a son." Abe himself could talk of nothing but Steve "in a manner," wrote one reporter, "that indicates that at any moment he will pull out his wallet and show pictures of the boy."

Steve's role in *The Honeymoon Machine* was again a comedy role, as though the producer (*a*) had never watched TV and had not quite grasped the subtleties of Steve's performances in "Wanted—Dead or Alive," or (*b*) was so impressed with the way he had played in *Never So Few* that he saw Steve as another Bob Hope. In the light of the offbeat, highly charged characters that he was later to play, in many of which he seems content to have achieved an effect of smouldering menace by just standing still and letting the camera almost swoon over him, Steve turned in a performance as vivacious and volatile as a newly sliced grapefruit. He is either a far more subtle character in private life than he is given credit for or a far better actor than certain static characterizations—in particular, the hard-up rodeo cowboy of *Junior Bonner*—of his later films would lead us to suppose. Steve appeared in *The Honeymoon Machine* as Lieutenant Fergie Howard of the U.S. Navy, who dreams up the idea of using his warship's computer to break the roulette bank at Venice. The plan looks as though it will succeed until complications arise in the person of the Admiral's daughter (Brigid Bazlen) and the former fiancee (Pam Dunstan) of co-conspirator Jason Eldridge (Jim Hutton)—which is nothing compared to the complications that ensue when the ship-to-shore signalling system intended to pass messages from the computer to those actually at the roulette wheel is intercepted by the U.S. Admiral and the Russians, each of whom decides it has something to do with aggressive designs by the other. In the outcome, the threatened World War III is averted, and love finds its way. On the whole, the film never quite succeeds, falling into too many sidetracks and ramifications to sustain what was basically a rather good idea. Steve made no particular impact at the time, and another look at the film still fails to show him as a potential star worthy of filling the shoes of the great figures of pre-war Hollywood.

The critics also found nothing particularly stimulating in his performance in another war film released the same year, *Hell is for Heroes*, even though it allowed more scope for his personality. The story is set near the Siegfried Line in the autumn of 1944. Steve, as Reese, joins a group of weary GIs unexpectedly ordered back into the line when on their way to a rest area. While most of the men withdraw from their positions facing a German pillbox at the far side of a minefield, half-a-dozen men are left to protect a wide front. By various ruses, they manage to convince the Germans that a large force is still holding the position. Then Steve leads two of the men in an unauthorized and unsuccessful attack on the pillbox, in which the other two are killed; and when the main platoon returns, he is threatened with court-martial. Rather than face the disgrace, and in an attempt to show he was right, he makes a one-man attack on the pillbox and, although badly wounded, blows both the Germans and himself up. Throughout, Steve gives, according to one critic, "an unvaried performance as a sullen, unshaven incarnation of the death wish in this conventional war story of the rebel against military authority who is finally justified." The same critic found the performance of the former bobby-soxer idol, Bobby Darin, "far more convincing."

Yet when we come to *The War Lover* (an Arthur Hornblow, Jr., production filmed in England, based on a novel by John Hersey and directed by Philip Leacock), we find he has begun to make an impact—albeit a delayed one—with both critics and newsmen. One well-known London film writer who had then yet to meet him, telephoned a Hollywood producer to find out something about him. The reply was, "I can't tell you a thing, except that Yul Brynner hates him." As Yul Brynner "only hates the most interesting people," the writer decided it might be worth doing a piece on him. "Nothing else?" he inquired hopefully. "He drives cars too fast," came the answer.

Steve was drinking tea and nursing a hangover in his London hotel, shirt off because it was a warm day. "Man, I'm still drunk," he announced to the film writer. "I went out with Stirling Moss last night and got stoned." Apparently he had downed a pitcher of ice water on waking up, and that had stoned him all over again. The image of a hell-raiser satisfactorily established, he rambled on about acting and car racing. As Moss's name had already popped up in the conversation, it was natural it should occur again. Steve said he saw himself as "a sort of poor man's Moss in America." He loved driving racing-cars. "Acting is all right, but it's car racing I love." What did studio bosses think of his racing activities? "They hate it, man. They think I've got a death wish or something. But I love it; it's my life. When I've made enough money, I'll quit acting and just race. Man, I'm a bit of a nut. Thirty years old and done everything. And I mean *everything*; the lot! But I didn't hurt anyone but myself. My wife and kids are taken care of—they have enough bread." All delivered, the writer noted, in an "audible stream of consciousness."

Stirling Moss had first run into Steve in 1959. At that time Moss was widely regarded as the greatest driver in the world. Says Moss, "Steve and his wife were living in a funny little house at the back of Hollywood when I first met him. He was then riding a motorcycle. When I next met him he had hit the high spots. He had a D-type Jag, among other things, and a fantastic house. I considered him a cool sort of guy. He didn't waste words—he believed in actions rather than words. Very keen to learn, very keen on things, interested to get advice and take it—which I consider very intelligent. I can remember that night we had out together in London around that time; I think Sammy Davis came into it at some stage. If you ask me the kind of things we talked about, that's fairly simple—girls and cars. Yes, in that order."

It was largely through Stirling that Steve heard about Brand's Hatch, the motor-racing circuit in Sussex, some 50 miles from London, scene of some of the most spectacular sports car racing in Europe. Most of the legendary racing drivers—Moss, Graham Hill, Jim Clark, Jackie Stewart—have drifted or slip-streamed their way around this circuit at one time or another. Although Steve had promised both Neile and his employers that he would never race again—and, indeed, kept to his resolution for several months—the chats with Moss and the attractions of so famous a circuit proved too great a temptation. He apparently decided to have a go.

He was lucky he did not kill himself. On one occasion it was raining heavily, and his borrowed Formula Cooper skidded crazily when he hit a pool of water; he went straight into the fence but relaxed his body just before the car impacted and escaped with shock and minor bruises. He commented afterwards, "If I hadn't relaxed, I'm sure I'd have been a goner," although, in fact, Brand's Hatch is famous for spectacular crashes from which most drivers seem to get up and walk away. The incident left him with a badly cut lip, which had to be stitched. He was due to appear in front of the cameras the following day as Buzz Rickson, pilot of a B-17 bomber. At first it seemed as though shooting would have to be held up, but Leacock, the director, got around the problem by getting Steve to wear an oxygen mask—a small anachronism which few who saw the film ever noticed.

Apart from the experience of driving at Brand's Hatch, enjoyable not only in itself but also as an experience that ensured his survival on far less dangerous tracks and against far less skilled opponents, Steve's British visit marks a significant turning point in his private behavior. He apparently decided to go the whole hog so far as racing was concerned. Like an addict returning to drugs, he bought an expensive collection of cars and motorcycles, which he had shipped back to America—a mini-car, a Jag, a racing motorcycle, a Cooper Formula racing car, and a jeep.

His racing injuries and the inevitable hangovers were hardly the stuff to make him remember his London visit too fondly although he insisted, in public anyway, in expressing the stock American admiration for it. "I dig London," he declared. He seems to have had some trouble in staying out of physical trouble during his visit. He was lodged in an expensive suite at the Savoy. It is a hotel, of course, which hardly expects its guests to do their own cooking— a mere quibble, perhaps, for an ex-hobo who has a compulsion to devour snacks at any time of the day or night. Anyway, Steve invested in a plug-in electric hot plate; and one night, when he had some of his racing cronies in for a drink, prepared cheese on toast. He was taking the third portion to one of his guests when there was a sudden yell, and turning around, Steve saw the curtains above the hot plate on fire. It had been a warm, humid night, and Steve was clad only in shorts. Without waiting to don trousers, he ran into the hotel corridor in search of a fire extinguisher. He grabbed it, rushed back, and put out the fire— not, however, before his behavior had been noted by other guests, who reported to the management that "a wild man is running loose in the hotel." Steve says he was asked to terminate his occupancy.

Steve with his present wife, Ali MacGraw, as they appeared in *The Getaway* (1972).

Shirley Anne Field and
Steve in a scene from
The War Lover (1962).

*Love with the Proper
Stranger* (1963), co-
starring Natalie Wood.

Steve as the hillbilly husband of Lee Remick in the psychological drama *Baby, the Rain Must Fall* (1964).

Appearing as a prisoner in a German camp during World War II in *The Great Escape* (1962), Steve established himself as a major film star.

Stills of the famous
poker game between
Steve and Edward G.
Robinson in *The
Cincinnati Kid* (1965).
The film also starred
Ann-Margret, Karl
Malden, and Joan
Blondell.

The trip, of course, was not all minor bouts of hell raising, hang-overs, car injuries, interminable conversations about cars (or girls and cars), and a small fire in a hotel suite. The primary purpose of the visit, after all, was to film *The War Lover*, which co-starred Robert Wagner and an English girl, Shirley Anne Field. Steve's role, as Buzz Rickson, captain of a Flying Fortress, was anything but an endearing one. Steve admitted that the part called for him to play an extrovert up to the hilt; and as part of his preparation for the role, he tried to turn himself into a total extrovert in real life. "I have to stay in character," he explained. "I always try to immerse myself in the role I'm playing—and Buzz Rickson was no shrinking violet. Let's get the facts right, man." As drawn by John Hersey, however, Buzz's character was much more than that of a simple show-off; he was more than just "a hot pilot." He was a man in-capable of love for other human beings because he was obsessed with a love for war. His mania was for speed, excitement, destruction, the bombing raid—aberrations that made his attempts at physical lovemaking with the opposite sex empty. "He's a complex guy," explained Steve enthusiastically, "not just another flying wise guy. He's selfish and selfless. He has the respect of a crew that pretty generally hates him. He's not the kind of guy anybody really likes. He's a helluva flier and can make a B-17 stand up on its tail and dance. But he's filled with repressions and deep complexes. All of that makes him an interesting guy to portray. Maybe next time I'll play a nice Madison Avenue soft-sell guy or a comedy cut-up. And that's what I'll be, on-stage and off. It goes with the part."

He talked willingly and frankly about himself, both as an actor and a man—and as a cult figure. He agreed that he was "a professional quick study," that is, that he was usually on top of his lines and need-ed little or no rehearsal, that he was simply a "natural" actor. He didn't mind the gibe that he was hardly an actor at all, that he simply played himself on the screen. "It isn't a slap at an actor to say he is completely the part he is portraying," he pointed out. He had already explained that he had been showing off a character privately in London that was not really himself; he was playing Buzz Rickson all day. As though conscious that this carried an implication that he had been behaving like a bit of a bastard at times, he said, "But you know, I'm not really as tough [meaning hard-bitten] as everyone makes me out to be!'' Oh, certainly he had been "a rebel." He had denounced authority, regimentation, conformity—all the pressures that sapped at a man's freedom and independence—and he probably saw no reason now to argue against the proposition that his success was due to this. "Since most kids are rebels, they seem to sense a fellow spirit in me." Rather more surprisingly, he verbally set out to destroy his "cool" image. He insisted that, despite appearances, he was "a nervous performer." He added, "I work myself up into such a state of nerves while acting in films that I use cars as a relaxation. The faster I drive, the better I feel. It helps me to unwind.''

He showed himself the perfectionist for which he had already established a reputation. Although he has shown a dislike for love scenes—and, indeed, despite his success with women— detestation of the kind of "mushy" films that are usually called "women's films," as it happened, four days were spent getting his love scenes with Shirley Anne Field just right. And as the lady pointed out with amusement later, she ended up with a cut lip, too.

The film itself was found by critics to be "a curious mixture of the authentic and phony." Some sequences were even badly photographed; yet other scenes held tremendous power. In particular, there was high quality in the shots of aerial combat. Buzz, the film showed, was a psychopath (no wonder the private Steve seemed "tough" in London). The story tells of his collapse when his confidence is broken. Originally he is a loud-mouthed womanizer, whereas his co-pilot, Bo Bolland (Robert Wagner) is something of an introvert who considers combat a distasteful duty. Buzz has few scruples; when Bo quarrels with his girl friend (Shirley Anne Field), Buzz calls on her in London and tries to seduce her. In repulsing him, she lets fly with a few home truths. The effect is traumatic. Shortly afterwards, when his aircraft is damaged in a mass raid on Germany, Buzz orders the rest of the crew to parachute to safety while he himself stays with the plane until it crashes into a cliff. The critics saw the character's end as "a mixture of suicide and madness" but had no doubt that Steve's performance largely supported the film. It was a performance bearing the hallmarks of a really good professional actor; yet it failed to make him a star.

Talking to a London newsman at this time, he revealed that he was confident of his abilities and knew that one day he would make it. He was only waiting for his big opportunity. "I guess I just go from one thing to another without bothering too much about the future," he commented. But then, with a prophetic grin, he added, "I think I'll recognize the big one when it comes."

Within twelve months his dream had materialized and his confidence in himself had been justified. By then he would be the "hottest property" in Hollywood, second only in box-office drawing power and stature to that durable monument to all who ride tall in the saddle—John Wayne.

9.

RACING TO SUCCESS

For three days Steve had been urging his motorcycle mercilessly around a tortuous circuit at Erfurt in East Germany as a member of the six-man U.S. team competing in the German championship trials—a tough, gruelling test of skill and stamina spread over six days and involving 1,500 miles of flat-out racing.

It was late afternoon, and pressing Steve closely were the East Germans and Finns with some of the Americans farther behind, including Steve's closest friend, Bud Ekins. For the first time since the trials commenced, Steve probably knew he had a chance of picking up a gold medal for an individual performance—an opinion enhanced when he came out of a tight curve and saw a straight road ahead leading gradually to a small hilltop. In contrast to other parts of the circuit, the road ahead was dead straight and well-surfaced and he must have decided, "I can let her go full throttle here and shake off these other guys." Tightening his grip on the throttle situated on the right side of his handlebars, he allowed the little machine to scream to its limit and hurtled towards the horizon.

The joy of taking part in such an event is that normal road hazards are thankfully absent—no oncoming trucks, no drivers hurtling
towards you at your own speed, no cows or pedestrians or farm
carts to create unexpected hazards. Although Steve would have been
unable to see exactly what was on the other side of the hill, he would
have known that officials had roped off the circuit and that the road
was clear. So he pushed the cycle to the limit. As he crested the hill,
the motorcycle leaped into the air like a skier taking off, and in that
instant, he got the fright of his life. A small boy had ducked under
the ropes and evading the eye of watchful officials was now about to
run across his path. In a crisis such as this, of course, there is no
time for thought. A rider must react intuitively. Steve had no time
to judge whether he would miss the boy if he kept on, or to decide
whether the boy was likely to make a mad dash across the road, or
whether he would duck back under the ropes: It is reflex rather
than intelligence that comes into play at such moments, and as Steve's
bike thumped down on the road again, he pulled it hard to the right,
zooming over a slight incline and into rough terrain dotted with trees
and shrubs. With his bike wobbling and bucking ferociously, he managed to avoid piling into a tree and then, spying a mass of thick foliage
ahead, let the bike run on. As he hit the foliage, he flung the bike to
the left and himself to the right, at the same time relaxing his body
sufficiently to break his fall. The jagged points of the foliage ripped at his
face, body, and limbs. When his head cleared, Steve found himself
covered in blood but fortunately with no major injuries. Despite a sharp
pain in his right leg—there was no fracture, only strained ligaments—and
although shocked by the toss, he decided to carry on. However, his own
bike was unusable; and despite pleas to officials, he was told he could
not take over another rider's bike.

That same afternoon, his friend Bud Ekins careened into a stone
wall and fractured his leg. While other members of the U.S. team
managed to win individual medals, the American team finished well
down the list, the East Germans winning the trials and Britain finishing second. Steve cheerfully announced his intention of taking part
again the following year: "I don't want to win 'em all—just one,"
he grinned.

It was 1964, and it is significant that although he usually insisted that Neile accompany him wherever he went, this time he was alone. It was the first time I had ever met him personally. He came through London on his way to East Germany. I found him a small, lithe, nut-brown, electric-blue-eyed man who listened carefully to whatever was said to him and pondered questions about his motorcycling and other activities with the gravity of a U.S. presidential candidate answering questions from the press on TV. He proved to be courteous and well-mannered, and it was hard to credit rumors of vanity and arrogance. The impression he gave was of an alert, if slightly suspicious, man who had reached certain conclusions about his own financial value and would actually prefer to be left alone. However, recognizing that there was a genuine public interest in him—one, too, that was rapidly increasing—he was happy to cooperate. He was a professional behaving as a professional ought to.

He talked readily about both his private and his public life and about the overlapping areas. He was proud of his children—for instance, before coming away he had spent "a full day" with them. He had taken them to the beach where he and Terri played in the sand while Chad went swimming in the sea. A little later Chad had returned surrounded by a crowd of kids and yelling, "Hey, I caught a shark!" He was holding something aloft, and Steve was delighted to see it was a baby shark. He was even more tickled when he saw the cuts on Chad's face and realized that the boy had battled like a man to overcome the shark—and had won!

He talked about his insurance difficulties: "Motorcycling is one of the most important things in my life. People interested in my career try to stop me. They never will. If I want to do something, I'll do it. I answer to no one except my old lady [Neile]." On the other hand this was costing somebody—presumably Steve—a few hefty premiums. He was insured for a million dollars against death; a half-million against the loss of an arm or leg. "Not that anything like that would stop me. I'd race again without it, that's all."

Was Neile scared when he raced? "No, she just asks me to be careful. She used to come along to the tracks and keep lap records for me. She used to tell me I was driving like an idiot."

It was said that he was a hard bargainer and negotiator, a toughie in business deals as in much else. What was the truth? "I know what

I'm worth, and I've no intention of losing a dollar to a movie tycoon. I wasn't born yesterday; and I've got enemies, plenty of them. But the young people like me, though—they like my mug, and I'm proud of that.''

And the future? Well, at thirty-four, he reckoned he was "still good for a few more years in films. I wouldn't mind an early retirement, though. I admired Gable and Cooper, but they made the mistake of not packing up in time. They didn't give themselves a chance to relax and enjoy life.''

Neile, I gathered, had told him that she did not want to see him race in East Germany. If he insisted on taking part, in risking his neck, she would rather not be there to see it. At this stage, of course, she had given up the struggle to keep him away from fast machines. Brand's Hatch had proved to him that he needed speed in his life, and when he returned to the United States, he was flattered by an offer from the British Motor Corporation to take part as one of their team in the twelve-hour endurance test at Sebring, Florida. It was the first time, of course, that an actor had been chosen to compete against professional racing drivers, and it is questionable if anything on earth could have stopped him from taking part, short of an act of God. Stirling Moss, one of his teammates, while not anxious to take away from Steve's achievement in any way, nevertheless thinks it only fair to put the matter in perspective. "They were only Healey-Sprites, you know, the speeds weren't very great.'' Steve himself has never tried to give the impression that this was racing on a Grand Prix or Indianapolis level. Yet it was an endurance test similar, if not comparable, to LeMans itself, and most of the competitors were world-class drivers. He turned in a creditable performance, leading his class for a time and finally coming in eighth, only three places behind the great Moss.

His performance in such company encouraged him to try out his Formula Cooper at Santa Barbara. He had an easy, stylish win, although the competition was scarcely world-class. This was in May, and it was his last race for two years. "The studio clamped down on me.'' he says, "and I had to quit cars. But in Germany for *The Great Escape,* I began racing motorcycles.''

This was the film, of course, that had changed everything for him.

It brought him back to his first love—the motorcycle. It brought him success—and with it some of the drawbacks of success. Suddenly, "you've got a lot of juice going for you, and in this town (Holly-wood) there are a whole lot of guys who hit on you." What he was saying was a familiar enough story. The successful man, particularly in show business, is flattered and fawned over. Powerful men who could have helped him when he needed it but would not give him even the time of day suddenly came forward with outstretched hands and beaming smiles and greeted him as "my boy!" Then there was the army of professional hangers-on—the leeches who fasten onto a major star, who gather when they smell money the way sharks gather when they smell blood. The boy from the reform school found it all too phony and embarrassing for words, even when he realized the attentions were necessary—an army of studio assistants combing his hair, pressing his suits, "powdering my nose."

He has insisted that he only managed—and can still only manage— to preserve his sense of proportion by competing in sportscar or motorcycle races. He likes his own "group of guys" in Hollywood, people he believes he can trust, men he has known for years, men with whom he can relax. "Our group of motorcycle racers is one of the best groups in town. I've known some of them for twenty years, and I'd trust them with my life. I could tell you a hundred times when these guys have done something really great for me, but I just can't do it. They'd never forgive me, never let up on me. They are the kind of men you can't even thank. They're not about to take any-thing off me. There are eight or nine of us, very tight; they've really got me and that's great. When you trust people, you can relax."

He was talking mainly of Bud and Dave Ekins, John Steen, and Cliff Coleman, who had taken part with him in the International Six-Day Bike Trials at Erfurt, East Germany. He likes to recall that when he first ventured among these fellows they were condescending toward him because he was only an actor—and actors, as everyone knows, can do nothing but act. "A lot of people think actors can't do anything but get paid lots of money for performing. I had to beat the actor's image to prove my capabilities in a sport that's always intrigued me." Undeterred because "they refused to accept me," he set out to prove he was as good a man—as distinct from an actor—as any of them, usually in desert scrambles. "After a broken shoulder, some smashed toes, a few stitches and a broken arm," he says, "these boys knew I was in there for real. They saw how thick my mud was, and dropped the actor label."

On the whole, perhaps, Steve's greatest asset is his integrity. In his private life, for instance, no one could have blamed him if he had surrendered to the more enjoyable aspects of success: hob-nobbing with other famous people; living it up stylishly; being seen in the best restaurants and at the leading social functions—no one can be blamed for giving in to some lionization. Yet he has stubbornly refused to become an integral part of the Hollywood social swirl or to join other actors in the endless round of parties. Actors per se simply do not interest him. "I'm not interested in actors' talk and they're not interested in racing cars, so what the hell can we talk about?"

Nor has success blunted his perceptions; if anything it appears to have sharpened them. Steve has admitted that being a successful movie star is a tough business. "You take a man off the streets and make him famous and he loses all sense of values. Believe me, it's not difficult to do. That's why it's important to have the right kind of friends." Nor was he easy to make friends with. "I guess I'm too suspicious of people. It's something to do with my childhood; I've been had too much and let down too often to trust people much."

When a sentence such as "You take a man off the streets and make him famous and he loses all sense of values" is underscored, one begins to understand what Steve means when he talks about "growing." He is aware of the dangers of sudden fame and success, particularly the kind that normally attends film stars. He has admitted about himself, "When you start believing everything that's written about you, there is a tendency to get too big for your britches. But when I start thinking I'm the cat's behind, my old lady says to me, 'What's your story, McQueen?' And I'm back to normal." Obviously he has had a struggle to maintain his balance; one explanation, perhaps, why there is such a division of opinion in Hollywood about him. He has said that when he first reached the top, he faced a problem that had destroyed many good actors; he wondered who he was. "As people wrote about me, I'd say they were bright enough to see that, then that's what it is about me. I started being a caricature. I got too big for my britches. I was on a big ego trip." Yes, he had seen the fallacy of it all, he claimed. Now he simply wanted to do what he felt like, take the time to live a bit—"and by that I don't mean discotheques"—to see something of the world "and not just movie sets."

It is easy to bandy words such as vanity, arrogance, ego trip about Steve; yet in the one field where his passions have been deeply engaged—racing—he has shown commendable steadiness. There is no evidence that he even considers himself a good racing driver or motorcyclist. He once said, modestly enough, "I don't figure I'm anything special with motorcycles, but I do it because I need it." Yet his aspirations were serious enough. He broke more than his promise to Neile when he returned to car racing at Brand's Hatch while making *The War Lover*; he roused the ire of the producing company, Columbia, who told him, "Risk your neck if you want to, but not during our present $3,000,000 promotion," an ultimatum that forced him to desist until the film was finished. Then what probably annoyed him most was not the ban by Columbia, it was the suggestion that he had a death wish. "I haven't any death wish like Jimmy Dean," he said. "But racing is no hobby for me—it's a dedication. I want to do something that has dignity, and car racing has the most."

It was more than a simple urge to indulge in speed, then. His words, in fact, open up some interesting vistas. There is the constant recurring McQueen theme about "dignity." He wants a "dignity" mere acting cannot give him. He has not only seen speed racing as a way of "proving" himself but as a way of imparting a "dignity" to himself that he seems to think acting cannot do. "There's no dignity in acting," he has said. "An actor is a puppet in the hands of the makeup man, the director, and the rest of the crew." Steve has Hollywood's usual fine disregard for writers, the men and women who actually *create* the story and dialogue, which are then merely translated into visual terms. Acting money was fine; however, he had taken up racing in 1958 because he wanted "another identification" besides acting. "If I can get to the class of top racing drivers, then I'll probably make a hobby of acting," he prophesied—rather rashly.

He actually said this while in Britain making *The War Lover*.

His only reason for agreeing to do the film, he claimed, was because it brought him to Britain, "the cradle of racing drivers" (he here shows an unexpected lack of knowledge concerning the pre-war racing scene, which was dominated by Germans like Rudolf Carraciola and Italians like Nuvolari). At this time, in fact, Stirling Moss thought he had a good touch at the wheel; and John Cooper, designer of the Formula Cooper, said that if he remained dedicated, "he would be a top-line racing driver within less than two years." By 1965, however, Steve was on a different tack. "I would like to have raced cars, but I'm too old now. Thirty-five is too late to start racing. I'm even slowing down in my private driving. It's been years since I went really quickly." Still his admiration and respect for racing drivers remained as high as ever: "Racing drivers are the only people I have ever really respected, I guess. They are fascinating to watch. Their concentration makes an actor's concentration look like a bowl of skimmed milk." His vocabulary, naturally, had begun to undergo fundamental changes; it now included words such as "smooth charger," "fast charger," and "shunt." Somebody once asked him what the hell a smooth charger meant. He explained that it was a racing term but that he had learned to apply it to his private life. "In the old days I tried to bluster through the pack. But one day I got a little advice from Stirling Moss. He told me to be a smooth charger. It's a guy who doesn't kick up any more dust than he has to. You look into your rearview mirror and you see him trailing the pack. Then he isn't there—he's at the finish line waiting for the field."

He said he saw beauty and passion in racing on a par with bullfighting. "There's a moment in racing when you're slipstreaming round a turn in the middle of the pack that's like the moment of truth in bullfighting—the moment that separates the men from the boys. And that's a lot of buffalo chips about racers having death wishes. Racing isn't a sport for kooks. If you think you're gonna get killed, you'll get killed. I've learned a lot about life from racing—the guys who pick their spots, the smooth chargers."

By 1964, then, Steve McQueen could look around him and see such dramatic changes in his life and circumstances that are the stuff of dreams for most men. He was world famous; his earnings were a reputed $300,000 a film, plus a share in the profits; he was happily married with two children, a girl and a boy; he had a garage full of fast cars and motorcycles; and he had his dream house.

He could be pretty objective about it all, however—in striking contrast to most of his Hollywood predecessors. No actor ever before had dared to discuss the reality of stardom with such candor, to rip away the gloss and show the business for what it really is—just another job, albeit a well-heeled one. "I don't go much with this emotional luxury of being a star," he confessed. "I have a tendency to go the other way. To search and make sure that nothing happens—that I don't grow too big for my breeches. When you suddenly get a corporation of love coming from all different areas because you're successful, the best people in the world can fall for this big star stuff. It doesn't mean beans. I love this business, but it's a job. My private life is something else. I go home. I'm pretty square about my family life; and other than people recognizing me, we lead a pretty normal life, do what we want to do. I don't live in the orbit of the theater or Hollywood. That's OK for some people, but we go camping, we go to the desert, to the beach, to the mountains. I don't want to knock Hollywood because, as a matter of fact, I feel a great responsibility for it. But if ever acting puts clamps on me, watch out! I'm not looking to get categorized—I'm my own fellow. If ever it gets too stuffy, I might just pack up, take my kids, my old lady, and go out and watch the flowers grow."

There is not much doubt that Steve is sincere enough when he talks like this, although like many people who have tasted fame and adulation, he might find them almost as addictive as heroin. Meanwhile, whether because of personal shyness, inner feelings of inadequacy, deafness, or simple dislike, as he insists, of formal gatherings (Neile once said that if he suddenly found himself in a room with more than five people in it, he would get up and leave), he has tried to keep away from the star routine, preferring the simple life.

The impression he gives, in fact, particularly when allied to his known attitudes of hostility and suspicion, is that, if only subconsciously, he sometimes feels himself beleaguered. A restless man, pursued endlessly by the twin demons of boredom and emptiness, it did not take him long to establish his personal fortress. Just as soon as he could afford it, he bought a place where he could find security and privacy and from which, on occasions, he could sally forth like his hero, Alexander the Great, to conquer the world. He once admitted, "It's important for people like me to have sanctuary and privacy. That's why we have this house. This is it!"

The house, known locally as "The Castle," sits on top of a hill at Brentwood and is Spanish-style, with a red-tiled roof. Set in three-and-a-half acres, it overlooks the great crescent of the Pacific Ocean and the pinks, greys, and greens of Beverly Hills and Hollywood. An unmarked driveway leads up a hill to a massive oak door recessed under a stucco arch where a visitor is—or was—asked to state his business to an electric buzzer. If the caller was expected, the door then parted silently in the middle and the visitor entered a broad driveway leading farther up the hill. The house itself lies to the left and could be glimpsed through the trees as the visitor ascended to different levels. A couple of sharp, climbing turns led to a gravel driveway from which a long staircase went upwards through a rock garden to a big door—the back door, in fact. The front is a huge circular flagstone leading to the main entrance. The living room is—or was—about twenty feet long, with a sloping roof and windows looking out onto a terraced lawn—a room elegant in the Mexican style but informal, with shelves of books and the inevitable stereo equipment. Two steps down in an adjoining room stood a huge Spanish billiards table with ornate legs, dominating the room. Over the fireplace was an animal skin with some old guns. The house, like the man, was pretty informal—very different from the image of a Hollywood star's home. Outside, the driveway and garage court were, until recently, littered with Steve's collection of bikes, cars, and pickup trucks, while inside the kitchen was a clutter of his motorcycle gear.

It obviously related to some inner vision Steve probably had once entertained about success. The first time he actually saw the place, for instance, he said to Neile, "Let's go home!" It looked expensive and was; but, "Man, my heart was jumpin'," so he bought it. Then he took a year off from work to get the place right. "At first Neile did all the buying. She never buys things just to buy them. Every piece of furniture, every picture had to be just right—what she thinks I am. They've become part of our lives, every chunk. Part of my blood, too.''

At one stage they almost had second thoughts—the place seemed *too* big. But gradually they settled down and found themselves pretty happy. Steve used to sit in his den overlooking the lawn with trees blowing in the wind, working or fixing up deals, or giving interviews. "This place is so great—milk and honey. And it's so good to have these trees," he told one caller. The grounds held myriad forms of natural life from ants to birds and raccoons, all carefully protected by Steve, who has never lost his farm-boy love for animals. On one occasion, a guest at the house suggested Steve ought to do something about a swarm of bluebirds that had nibbled away all the ripe fruit on the peach trees. Steve turned angrily on him: "What the hell are you talking about? Those birds have more right to those peaches than we have!"

It was all homely, comfortable. One might see Steve working in his workshop, or padding around the living room without shirt and shoes. Then, Neile might return home from a shopping expedition to Beverly Hills with a sack of popcorn and candied nuts for the children and a carton of Mexicali beer (his favorite) and some Mexican hors d'oeuvres for Steve.

Here he often reflected on life and his way of pursuing happiness. "Sometimes I look at those rich guys cruising by in their Cadillacs, paunchy-looking and soft, and I think, 'Not for me!' I take care of myself. Thirty minutes' workout every day to flush the blood around. No booze—I'm the cheapest date in town; four beers and I'm whacked! And I watch what I eat. Organic vegetables and brown flour. It's no good eating white bread. They bleach the flour white so the bugs won't touch it—and if the bugs won't touch it, why should I? I was a vegetarian for a year, but it didn't work. I lost all my strength. Yeah, I got very chippy, indeed. Now, I'm back on my meat and feeling fine.''

Neile, perhaps unwittingly, drew a slightly different picture. According to her, it was the motorcycle that kept him "in shape," though in fact, he did not worry all that much about keeping fit, and he never even gave much thought to his appearance. "He can eat anything he likes," she revealed. "Mind you, he does get a little thick around the waist sometimes after drinking too much beer, which is all he does drink nowadays. But a few hours on his bike and it's all gone.'' As for the daily workout, ''We've a temporary gym in the room off our bedroom, and he fiddles about there with light weights.''

With a glass of beer at hand, Steve liked to relax in the den or on the front porch and chat easily about his life. It seemed a far cry from the ''living it up'' style favored by Frank Sinatra and his friends; even a far cry from the conventional picture of the superstar leading a— as always unspecified—glamorous life. His friends were ''doctors, businessmen, attorneys, working stiffs, mechanics,'' the guys he raced with, in short. ''These are the people we spend most of our time with, our personal time. The guys bring their families along. We don't do that flat-track stuff—nothing really dangerous, just over hill and dale.

''A very tight friend of mine is Bud Ekins; he's a racer and he's got this little girl, Donna, the same size as my boy Chad. The two of them play a lot, and there are other kids Terri's size. We get in the pickup truck and the bikes are in the back, and off we go. They're clean-cut people who work hard for their dough, and they don't compromise. I'm the only movie guy, and they don't hold it against me. I don't think they hold it against me except when something happens like that fashion layout (when a woman's magazine published a spread of Steve with a group of fashion models). You should have heard them then: 'Hey, McQueen, we sure like those bracelets on your arms!' Man, they sure put me on!

''Some of my friends have money and some of them don't, and nobody feels funny because others make some dough. Of course, the way we live, I don't have any money at all (he never wears a watch, either). In fact, it's normal to assume that I'm going to be broke and someone's going to have to stake me on our bachelor nights out when we go somewhere for Mexican food. I just never have any money on me. I had a hundred dollar bill once and carried it around for emergencies but lost it long before the first emergency. It's just sort of my nature to travel light—no rings, no excess baggage. Weekends, the wives and kids get together out in the desert. The kids play in the sand, and the ladies kind of root for their guys and talk fashion. I've come back from a race smelling like a goat and they'll be discussing something from a swank store.

"It's pretty involved—what makes people friends. There's something almost chemical to start with, some interests and experiences to share together. In any activity, someone comes across, and you come across, and the relationship progresses. But these buddies of mine are the ones you can count on when you get right down to the real nitty-gritty. If I'm right, they're with me. If I'm wrong, someone nails me—quick!"

What he had sought—and believed he had found—were people who liked him for himself and for what he could do outside a movie studio, people, he liked to believe, who would still be his buddies if his wealth and fame disappeared overnight.

And the life he led with them—well, it was not sophisticated. It might, indeed, sound a simple and even purposeless way of filling in time between jobs. And yet is that a pretentious notion? He had the open air, the sun, the desert, his friends, and the sensation of action—of going somewhere and going fast. And if Steve was not a man to stop and wonder: "I'm going fast, but am I really going someplace?"", whose business was it but his own?

Between 1963 and 1965, Steve McQueen made no fewer than five films: *The Great Escape; Love with the Proper Stranger; Soldier in the Rain; Baby, the Rain Must Fall*; and the excellent *The Cincinnati Kid*.

Neile, who later declared, "We believe in working together. Our lives were nothing before we met," accompanied him to New York City, where location scenes were shot for *Love with the Proper Stranger*, directed by the distinguished Robert Mulligan from a screenplay by Arnold Shulman and photography by Milton Krasner. Costars were Natalie Wood and Edie Adams. The critical opinion of it on release was that it was "an uneven but undeniably likeable little film."

The story, set in Italian Brooklyn, displayed many cliches; however, Mulligan won praise for his warmth and sophistication, although inevitably one must wonder just how much such qualities are due not to the director but to the scriptwriter. Natalie Wood plays Angie, a salesgirl in a New York store who, already suffering from the restrictions imposed on her by her conservatively-minded Italian family, catastrophically finds herself pregnant after a night spent with an irresponsible musician called Rocky, played by Steve. She goes in search of him, finds him in a musicians' hiring hall, and demands his help—not, as he first supposed, to marry her but to help her find an abortionist. Rocky is rather pleased with this approach and agrees to help. At the last moment, however, he refuses to let her go through with the abortion and stops it. She is thus left in the predicament of having to marry an Italian restauranteur she has always disliked, simply to give the baby a father—for Rocky's refusal to permit the abortion did not involve a pact to marry her. Rocky, in fact, hates the idea of marriage, but suddenly he recognizes that he loves her and deserts his stripper girl friend, played by Edie Adams. Angie at first refuses to marry him, though, believing that later he will feel he was trapped, but in the end she gives in to the marriage.

Critics found echoes of the successful *Marty* in the film, mingled with some of the comedy and toughness that marked the early work of Billy Wilder, and overall, despite a certain unevenness, it had "a delightful freshness" about it. Once again, although the mountainous Nina Varela as the Italian mother tended to steal every scene in which she appeared, Steve emerged as a very strong actor. Essentially, this proved to be a woman's picture and its success confirmed Steve's success at the box office with both men and women. Exposed to the full flood of his raw masculinity and sullen good looks, women began to fall over themselves to see him on the screen. *The Great Escape* had made him a man's star; *Love with the Proper Stranger* gave him romantic status. It was after this—Neile's favorite film—that Steve declared ringingly, "I've got loot, a family, property; and I'm heading for the big apple, stepping on the gas, you know . . . the brass ring."

Soldier in the Rain, on the other hand, was almost wholly a disaster—as a film, that is, but for Steve it in no way damaged his growing reputation or popularity. However, Jackie Gleason, as Master Sergeant Maxwell Slaughter, out-acted him on points, and indeed, held the whole film together. Gleason, incidentally, got on well with Steve and was at pains to dispel the notion that he was "difficult" to work with. He announced, "He's a conscientious kid, and he works hard. There's very little horseplay when you're working with him. He wants to get the job done and go on to something else." This was considered a tolerant and even charitable gesture by Gleason; for one director, talking about Steve a little earlier had emphasized, "He's always taking his own time and trouble to do his interpretations. He says he has to 'feel' his way into a part, and this causes production delays." Robert Mulligan was another who was quick to refute this: "I've heard all those stories about how difficult Steve is to work with, but I didn't find him that way at all." Steve, of course, is a man of many moods and whims, and it would be odd if part of his unpredictable nature did not spill over into his job.

The film ought to have been better than it was if only because it was based on a novel by William Goldman. The screenplay, credited to Maurice Richlin and Blake Edwards, the producer, failed to do justice to the book. Not that the film was without its good moments, although some critics found Ralph Nelson's direction at odds with the obvious intentions of the narrative.

The film opens promisingly enough along the lines of a familiar U.S. Army farce. Sergeants Maxwell Slaughter (Jackie Gleason) and Eustis Clay (Steve) play out the comedy of a rather hapless pair who have found a comfortable berth for themselves in the army, one where Steve as supply sergeant is able to use his stores for the purposes of bribery and barter. Due for discharge soon, Steve tries to persuade Gleason to quit along with him so that they can both go into business together. He is so full of wild schemes for making enough money to get together a stake that Gleason spends all his time getting Steve out of trouble. Eventually Steve persuades Gleason to take up golf and even introduces him to a smashing gum-chewing girlfriend (Tuesday Weld) as a sample of the joys awaiting him in civilian life.

The film might have actually managed to get somewhere if it had been content to proceed along these comedy lines; instead it attempted also to touch the realms of poetry and mystery, to make a statement on the theme of private dream worlds and loneliness. Sentimentality in the shape of a pet retriever and a tropical island to which the partners intend to retire is allowed to creep in, and although there are touching moments as Gleason and Tuesday Weld develop their incongruous relationship, the film ends rather incoherently. Gleason, as the principal star, was hailed, however, for a beautiful performance, and while both Tuesday Weld and Steve earned top marks, at least one critic felt Steve had been let down by the direction. Neither the film nor the role could be described as among Steve's favorites.

In *Baby, the Rain Must Fall,* Steve once again found himself under the brilliant if erratic direction of Robert Mulligan in a film based on the play, *The Travelling Lady* by Horton Foote, with Lee Remick as his costar. Again it was an offbeat part that ought to have suited Steve, at this time rapidly building a niche for himself as the proto-type of the "new star"—the non-hero. In fact, although his performance was acclaimed by the critics as "intelligent and attractive," Steve was miscast as the confused hillbilly husband of Lee Remick, the "travelling lady." Released on parole from prison, where he had been sent for a stabbing incident, Steve is joined by his wife (Remick) and small daughter. He tries to earn a living by working as a handyman in the daytime and as a jazz musician in the evenings. His domineering foster-mother, however, interferes constantly with his musical aspirations. And his domestic stability is also continually threatened not only by his own outbursts of violence, due largely to his sadistic upbringing, but also by his foster-mother's threats to have his parole revoked if he does not give up his music and go to night school instead. Following a severe beating in a dance hall brawl, he decides to follow his foster-mother's wishes until, with her death, he again changes his mind and is then found at her graveside, frenziedly plunging a knife into her coffin. Arrested after a fierce struggle, he manages to escape only to be caught again and this time sent back to the penitentiary for having broken his parole. Meanwhile, his wife and daughter, their lives again uprooted, are forced to move on.

Both the photography and many of the sequences are extraordinarily well done; but the film, largely one of mood and atmosphere, never quite makes up its mind where it is going, and the reflective passages and occasional lyrical sequences are always at odds with the strong psychologically ridden plot. Although generally regarded as a likeable film, the distributors did not rate it sufficiently highly to give it a press showing—at least in Britain.

Steve's career had now begun to roll in earnest, and the scripts were pouring in. And by almost any calculations, it seemed an odd time to take a year's holiday. Steve, however, seemed obsessed with his new house, with buying all the right things for it, and getting it just as he wanted it—besides living up to his reputation for unpredictability and vanishing from the scene just when the demand for his services was at its height.

He had his own good reasons, of course, and they were not just because of the house. There was his marriage—and his relationship to his children. "We hadn't had enough time together for a couple of years," he said, "so I took off, and my wife and I had a ball." They first went to Paris where Steve was astonished to find that he was as big a cult figure there as in America. In order to walk down the Champs-Élysées, for instance, he had to be equipped with a moustache, goatee, and beret by de Gaulle's makeup man. After Paris, they rented a car and drove through Belgium and Germany (they still had fond memories of the chalet outside Munich where they had stayed during the making of *The Great Escape*) before finally ending up in Spain. There, "We took the boat to Majorca, stopped and bought stuff for the house, got lost, and ate wonderful food." It was the first real holiday Steve had ever had.

The holiday, in addition to the time spent working on the house, stretched to almost eleven months. Steve seemed content to bask in his success a little, taking it easy, relaxing, and looking for the right script to go to work on next. Early in 1965 and after he had recovered from his bruising during the East German motorcycle trials, he began work again, learning how to be a card expert for his film *The Cincinnati Kid*, which was to costar Edward G. Robinson, Tuesday Weld, Ann-Margret, and Karl Malden.

His crash in the East German trials had highlighted a distinct ambiguity in his situation. Never before had a hot Hollywood property gone seemingly so deliberately out of his way to ignore the normal precautions suitable to his position. Previously, big stars, of course, had either died or killed themselves while still at the zenith of their popularity—Valentino and Jean Harlow from natural causes, Carole Lombard in a plane crash, James Dean in a car crash, and Marilyn Monroe committed suicide. But no other star had ever gone out of his or her way in such an outrageous manner apparently to invite disaster. Asked about his dilemma, Steve answered, "I have to hang up my racing when I go to work. I have it in my contract because that's the way I want it. I'll stay off every-

thing from pogo sticks to roller skates for six weeks before we
start shooting and for two weeks afterward to give them leeway just
in case they have to reshoot a scene." However, there was no point
in anybody trying to coax or coerce him to give up racing altogether.
"Racin's part of my life," he announced firmly.

Neile then was asked how *she* felt about the crash in Germany.
Loyally she stood by her husband although she was unable to completely conceal signs of the strain and turmoil within her. "I married
Steve because I love him. I didn't become his wife to take anything
from him—only to give my love. I worry, but not with hysteria. I
want him back safe, of course, and I wouldn't be all that unhappy if
he gave up racing. But he loves it, too. I think some women overlook
one fact which should be obvious to us all. Every man has another
love besides the woman he cherishes. And whatever the object of
that second love might be, he must be allowed his chance to achieve
it. It has nothing to do with how he feels about his wife or his family
or his job. It is something he wants privately, for himself, without
help or hindrance from anyone."

It was probably an honest summary of her feelings at the time;
yet she would be hardly a woman, or a wife and mother, if she did
not change her mind. Only a short while afterwards she made him
promise once again to give up racing, and we have to feel a considerable
degree of sympathy for her in her plight. Steve said nothing at the
time but much later revealed that he was not impervious to her
situation. "Sure, she suffers every time—and I suffer for her suffering," he said.

By any standards, certainly it was an extraordinary marriage, and
one that would have created a nervous wreck out of most women.
Hollywood thought Neile was a very clever and patient woman and
recognized the major role she had played in Steve's success, if only
for the way she had carefully cared for him and given him that constant reassurance and affection that his nature and temperament
seemed to demand. Steve himself made no bones about his debt to
her. "I knew nothing of real pleasure and happiness until I met Neile,"
he admitted. Again he said, "She is everything to me. I don't think
I'd have worked nearly as hard or got so far if I hadn't been married to
her. We feel as if we're part of a team, working for each other."

Neither of them ever attempted to diminish this need of his. They admitted more than once that after a particularly difficult filming session, Steve would go home, thoroughly upset and ruffled, and spend a full ten minutes "barking" and "sounding off" in order to get rid of the day's frustrations. When Neile wasn't in the mood to put up with this, Steve would jump on a motorcycle or into one of his fast cars and drive and drive until he had "worked out the kinks."

One cause of his fearsome reputation, of course, arises out of his intense desire to get on with a job—part of his "hurry, hurry" philosophy now almost ingrained in his nature. Steve is often seen at his most petulant when subjected to delays. He shows a total impatience with red tape and with those interminable conferences endemic to all filming—when points are gone over again and again, although a decision seemed to have been already reached. It was at times like these that Neile appeared to fulfill an indispensable function for him. Once, in public, he came over to her, a determined-looking hombre with his chin jutting out, shoulders hunched as though ready for a fight, and growled at her, "I just can't stand it! When the baloney brigade brings everything to a stop because they want to sit down and talk about problems that haven't even come up yet!" On this occasion, she took his hand and said gently, "Honey, hasn't anyone told you, you don't have to fight so hard any more? You've won. The battle's over."

He cooled down sufficiently to think about this; then came back at her with the disenchanting question: "Yeah, but what happens to a man who's spent his whole life fighting and suddenly discovers that there isn't anything to fight anymore?"

Herein, in fact, lies one of the main problems now facing Steve McQueen; the sudden sense of letdown after he has fought like the very devil to scale at a height and then doubtless realizes he has come to a dead stop. It is the old Alexander the Great syndrome all over again—realizing that there are no more worlds to conquer. Steve spent at least a decade of his life fighting tooth-and-nail to become a success and then suddenly discovered that the hustling and battling were, in his case at least, anachronisms. "It's the hardest thing about this business—once you've established yourself professionally, you suddenly wake up and realize you're a success and you ask yourself, 'What now?''

"You've been so busy trying to be successful that you haven't had time to grow up and adjust to your new position in the world. That's the really tough part—when you realize that the world isn't there for you to turn on its ear. You've got to understand it. And before that, you've got to understand yourself. The only education I had was in survival, and they don't pay any extra goodies for that. I used to be the guy who always banged his head against a stone wall. But things have changed, and even success can be a problem, too.''

Yet if professional achievement had solved one problem in his life only to create others, he had the consolation of being backed now by something for which he had longed all his life—a tight, integrated family of his own. He declared himself very happy that his family "was very, very tight." He no doubt felt very protective and concerned about it, yet somehow he was able to see it as a vulnerable point, a possible chink in his armor. One of the things that apparently "bugged" him about the film business was how some people "try to get at you through your wife and kids." Steve comments that he wanted Neile and the kids "to be people in their own right and not shadows reflected from a movie star"; he did not want anybody looking at Chadwick and saying, "That's McQueen's kid." His view was: "I want them to have their own identification and not grow up in the shadow of some movie-star image."

He apparently took his parental duties seriously and seems to have had firm, clear-cut ideas as to what a father's role ought to be vis-à-vis in children. Friends said he was always ready to play with them, to point things out to them, to stimulate their interest, and to answer their questions. But he was seemingly not the type to be an indulgent parent who lavishes toys and other possessions on his children in an effort to make up for anything he might have lacked in his own life. He was a traditionalist, and traditionalists do not curry favor with their children. What he seemed prepared to give them instead was a focus of strength, security, and decision. When he issued an instruction, then that was that. The story goes that once young Chad wanted a toy similar to one he had seen in another boy's house; Steve refused to let him have it—probably on the grounds that his children had to learn the value of things. Chad bawled his head off, but Steve remained firm. When the children needed a spanking, Steve did not shirk his duty—they got it. Although Neile says that after Steve had given Terri her first spanking, she found him sitting on the back stairs "fighting back the tears." Still, with all his money and resources—and his memories of his own youth—it was inevitable that both Terri and Chad should be spoiled to some extent.

Nonetheless, he still seemed to see them as hostages to fortune; as another route by which people could get at him or in some way injure him. "Let's get one thing straight," he declared, "because I talk hip and was a hard case as a kid, some ding-dong puts me down as a kook. Well, believe me, I'm not feeling sorry for myself. I got my cake and I'm trying to eat it, too. I'm not a kid anymore. I've built a life for myself and my family. The kids are off limits. They can't fight for themselves—I have to do that for them. If anybody hurts my family, I'm gonna put them down in a little black book."

Early in 1965, however, the ruminating and philosophizing came to a temporary halt as he threw himself with renewed fury into the process of making another film. Probably as a symbol of his growing success, he allowed himself the luxury of a present—a new caravan dressing room. It had an expensively furnished living room, mini-office with three telephones, bedroom, kitchen, bathroom—and, of course, a bar. It also had a TV and stereo equipment and was equipped with a host of electrical gadgets. Then he settled down to make *The Cincinnati Kid*, one of his most esteemed successes.

10.

"Shaping Up"

I~t~ could be argued that it was a gift more likely to thrill Steve himself than Neile. Yet there it was—her tenth anniversary wedding present. And unquestionably expensive! A dark green classic Jaguar SS Excalibur, wrapped in blue ribbon.

She had been up early that morning as usual to prepare Steve's breakfast and see him off to work. (He once listed among his pet hates: "Waiting around for breakfast. If I don't have breakfast the instant I wake up, I rage like a tempest. As soon as I've had my tea and oatmeal cookies, I'm calm and sweet-natured again.") She knew it was their wedding anniversary; but Steve, like many men, had given her no indication that he remembered it. He had kissed her as usual, winked and rushed off saying, "See you later." She felt neither peeved or disappointed; she had long ago reconciled herself to the fact that Steve would, in so very many ways, hardly qualify as an ideal husband. Anniversaries, birthdays, and all those other little holidays, pseudo or otherwise, were the kind of events that just naturally slipped his memory.

She had just got up for the second time that morning when the maid entered her room carrying a bunch of violets. They had been handed in at the door by the delivery boy. Neile sniffed the violets, then opened the tiny envelope that accompanied them and read Steve's familiar scrawl. All it said was, "Good morning, baby," but she knew exactly what he meant; he *had* remembered the anniversary.

Later, when she reached home after picking up the children from school, Steve himself came to the door instead of the maid when she rang the bell. He stood and stared thoughtfully into her face for a moment before leading her around to the front of the house where, parked in the court, was the Excalibur.

"It's yours, baby," he said simply.

Neile admits to feeling flabbergasted—as much by the care he had taken to tie it up with blue ribbon as with the car itself, or even the money he had obviously spent on it.

Steve's marriage to the girl he always called his "old lady" has been dissolved since 1972, and so many of the comments they both made from time to time now have a hollow ring. Yet the marriage did last for almost fifteen years, and in the show-biz *milieu* in which they both lived, this is a remarkably long time—even given Neile's Catholicism and consequent aversion to divorce.

While women the world over certainly envied her possession of this attractive man who has been likened to "a shy rapist," not to mention "a latter-day Bogart with a hint of old-fashioned Jean Gabin," or simply "the world's most potent male sex symbol," one has to conclude that it was far from being cider and sweet apples all the way. There were at least four areas of tension within the marriage that must have caused her nerve-wracking moments: (1) coping with Steve in all his wild and unpredictable moods; (2) his obsession with speed and danger; (3) a knowledge that predatory females were continually trying to take him away from her; and (4) the claustrophobic nature of their private life—the absence of a varied social life involving parties and other formal gatherings; women, after all, do like dressing-up and being taken out somewhere.

A marriage is an exceedingly private affair, and it might well be argued that it is none of our business to analyze Steve and Neile's. Our excuse is that neither of them was reticent about discussing it when they were married, and some knowledge of it helps our understanding of Steve's character.

Nearly all male movie and TV stars find that a major obstacle to a stable marriage is the adulation they get from female fans, sometimes leading to quite open invitations to commit adultery. Many movie wives accept this as one of the hazards of the profession and simply turn a blind eye. It is true that both Steve and Neile were aware of this partic- ular danger, and it was one of the reasons they were at pains to go on location together. I possess no evidence that Steve ever was unfaithful; indeed, I have heard it said by one of his intimates that although Steve had the opportunities, "he never played around." It would be in character if this were literally true. However, London Journalist Michael Housego who interviewed Steve at LeMans got the following ambiguous statement: "It's very hard to say 'no' sometimes. Some of them [women who offer themselves] are very beautiful. I'm no saint, by any means, but I try very hard to retain the dignity of my wife. She believed in me when I was down—a nothing. She's my lady. Marriage is very diffi- cult when you're in the public eye. It becomes abnormally abnormal, and you're exposed to so many problems and rumors about other women. Neile is under great pressure constantly because I'm a movie star." So, whether they were justified or not, Neile faced the task of living with rumors; even if she succeeded in convincing herself that they *were* only rumors, she also had to live with the knowledge that somewhere in the wings waited a younger woman who might snatch him away from her. It could not have been a comfortable posi- tion.

His mania for speed and danger gave her many sleepless nights. At times she did summon the courage to demand that he give racing up, but she must have been constantly torn between the fears and her recognition that "racers," as he insisted, "are not courtin' death—they're courtin' being alive." She knew what he meant, recognized what he needed, probably wanted him desperately to feel that he was free. And yet, however she worked it out mentally, she had, from time to time, to insist that he must stop. It was an appalling dilemma.

Steve himself always indicated that he appreciated her position, and he certainly made gallant attempts to minimize his involvement in really high-speed racing. On the other hand, one part of him was an incorrigible "ham" who could never resist playing up to an audience. On one occasion, for instance, Dino, son of Dean Martin, took a drive with Steve near "The Castle." "We just took off suddenly like a scalded cat," declared the impressed youth. "I've never been so fast around suburban corners in my life. I was nearly scared out of my pants. Boy, he's wild—real wild. But he can handle a fast car, make no mistake about that." Furthermore, according to Dino, policemen waited in hiding just outside Steve's gates, hoping to pounce on him but always losing him on the first bend. One cynical writer suggested that either Dino was allowing his imagination to run riot or: "Steve must have enough speeding tickets to paper his living room."

Confirmation of Steve's predilection for impressing passengers comes from an *Esquire* magazine writer who records that during a spin with him, Steve drove his Ferrari into blind curves at between 60 and 70 miles per hour—although "it was quickly apparent that he knew the road well . . . knew in advance how much to brake and how far to gear down . . . and was satisfied to drive well below the speeds which the car could, in fact, have negotiated the road. . . . I relaxed." On this occasion, a motorcycle cop caught them and Steve remarked, "If you play, you pay." The cop for his part, finding he had snared the great man, was apologetic. "Steve . . . if I'd knowed it was you . . ." Steve, soothing the man with the comment that he had his job to do, then got immersed in the technicalities of the cop's bike and accepted the speeding ticket with grace. When he had gone, begging, "Wait till I get out of here before you open that thing up again, will you?" Steve remarked, "Those guys aren't so bad, you know. Some of them are okay."

It is also true that when a London reporter turned up for an interview with Steve at Le Mans, Steve insisted on racing round a field on motorcycles. This, of course, was partially due to his apparently insatiable need to "milk an audience," even if only of one. Yet there is no doubt that he was deeply aware of his responsibilities and on occasions tried desperately to stick to his good resolutions. One of these was to race his bikes less often and stick to cars and, after 1967, to "dune buggies," especially designed machines for travelling fast over desert. "He's cut down a lot on his motorcycle driving," explained one of his intimates, "the whole daredevil bit. Oh, sure, he still likes to take the bike out for a little spin, but he's acting more like a Sunday rider than a hot-rodder. I guess he's worried about his family now.''

Steve, however, is a fellow who seemingly has to show what he is made of ''when the chips are down.'' There is a scene in *The Cincinnati Kid* where he dashes across the train tracks with the Super Chief rushing down on him like a juggernaut. Neile declared, ''I've never been so scared in my life. I had to look at him and touch him and be sure he was right there beside me.'' Steve's comment: ''I told you when I shot the thing. I came home and said I'd done a stunt today. You didn't take it very big.'' He seemed to feel she should not have been surprised or scared—that it was a hazard of the game. She *knew* he expected to do most of his own stunts, and he had it all carefully worked out, anyway. ''I had to run across thirty-five sets of tracks for this scene. I talked with the engineer of the Super Chief and asked him how many yards he needed to halt this thing, and he assured me he couldn't possibly halt it, so I was aware of the setup and used my own timing.'' Neile observed, ''He likes standing like inches away when the train roars by.''

As soon as she had got over one thing, there was another. In 1965 he and John Sturges planned to produce a film about sports-car racing, starring world champion Jackie Stewart and with Stirling Moss as technical adviser, called *Day of the Champion.* Sturges declared that it would make *The Great Escape* look like a schoolgirl's picnic. Fortunately for Neile, several complications, the major one of which was the unconscionable time spent on *The Sand Pebbles,* led to its abandonment.

Nothing, of course, could keep Steve away for long from the famous Baja 500—an extraordinary race that has no counterpart anywhere else in the world and that would wreck any ordinary production studio however specially stressed and structured. The track grinds its way down the entire Baja California coast in Mexico, takes thirty hours, and creates unique dangers. Much of the race is run over open desert or along donkey tracks. The entries are specially designed cars, often made by the entrants themselves and looking like Rube Goldberg contraptions but with powerful engines and sophisticated suspension systems that enable them to be driven like bucking broncos. Any kind of contraption, including motorcycles, can enter. Along with his cronies

Bud Ekins, Chuck Coy, and Cliff Coleman, who were members of the team that had competed with him at Erfurt, Steve went off to Baja, "just to hang out and have a good time." They "slept in sleeping bags, got drunk, yelled at each other, and carried on. And then we ran the entire five hundred miles on those bikes. I loved it," says Steve.

The spectacle of specially designed "dune-buggies" bouncing over this notorious track whetted Steve's appetite for this form of racing, and in June, 1968, he took part in the Stardust Off Road Championship at Las Vegas in a similar contraption. Neile was waiting for him at the finishing post and got into a panic when he failed to arrive. She could not keep believing the worst and was in a state of agony until word finally reached her that he had merely broken an axle of the car and was himself OK.

Steve continued to run dune-buggies in the wilderness near his desert home at Palm Springs. On any one of these occasions, he was theoretically liable to break his neck or severely injure himself, although the dangers can be over-stressed. With practice, any young, alert man with a "feel" for machines can hurl motorcycles, cars, and even dune-buggies around like old shoes. Women, however, tend to see only the dangers; and there is no doubt that Neile suffered more than most wives, if only because Steve had the time, money, and enthusiasm to spend more time in dangerous machines than most husbands. Steve's passion for dune-buggies, incidentally, was not restricted to racing them; he formed a company to manufacture them, and the sleek, powerful buggie he drove in *The Thomas Crown Affair* is reputed to have been designed by him personally.

Probably the worst strain Neile had to undergo was when Steve made *Bullitt*—famous for its hair-raising, car-bashing stunts along the switchback roads of San Francisco. When Neile, who had stayed behind in Brentwood, found out that Steve was doing his own driving in the film, she telephoned the producer, Robert Relyea, and demanded that he be replaced by a stunt driver instantly. As all the dangerous stuff had been already shot, her plea was too late.

Whatever she said to Steve in private at least had the effect of reminding him that he had a family dependent on him and that he was not quite the free agent he would like to be; certainly after *Bullitt* things calmed down a bit around the McQueen household. Then, in 1969, he discovered yet another form of competitive racing. This was jeep racing at Ascot Park, a Los Angeles dirt track that stages night races— spectacular events involving 25-feet jumps over poles and a great deal of fender bashing and end-over-end crashes. Steve strapped himself into his own Jeepster, and the crowd of four thousand who packed the stands one night saw him fling his machine through a pack of howling vehicles and clouds of dust to win. He turned out again at this event fairly regularly—at various times running out of brakes, chipping his teeth, crashing, and spinning. In November, 1969, he made a full-scale attempt on the gruelling Baja. He drove an extremely powerful machine, which he called "The Boot" and which had a 450 horsepower engine under its truck-like bonnet. Steve left the starting line with the cheerful declaration that "she rides smooth as a Caddie," but the rough track took a front wheel off and ended his attempt.

Although his plans for *Day of the Champion* had proved abortive, he had apparently never quite put the idea out of his mind of making an epic film based on one of the great European classics. The success of world Grand Prix champions such as Jim Clark and Graham Hill at Indianapolis had brought home to Americans the supremacy of European cars and drivers in general. Steve himself was under no illusions as to what Grand Prix and European endurance races were all about—the greatest test of driver and car in the world. In particular, having sampled the Sebring twelve-hour endurance test in 1962, he said he was fascinated by the extraordinary event that took place annually at Le Mans in northern France: a round-the-clock event along ordinary arterial roads, with twists and bends, against machines capable of doing over 200 miles per hour, and in totally unpredictable weather conditions. "I got to thinking about Le Mans and the film I wanted to make there," said Steve. Cinema Center Corporation agreed to back the film, which Steve's own company, Solar, with the enormously successful *Bullitt* under its belt, would produce. "I needed to sharpen up for *Le Mans* in a piece of hot machinery, so I wrangled a 908 Porsche."

He gave the new car a tryout at Holtville and won. At Phoenix, Arizona, he set up new lap records and came in first. At Riverside, he did a Stirling Moss—that is, he drove the car a bit too hard. As he led the pack toward the first turn, changing gears rapidly, the gearbox blew up, throwing bits of twisted metal in all directions. The Porsche slid helplessly across the track at over 100 miles per hour while up in the stands Neile watched petrified. Steve managed to bring the car to a smoking stop but admitted, "That one scared me plenty." Shown photographs of Neile's face, he commented, "I got the message." Later he was impelled to point out, "Maybe the publicity in my case has got out of hand so that the public thinks I'm a super driver of sorts. I'm not that; I'm simply a guy who loves the sport"—an example, incidentally, of his talent for modesty against all the expectations his behavior can arouse.

The incident was of such a nature that Neile, despite herself, had to protest yet again and plead once more that he jettison Le Mans. Yet Steve had once said clearly, "I live for myself." Anyway, she knew that if he were to give up the sport, what, exactly, would he have left? How would he occupy himself when not making a film—this restless, itchy-footed man who had driven himself remorselessly to success and could not easily gear down? What does a man with no intellectual interests do when he can no longer indulge his desire for action? How does a man who lives for purely physical sensations find alternatives to erase the *ennui* that has always threatened to engulf him?

There is little doubt that Steve would have given anything to please Neile. As he matured, "shaped up," mellowed, he was more and more aware of his responsibilities, yet he remained a prisoner of his past— he had no cultural or intellectual pursuits. Whatever his wife said, whatever his managers advised, whatever his responsibilities, Steve saw no option but to proceed with the great project—*Le Mans*. He attempted to explain his feelings: "A lot of actors give racing a bad name because they're not legitimate about it. In other words, they're nothing but amateurs who make phony movies about themselves and racing, taking the publicity and the profits and then running without giving anything back. To me, it matters what people are thinking of me, whether it's in southern California, the movie scene, the motorcycle world, or the car world. I've gone through the mill, and if a guy beats me, he's a better man than I am. If I beat him, I'm a better man than he is. That's the game. When I turn 'hare and hound' in the desert, it's the same situation. A number of times I couldn't even qualify. When I started winning, I was accepted. But you've got to make it yourself. People know I'm serious about racing. I care about it, and I would never shortchange a sport that means a great deal to me and to tho: e people who relate it to me.''

Good, fine words, in short embodying much of his philosophy. The Game was competing against others; accepting that if you win, you're better, if you lose, the other guy's better; becoming ''accepted''; making it yourself in the good old American way; not shortchanging people; having ''integrity.'' They were only cold comfort to Neile, however, particularly when Steve announced that as a preliminary warm-up for the film, he intended to have another shot at the Sebring twelve-hour endurance test in March, 1970. To ''build up my endurance'' he first entered a motorcycle race at Lake Elsinore. ''It was a rough grind,'' he said—one hundred miles of all-out riding embracing desert trails, drainage jumps, sand washes, and a mountain trail with a 500-foot drop—''a really good workout.'' More than five hundred other cyclists took part in the race, and Steve overextended himself. In an effort to keep up with the leaders, he throttled into a road dip too fast and was thrown from the bucking bike into the crowd. Instead of breaking his neck, he got away with breaking his foot in six places. He somehow managed to ''climb back on and finish in the top ten, but it hurt a little,'' proving, certainly, that he has guts. The foot was encased in plaster immediately after the race, and he was warned to take it easy for a while.

It is impossible to seriously question Steve's nerve or courage, if not sometimes to doubt his sanity. It has been said that Steve actually entered Sebring because doubts had been expressed to the effect that he had not done his own stunts in *Bullitt*. It is typical of the man, perhaps, that he would insist on quashing such doubts in the most public way imaginable. Yet even the doubters must have been taken by surprise when Steve limped out onto the starting grid at Sebring with his foot still encased in plaster, joking that this was his ''ghoul foot,'' or ''Frankenstein Boot.'' He says, ''I went through several casts and a variety of special shoes and boots, trying to get the right combination for driving at Sebring. In Florida they passed me at the medical, even though I was on crutches. I convinced them that I could handle my end of things. Pete Revson was my codriver, and we took turns behind the wheel for the full twelve hours. And I guess you could say we were lucky.''

This, of course, is the quirky side of the McQueen nature for the resulting achievement cannot be all that easily discounted. In fact,
competing against some excellent European and American cars, Steve
and his codriver won their class in their 908 Porsche and were only
twenty-two seconds behind the overall winner, Mario Andretti. By any
standards, it was a success of which any driver could have been proud;
but for an amateur, with one foot in a plaster cast, it was more than
good. And few people had any idea that the wracking pain had been
such that on several occasions during the race, Steve is reported to
have come near to blacking out completely. Neile watched it all and
suffered every minute. Steve himself, flushed with success—it was his
biggest achievement in racing ever—characteristically shrugged it off
with the remark, "Heck, it was nothing—my plaster boot was too heavy
to lift off the throttle!" (Later he modestly elaborated, "We only came
in second because everybody else dropped out.")

Well, that was the funny side, ignoring the pain. Yet there were con-
flicting reports of how Steve had really felt. There was the newspaper
quote, which seemingly owed more to a publicity source than Steve himself: "This is all too fantastic for words. Like a dream. I had no idea
we could achieve anything so staggering." On the other side, there was
the man in the pits who was heard to say, "That's a great driver, all
right. But Christ, look at him. He's scared the pants off himself!" Perhaps the truth lies in a mingling of all these aspects—that Steve suffered
pain; was scared some of the time; was proud of his achievement; considered it fantastic (or at least, beyond anything he had ever hoped);
and that he had done so well and "proved" himself.

Whatever the truth, one thing was certain: nothing on earth could
stop Steve from making a film on Le Mans, and it was this more
than anything else, that was to prove a breaking point in his marriage.

Steve McQueen appears to get by, both in his private and public life,
with an extraordinary economy of words. Apart from his early light
comedies in which he spewed forth words with the rapidity of Groucho
Marx, he has made almost a feature of inarticulateness, or better,
controlled silence. I personally found him both terse and hesitant in
answering questions, but many other writers who have spoken to him
say that he speaks very well when he wants to. It would be clearly

unfair to suggest that he has been influenced by Marlon Brando, but he has obviously utilized certain elements of Method acting that he considers of special use to him. Certainly, film by film he has said less and less until he reached a nadir in *Le Mans*, in which the camera spent an inordinate amount of time just standing there worshipping him as he just stood there worshipping it back. No doubt some women found this enchanting enough—preferable, anyway, to gazing at bits of metal shaped to look like cars flashing across the screen.

The technique is one unique to Steve and is subtly different from the old strong-silent-man attitude of, for example, Gary Cooper, who could get by for several frames on a single "nope." One never felt that Cooper was anything but a hero who was bound to win, even in the classic *High Noon*. Steve, however, is man matching fate, a man dumb and inarticulate in the face of forces continually threatening to overwhelm him. Always the dice is seen to be loaded against a man who can never win. It is a portrait of a kind of dumb suffering. Neile has explained the technique: "Steve dislikes open emotions. He believes that the true nature of man is how much he can feel without showing it." It is very effective on the screen, certainly, and he emerges as a calm, controlled, "cool" person who recognizes the odds and simply does not flinch.

Yet Steve, in real life, is probably far from being what he seems on the screen. Neile has said. "Inside he seems like some great angry sea in a storm." Part of her wifely duty was to weather those storms. She was very frank about it: "There are times at home when he doesn't do very well at keeping his temper down. I have a number of hideouts in the house, and when he explodes, I fly to my nearest secret niche and curl up until the storm I married has raged himself back to calm. It's the best way, believe me." None of this emerged from Steve himself; all was now wonderful in a really wonderful world: "I have a great home and a great wife and great kids. I am grateful for everything I got. The only trouble is I don't know who to be grateful to." He made it sound idyllic, and, no doubt, he believed it. "To me marriage is a sacred thing—it's *heart*. That's where it's all at it's sharing your roof and bed." When questioned about the relative longevity of his marriage, he could never offer any explanation: "Everybody's got their own life, and they've got to lead it. If a guy's married the wrong chick, he's got to live with it or find himself another lady. If the chick's unhappy, they're gonna split. Either a marriage is compatible or it isn't. I'm always put in the position of coming up with hard statements. Somebody asks, 'How come an actress can't stay married?' I've no idea. All I know is I've got good vibrations with my wife. She's my wife, and I love her. We're not supersonic people when it comes to marriage. Basically I'm a lot more conventional about marriage than a lot of people who have nothing to do with show business."

At this time, Neile concurred. "Wild and unconventional though Steve is, he's really rather conventional about marriage." He did not, according to her, "like to see other men fooling about with other women. He doesn't believe in that. To him, what was 'right is right and wrong is wrong.' " Everything either of them said seemed to enhance a paradox. Success, for instance—was he really so "cool" about it? Yes, their basic mode of life had not changed. "We've more of everything—a bigger house, more clothes, the children can go to good schools, and Steve can buy fifty pairs of corduroy pants and drawers full of socks (he has a thing about socks). And I love antique Spanish furniture. But basically our life is the same."

She must have tried to change him, though? "Why should I? I was enticed in the first place by his difference." She hoped fervently their children would grow up to be like him: "a human being who's done a lot of living and learned, absorbed, from everything, the good, the bad, the beautiful, the ugly, who's grown from but not relinquished his past." Pleasant sentiments. And we have Steve chipping in with comments on himself in the role of father and how it had helped him to "find" himself. Not knowing his own father was a help, not a hindrance: "It was kinda like me trying to give the kids all the warmth and companionship I wanted when I was their age. Maybe it didn't turn out too badly after all. I lost my father, but I found myself." All part of "growing" and "shaping up." He *had* changed, in fact, he insisted: "I've learned to talk things out and to compromise instead of blowing my top. I used to throw away money, now I throw away pennies as though they were manhole covers. I'm a businessman now. I take care of my health, avoid self-indulgence; I watch what I eat and drink; and I don't pamper the kids. When it's bedtime, they go! I believe in a lot of love, security, and discipline. I'll never be able to see my own father in this world, but at least I can be a good father to my own kids."

It was all fine and commonsensical—so far as it went. And, of course, it had its modicum of fun. Neile, indeed, could talk about it all being "a ball," but she had to mollycoddle him a lot, and his whims and sheer restlessness could not have been always easy to live with. He was lost if she were in another room, for instance. "I do everything for him," she once said. "He's like a child, he just likes me to do things for him. He can't make a pot of hot water. I don't mind except when the help is off, and I'm cleaning the house, and I'm all mixed up getting the children to school and all that, and he comes and says, 'Would you bring the coffee up to me?' " On such occasions she behaved, if not like a member of Women's Lib, at least with a show of independence. When she refused, he would go back upstairs, either back to bed or to his den where he would sit and make phone calls until Neile brought him the coffee. Nor did Steve like to eat by himself or to be served by anyone he didn't know. "That's really why I don't work," she explained.

She has said he was possessive to an inordinate degree—possessive and demanding. For example, when she starred in the theatre-in-the-round performance of *Pajama Game* at Covina, she had to drive there every afternoon and return home each night after the performance, although the rest of the cast sensibly lodged there. Even so, Steve must have been mildly petulant about her absences—to such a degree, indeed, that one night he left a note on her pillow saying, "I love you—your pen pal." Neile said she understood his attitude—it was hard on him to get home from the studio after a difficult, possibly quarrelsome, day to find she was not there. "The rest of the cast stayed at Covina, but I'd just drive back to be with him and keep peace in the family. On weekends, when we had two shows on Saturday and two on Sunday, and I had to come back on Saturday night and go back the next day, I wasn't too crazy about doing that."

Often she arrived home to find Steve asleep, so she would leave a note to say she loved him, then go to bed. She would get up at 7:00 A.M. and slip on a robe and see him off to the studio before going back to bed. Loyally she claimed that none of this upset her: "I once had a maid who put it very well. She said, 'As long as the man of the house is happy, then I'm happy.'" She took good care, too, to make it apparent to all that it was Steve who wore the pants in the family: "I ride back seat." She helped him in his job: "I'm a sounding board." Whenever a script was offered him, he always consulted her. "If I don't like it, then he's swayed by me." She had read *The Sand Pebbles* and told him, "It's perfect for you," and he took her word for it.

Friends have said the couple had reached a happy *modus vivendi* in their marriage. Now and then, they contrived a little therapeutic breathing room; Steve went off by himself to their house in Palm Springs where he would "just lie about in the sun and think, things like that."

Although careful with his money, he demonstrated his affection for her by presenting her with many valuable gifts. There was the Excalibur SS; there were Italian earrings and an amethyst cross he picked up on their European tour. He appreciated the value of every coin, but he was capable of bidding $10,000 on a gift for her at a charity auction. As the story goes, Steve paid the money for a diamond ring although he was under the impression that he was bidding for a fur coat. Neile listened in apparent amazement as the bidding rose and rose, and when it reached five thousand dollars, she remarked to James Garner who was beside her, "He's bidding $5,000 for that damned coat, which I could get for $600." When she heard the bidding closed at Steve's $10,000 bid, she almost wept. "Isn't it terrible," she is reported to have said to Garner, "and I don't even want the coat."

According to the story, when the ring, a square-cut diamond circled by a myriad of baguette diamonds, was handed over to Steve, he said, "I don't want that—I want the fur coat." "But you bid for the ring," explained the girl messenger. "Well, OK, then." Later, when Steve handed Neile the ring (until then the only ring she wore was the band of twisted molten gold that was her wedding ring), he reportedly growled, "It's the last time you'll get anything like that." One suspects that Steve knew quite well what he was about and simply wanted to surprise Neile.

As though to make up for his careless forgetfulness about birthdays, anniversaries, and so on, he often surprised her with little tokens of affection. Once she walked up the drive of their home to find Steve waiting with a bunch of flowers for her. Whenever they did go to parties, he frequently came over and put his arm around her. If they were at different ends of the room, Steve would suddenly look across and smile at her. He liked to show his affection in public, to touch and be touched by her—but not by other people.

She made no secret, however, of the obverse side of the coin—the squabbles, the shouting and "hollering" at each other, the lapses into mutual pique. "But he knows when he's wrong and I know when I am—and we apologize and say 'I love you.' " She was meticulous in pointing out that all the changes that had taken place in his character were for the good. He was no longer as wild as he had been, and he was more relaxed and seemingly content. His greatest "vice" was sheer restlessness—the inability to keep still or stay in one place very long. The restlessness was one reason why he had "a terrible time" keeping his weight down; because he could not sit still, he ate constantly. The restlessness was there at all hours of the day and night. Once, when she remarked, "How lucky we've been," he replied, "Luck and hard work, lady." And like him, she always had a sneaking feeling that the luck could not last. The idea that he might even leave Hollywood was not always that remote, either. Neile has said that he often repeated, "I'd like to try Australia. I've got itchy feet," Australia probably represented some vision for him; it is a motif that actually turns up in the film *Junior Bonner*. Loyally she claimed that Steve was "no pigeon for boredom." Steve himself claimed: "I've never been bored except when sitting in an office. I guess Neile and I aren't the kind of people who get bored easily. There's always someplace to go, someplace to see, something to do. It's as simple as that." Boredom may have been Steve's problem; it was not hers—it was his incorrigible restlessness. "If he wants to go out at three in the morning, I won't stand up and say 'No.' I believe it's his right. Sometimes he gets up at 1:00 A.M. and says, 'Let's pack up and go to Palm Springs,' so we pack up and go to Palm Springs." She added, "I can't see why I shouldn't go to Palm Springs at one o'clock in the morning, anyway."

On another occasion she said that he planned to take an entire year off after making *The Sand Pebbles*, but he was so restless without work that he was soon back filming. "It's not that he goes out with the boys too much—although he does sometimes—he just can't relax. We're constantly going backwards and forwards to our other house in Palm Springs. We no sooner get to Palm Springs than he says, 'Let's go home.'" What he seemingly needed constantly was "something concrete to occupy his energies." The night journeys helped Steve "to unwind." He seemed more restless between films than when actually working. "We go to bed, and I fall asleep. He *hates* it when I fall asleep and he can't sleep, so he wakes me up and talks to me. I plead, 'Oh, no, *please* leave me alone.' And he says, 'I'm hungry.' So he gets up and raids the fridge. Or he'll wake me up with 'Get up and pack. We're going for a moonlight picnic.'" What did she do about it? She might easily reply that she had no choice. Sometimes they went down to the beach and careened around in go-carts or on the motorcycle. Sometimes, by day, he went off on long drives by himself, to get back into his own mind, to take out any frustrations he might have, because "it has an emotional release." From time to time, he took the family along because "it gets us away from the world for a while, together as people."

Steve paid his tribute: "She's as game as hell. If I get up off the couch at twelve o'clock at night, which I've done, and say, 'Let's go,' we take off. Before we had kids, we could go at a moment's notice; now I sometimes have to wait to get them out of school." Neile commented, "Ours is not the cozy family life where everything runs like clockwork. Nothing is predictable with a man like Steve."

A bluntly spoken man, he apparently weighed his words or considered if they were tactful or impolitic; and he had thoroughly old-fashioned ideas with regard to marriage and the role of women. In his eyes, the man of the house *had* to wear the pants, no question. If he did not, then he was henpecked. "Man, nobody's gonna tell me what to do. If my old lady wants me to do something for her, that's fine, I'll do it for her, not because I'm afraid of her but because I love that woman and want to make her happy. And even then, if what she wants me to do really conflicts with what I want to do, like race my bike, I just won't do it." Over the years she suffered with that bike, and because of it, she probably felt little sense of tranquillity and security in the marriage. From the beginning, of course, Neile had realized that she had a part-boy, part-man on her hands and that when it came to his beloved bike, he would never quite grow up. In fact, possibly to her surprise, he at least gave up racing as he approached his fortieth year, yet he still careened around fairly furiously on his bike. "Remember this," producer-director Robert Wise once observed with a certain obscurity, "Steve is desperately anxious to maintain his own identity. That's why, though he will never race again, it is important for him to use his bikes. He wants to hang on to some part of being an average guy."

Neile was frank about Steve's moods. "But I understand him now and know him well. He is terribly moody—one word can change his whole mood—but it only annoys me when I can't understand it." One thing she never worried about was other women: "If I did, I'd get old before my time. If it's going to happen, it'll happen, whether I worry about it or not." She agreed, however, that it was unwise to be apart from him for more than a couple of weeks at a time. "I don't think a married man should be left alone for more than two weeks."

He could display jealousy. When she said she was going out on her own, he wanted to know exactly where she was going. He did not like her going out, even with a girlfriend, when he was at home (when he was on location and she was unable to go with him, he arranged that they call each other twice a day). If he did allow her to go out with a girlfriend, he insisted on knowing exactly where they were going, and invariably when she got there, Steve would be waiting. Just after they returned from Taiwan (where they were shooting *The Sand Pebbles*), they were invited to a party. As usual, Steve insisted he didn't want to go, so she asked him if it would be all right if she went along with Rick Ingersoll (Steve's former publicity man) and his wife. "Well, we hadn't been at that party for five minutes when Steve showed up!" Steve admitted that they clashed over such things as parties and, for people in their position, their relatively restricted social life. "Neile gets uptight because I don't take her out much," he said. "But I don't like going out."

To be fair, however, he did occasionally allow her off the leash. Sometimes she went to their Palm Springs house by herself. "A housewife has to do something for herself. I need silence sometimes, and there I just read, laze, sunbathe, swim—but never for more than a day or two. Steve frets if I'm away too long."

So there it was—a restless, itchy, and in a strange sense, claustro-phobic existence, lived on a hilltop. One can envision Neile waking up to hear Steve pacing about their bedroom, slipping on slacks and sweater, and zooming off behind her husband at 3:00 A.M. among the black hills of Mulholland Drive, feeling "as though the world were ours." The stars were watching them as they drove on and on through the countryside until dawn, without exchanging a single word, just feeling "a great togetherness." Steve, on their return, stretched out his arms wearily and with a slow grin, declared, "I feel wonder-ful. All the kinks are out."

She knew him all right: "Every wife has to know her man and how to make him happy." Nonetheless, there was the racing, and everyone knew that she suffered. But again loyally, she insisted: "I learned long ago that I must let the man who's my husband go-go-go in order to make him happy. I can't tie him down or say no to him. My hus-band is like some magnificent wild creature—he can't be tamed. He must have an outlet and his is racing. So even if my heart might be in my mouth, I let him go. If possible I go with him, but I never get in his way. I'm just there."

Two years before he made his biggest success, *Bullitt*, she took him aside and had a showdown with him about his family responsibilities. He then made her a promise to ease off, and to a large degree, he did so. Yet he seemed unable to resist temptation. He had promised once before and had then broken his promise once he saw Brand's Hatch. When he made *Bullitt*, nothing could stop him from driving in some of the most hair-raising car sequences ever filmed. "Those sequences for *Bullitt* were the hairiest things I've ever done," he ad-mitted. Someone, of course, "blew the whistle" on him and told Neile, who flew up from Brentwood "and gave me hell. Called me a sonofa-bitch in front of everyone." They had then been married for twelve years, and he added, "I guess she deserves some kind of Iron Cross for staying with me." With persuasion, he was ready to show the twenty-seven stitches on the inside of his lower lip caused by his Brand's Hatch crash. But he insisted that "at thirty-eight I have de-finitely started to change gear, to slow down. I've kept my promise to my wife to give up competition driving, and if I pace myself and keep up my coordination exercises, I should be able to go on at some speed until I'm forty-five.'' As a throwaway, he added, "Keep your body cool, and you're on a natural high all the time.''

Neile, almost with the submissiveness of an Oriental woman, apparently treated him in a way most Western women would find difficult to accept (and which will create a few problems for Ali MacGraw). She had evidently studied her man and recognized the boyish factors that remained in his makeup. This granted, even she could not predict how he would behave or what he would say next. "He will tell me at noon when I'm wearing a simple dress that I look beautiful, then at five o'clock say 'You look awful. Why are you letting yourself go this way?' And this when I'm looking my best!''

She continued to make sacrifices to keep the marriage going. She had missed her chance to play *West Side Story*. Now again, she turned down the lead opposite Marlon Brando in *Southwest to Sonora* because taking it would have meant being unable to go to Taiwan with Steve for *The Sand Pebbles*. Heaven knows what he might have done had she not gone, for it proved the longest and most arduous film of his career. She went along, however, and had the satisfaction of knowing that this film opened up a whole new dimension for him. She thought at the time, "No one could live with this man but me. He's a man of so many moods. He may suddenly wonder 'why did you do such and such,' referring to something that happened four months ago!'' On the whole, however, she seemed happy. In 1967 she declared, "This is our happiest period—these last five years. Not only because of the security Steve's success has brought us but because our personalities seem to be maturing together.'' Steve himself commented that he had "shaped up" and had more time to think about who he had been and what he had become: "You see, I don't believe in that grabbin' and grabbin' and stuffin' yourself and not givin' anything or puttin' it back. I'm not just a star—I'm a businessman now, able to make a great deal of money and to do things on a productive level, not just to help myself acquire the sanctuary I need but also to be able to handle it, to be able to feel responsibility. For openers, I'm a goof-off. I know it. I've always been. That was my thing, my *shtick*. But now I'm in a position where I have to be a businessman. I have to be prompt, I have to be the first one there and the last to leave. Also I have to be very considerate, very tolerant. I can't get mad any more. See, it's like all these things are makin' a man of me in an area where I never was. Now I'm stuck with a thing I always really wanted, and I'm a bit frightened of it. And yet I like it. I like being responsible and having two beautiful children and the old lady and the house and, you know, man, work every morning at 7:30 and back at 8:00 at night. Today, what I used to hate, used to rebel against, why, man, it's now part of my life." Even more grandiosely, he seemingly saw himself almost as a symbol of American democracy—"the guy who was hip when he was young and still managed to score," who hoped "maybe they (meaning the younger generation) will get the message."

11.

STAR INTO BUSINESSMAN

Sᴛᴇᴠᴇ McQueen, like so many stars, becomes transformed into a bundle of uncertainties when he sees himself on the screen. At a rough-cut of *The Cincinnati Kid* screened in MGM's studios, he "seemed to panic," according to people who were there. He has admitted: "I'm suicidal when I see myself on the screen. I get trapped in that room, and there I am twenty-four feet high on the screen, and I'm in a cold sweat."

He "suffered" so much, indeed, that when he and Neile eventually left the projection room, he dented the left front bumper of his car trying to drive out of the parking lot.

To this day, he can scarcely bear to watch *The Great Escape*. It was a spectacular part and he recognized what it had done for him, but although the character he played appeared to "represent" unquenchable rebellion, Steve himself actually disliked the character's philosophy. He simply would never have butted his head in vain in that stubborn way the Cooler Kid did. He is, in fact, filled with doubts about every film he makes—even when others acclaim him. He won an Oscar nomination for his role in *The Sand Pebbles*, yet he absolutely hated himself in it. However, he makes a practice of jumping into a car and driving to a cinema in some small town. There he will sit in the back row unnoticed to study the reaction of a disinterested audience in order to obtain a proper appreciation. When he viewed *The Sand Pebbles* this way and heard the music that accompanied it, he changed his mind and announced, "Hey, it's not so bad, really."

When Steve heard he had been nominated for an Oscar, Neile exclaimed, "God forbid you win it." This had nothing to do with him growing "too big for his britches" but with his neuroses. "If he'd won, he'd have been impossible to live with," said Neile, "not because of a big head but because he'd be worrying how to top himself next. I prayed he wouldn't win it. To be nominated was marvelous. It was just great to get near the target; this way he still had something to aim at."

It seems inevitable that Steve must collect an Oscar someday—if only for the very range and intensity of the roles he has played. These have been described as "offbeat," yet even when analyzed quite cursorily they are little more than the kind of naturalistic roles familiar in most European filmmaking. In McQueen films, the hero is not necessarily a knight in shining armor; he does not necessarily win. Although Steve no longer thinks of himself as a loser—is, indeed, emphatically a winner—he is only too ready to play a loser's role (although he is always the winner of some unexpressed private battle). Typical was *The Cincinnati Kid,* which he made in 1965 under the direction of the distinguished Norman Jewison. The story, based on a novel by Richard Jessup, is set in New Orleans in the late thirties. Steve plays a young stud poker player known as The Cincinnati Kid who "takes" all the local gamblers—honestly, of course—and is then matched with Lancey Howard, played by the patriarchal figure of Edward G. Robinson (The U.S. champion in a competition for the title "The Man," which Edward G. has held for thirty years against all comers). The dealer is Shooter (Karl Malden), widely respected as a fair and honest man. Just before the big game, Steve's woman, Christian (Tuesday Weld), leaves to visit her parents and, taking advantage of her absence, Shooter's woman, Melba (Ann-Margret) tries to seduce The Kid, who rejects her. In the meantime,

Slade, wealthy owner of a New Orleans brewery, is promoting the game, urged on by Lancey. He brings pressure to bear on Shooter over certain debts and orders him to fix the game by giving The Kid bad cards. During the game, The Kid notices what Shooter is doing and asks Lady Fingers (Joan Blondell), an old hand at the game, to pass the cards in his stead, claiming that Shooter, his old friend, is ill. At this point, as in the conventional Hollywood film, the hero should win. Instead, Edward G. bluffs his all on a single card and The Kid is beaten.

Originally the film was to have been directed by Sam Peckinpah, who directed many of Steve's later successes. Jewison unquestionably made a fine film, full of tension, with concentration on the atmosphere of the card table, and with excellent gambling dialogue written by Terry Southern and Ring Lardner, Jr. The acting throughout was extraordinarily good, with Edward G. out-performing everyone in sight, including Steve—a massive *tour de force*, alongside which Steve's own cleverly calculated performance seemed overshadowed. Yet his youth and animal magnetism were always there, counterpoint to Edward G's basso profundo.

The Cincinnati Kid was followed by *The Sand Pebbles* in 1966, which provided Steve with one of the experiences of his life. The night before Steve and his family left for Taiwan (Formosa), they had Paul Newman and his wife Joanne Woodward up to dinner at The Castle. Steve's last word that night as he saw his visitors off was, ''I really hate the thought of going to the Orient for nine weeks.'' This proved to be the understatement of the year; all in all the McQueens were to be abroad *seven* months. Bamboo vipers whose bite was almost immediately fatal were only one of the *small* problems they had to face.

The Sand Pebbles, produced and directed by Robert Wise, was Steve's first ''epic,'' in other words a ''big'' subject, with elaborate sets and locations, a stupendous budget, large cast, and eventually 16,380 feet of film, which took exactly 182 minutes to run. By any reasonable critical standard it was an enormous waste of time and effort, sinking effortlessly into mediocrity. And yet Steve, albeit looking curiously plug-ugly, even unattractive compared with his later image, because of his close-cropped hair and the over-frank photography, gave one of his best performances.

Shooting proved a traumatic experience. Afterwards Steve admitted, "Everything I ever did wrong, I paid for on that baby. That was *work*." Warned about the vipers, he had taken a heavy duty thirty-eight revolver with him to protect his family. It was impounded by customs, and he had to settle for a Chinese goose, which they christened Ha Ha and which paraded up and down in front of the house like a sentry. Geese were the local method of containing vipers, and Ha Ha was kept busy while Steve and family were in residence.

The story, costarring Richard Attenborough, centered on the task of an American gunboat, the *San Pablo*, in evacuating U.S. missionaries from their post on the Yangtze River during fighting between rival warlords in 1926, which saw the emergence of Chiang Kai-shek's Nationalist China. A great chunk of the $8,500,000 budget was spent constructing a miniature gunboat, 150 feet long, one of the most costly props in history. Made in Hong Kong, it was later sold to South Vietnam. Wise was able to spend what he did on the prop by shooting on location— the cost of creating fake backgrounds and sets, with junks, sampans, and thousands of Chinese extras would have been prohibitive in Hollywood. Yet if he effected budget savings, he had to contend with other problems aside from the ever-lurking vipers. There was the weather. Filming was scheduled for Keelung, which, regrettably, has an annual rainfall of 200 inches. Weather changes were even more extreme and temperamental than in Britain. One day a sweltering 90 degrees, the next a cold wind sweeping down from Manchuria bringing sleet and rain and zero temperatures. One day the *San Pablo* rode high in the water, and the next day it lay stranded on a dried-up riverbed. Days were full of unrelieved boredom as everyone stood around waiting for the right conditions for shooting. Once, just when shooting had recommenced after a long delay, real guns from the Communist China mainland opened up and again stopped everything.

Steve relieved the interminable boredom by zooming around the island on his Japanese-made motorcycle or by playing his favorite game, pool, in the Green Beret headquarters at Taipei. He never neglected his family, however, taking them for almost daily drives around the island. At intervals both Steve and Neile got sick, and an additional worry was the fear that the children might contract an obscure dis-

Steve's performance as Jake Holman in *The Sand Pebbles* (1966) won him an Academy Award nomination.

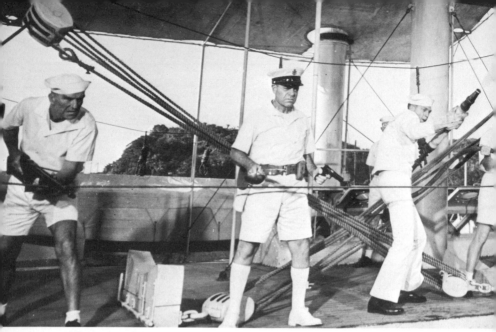

(Top photo) In a scene from *The Sand Pebbles* are (l. to r.) Ford Rainey, Barney Phillips, Steve, Richard Attenborough, Gavin MacLeod, and Charles Robinson. (Bottom photo) Steve cheers on his shipmate, Simon Oakland, in a fight with Mako.

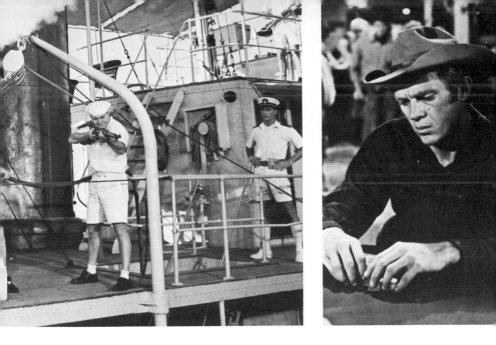

Although it was not a critical success, *Nevada Smith* proved to be one of Steve's financially most successful films.

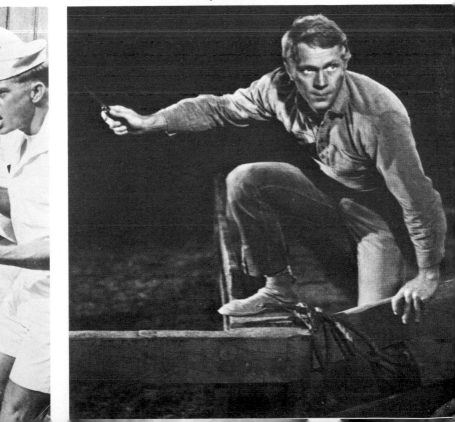

In *The Thomas Crown Affair* (1968), Steve played a Boston businessman who successfully engineers an ingenious bank robbery.

ease. Neile became very fed up and suggested she go home; but, presumably half-jokingly, half-seriously, Steve told her, "You gotta stay right here with me, baby, and earn your money." A disappointment for Steve, but a bonus for Neile, was the shelving of Steve's cherished project, *Day of the Champion*. "I've been rarin' to make an honest down-to-earth movie with lots of action behind the wheel of a racing car," said Steve, "but an actor's life is one of gambles and unexpected twists of fate. So let's just say I hope to make that movie someday." Meanwhile, he sat around in sneakers, brown sweater, and crumpled cream slacks, talking with his right ear inclined forward so that he could pick up the answers and drinking a beer brewed in Manila and smoking a lot (a habit he later abandoned). He was bored beyond belief with the everlasting, frequently torrential rain; the interminable shooting delays; and above all, perhaps, the anti-American attitude of the Chinese. From what we can gather, as he grew more mature, Steve found out something about himself he had never dreamed of— he was a patriotic American who loved his country dearly, who could not stand to have it knocked.

His only compensation was playing Jake Holman, ship's engineer in charge of the *San Pablo's* engine room. His love of machinery transmitted itself to audiences and to the critic who hailed his performance, "McQueen dominates every foot of the film on which his image is imprinted." Robert Wise declared, "The part of Jake might have been written with Steve in mind. It really hit him where he lives. I've never seen an actor work with mechanical things as he did with that ship's engine. He knew everything about it, and the warmth of his relationship to it showed. He's marvelous in the picture because he has the attitude and looks to carry the dialogue. He's not only an emotional and instinctive actor, but a *thinking* actor." Certainly Steve's empathy for machinery was clear-cut and striking. It was also extraordinary how well he performed considering that among his pet hates is "hanging around doing nothing on a film set."

The Sand Pebbles opens with Jake joining the *San Pablo*, one of the innumerable gunboats patrolling the Yangtze at a period when China lacked a stable government and the country was overrun by warlords. He finds the engine room run by coolie labor with the tacit connivance of the ship's officers and makes immediate enemies by deciding to run things himself. The film is largely the story of a man obsessed by machinery coming to terms with the idea that Asiatics could operate it (as recently as 1926, it is laughable to recall, the idea that Asiatics could handle technology was considered absurd). Richard Attenborough, as Frenchy, has a strong part in the film as the white man who falls for a virgin Chinese girl up for grabs in a whorehouse and marries her. Much of the film is concerned with this affair and shows Jake forsaking his beloved machinery long enough to help his friend. When the coolies, under a blackmailing threat from Chiang's army, withdraw from the *San Pablo* and leave her in a state of siege, Frenchy jumps ship at night and swims ashore to spend a night with his bride, only to be rewarded with pneumonia and death. The Chinese seize the girl and murder her for consorting with a foreign devil and then demand that Jake, who had visited the house where Frenchy lay dead, be handed over as her murderer. The captain slips the gunboat downstream, away from the demonstrators who insist that Jake be handed over, and then learning of a worsening of the situation, turns back to rescue some U.S. missionaries. At the film's climax, the *San Pablo* breaks through a boom the Chinese had flung across the river and reaches the U.S. mission. The missionary and his girl assistant, however, both refuse to be evacuated, insisting on the essential goodness of the Chinese; but when the missionary is killed, the girl finally agrees to leave. Jake draws the Chinese fire to allow the girl to escape and in the end is killed, a sacrificial victim, laying down his life for the others. There is no doubt that Steve gives a magnetic performance; yet the film itself was disappointing, with Wise rather unwisely interpolating a symbolic association with U.S. intervention in Vietnam in an attempt to give topicality to the story. If it had been more tightly written and directed, the film might have been a good, straightforward, action-packed narrative and consequently more successful. Nonetheless, until *Bullitt*, Steve regarded *Pebbles* as his favorite film and his performance as Jake as perhaps his best. It was some recompense for having to abandon *Day of the Champion*.

The experience was trauma-inducing in other ways. During those long, boring days, Steve appears to have made up his mind about one thing—his identity. Perhaps he had never believed his success as an actor was anything more than ephemeral and sought a second career to fall back on in car racing. After *Pebbles*, however, he declared, "I'm going to try to put the energy I used in competition racing into my work. Racers always end up screaming. I got a lot of stuff out of my system by doing it. Now the question of my identity is resolved. Neile taught me responsibility; I recognize my responsibility is to my family. Racing is for professionals. My profession is acting."

Yet to come, of course, were *Bullitt* and *Le Mans*.

His experiences in Taiwan had cost Steve a good deal of energy and enthusiasm, and it was time for a holiday again—and to take stock. He was a much different character from the bum who had hit Hollywood in 1956. His speech patterns had changed and were no longer solely those of hipsters and hucksters and the have-nots. He had taken to eating more sophisticated meals and was hooked on organic foods, such as brown bread. His circle of friends had changed a bit, although he still remained close to people like Bud Ekins. He was prepared to take an interest in other people besides himself, in other matters beside car racing and movie making. He was still in a hurry. Neile made it clear what he was after now: "He wants to build an empire."

This was a reference to his film company, Solar, which had been originally formed in 1961 as a legal method of diminishing his tax liabilities. Gradually it had become an umbrella for several ventures including a restaurant and a plastics factory (Solar Plastics Engineering), which, at Steve's insistence, hired Mexican-Americans, part of his charitable and good-citizen-of-the-world feelings. Despite diversification, Solar, however, remained basically a movie company with Steve himself the major asset. Before the holiday, there were bits to tidy up on *Pebbles* and talks about new films. Solar had coproduced *Soldier in the Rain* as far back as 1963 and was a coproducer with Argyle of *The Sand Pebbles*; it was planning its first big solo effort, *Nevada Smith* (based on a story by John Michael Hayes, which itself was taken from a character in Harold Robbins' *The Carpetbaggers*).

But first, the holiday. "He planned to take a year off," said Neile. And one day he walked into the house and said, "OK, baby, let's go.

I've got the camper serviced. You get the kids out of school." As impulsively as that. So they set out for Alaska via the Rockies to see what Steve called the Big View. Neile drove part of the way because he was tired. "I never thought I'd drive with a dame; I always thought it meant ending up on somebody's front porch." They stopped at a small store for groceries, then Steve took over, and they drove up to Flathead Lake, where they camped beside a waterfall in a heavily wooded spot. While Neile rested, Steve took the kids off into the woods. They returned with the news that they had met a fisherman who said the yellows were running good so that they could start bright and early next morning to catch golden trout. Hopefully, Steve would be lucky this time. Neile reports that the last time they had gone camping, Steve was the only one who had not caught anything.

The trip was successful. Like many men trapped in towns and jobs, Steve evidently always dreamed of the great outdoors. He had once promised Neile, "Someday I'm going to take you and the kids and blow right out of town, get somewhere big and out-of-doors"; yet he was soon aching to get back to work. The same thing happened after he finished *Nevada Smith*. Again he planned to take a whole year off, "but after four months he was almost out of his mind and couldn't wait to get back to work," Neile reports.

Nevada Smith was an ambitious film and Steve's first Western since *The Magnificent Seven*. It purported to tell the story of what happened to Nevada Smith, son of a white father and an Indian mother before he met Jonas Cord (the Howard Hughes central figure of *The Carpetbaggers*) and before becoming a film star in Hollywood. Young Max Sand (Smith's real name) finds that sadistic killers have tortured to death his parents, who lived isolated lives in the mountains, and he vows to revenge them. He meets Cord, a travelling gunsmith, who shows him how to use a gun. The boy then sets out to find the killers. He comes across the first in a saloon and, although wounded himself, kills him. He finds the second in a Louisiana prison camp to which he gets himself sent in order to engineer the escape of the man he wants to kill. During their break for freedom, he kills the second man, although he has to watch the death by snake bite of an Indian girl who had befriended them and helped them escape. The third killer is the leader of a gang of outlaws and suspicious of all newcomers, but Nevada still manages to get enrolled in the gang, only revealing his true identity and purpose during an ambush on a gold shipment. With the last man at his mercy, Nevada is overwhelmed by his conscience, realizing that he is in danger of becoming as bad as the men he has killed, and instead of killing his final victim, he merely shoots him in the leg to maim him for life. One of Hollywood's most distinguished directors, Henry Hathaway, directed the film and made the most of the visual scenes. Critics, however, thought that Steve had been badly miscast, that he had been unable to convey the impression of an illiterate halfbreed. Artistically the film was considered second-rate, and no one thought Steve had done anything to enhance his stature. Yet financially it turned out to be one of his most successful films. In addition, he *enjoyed* making it. It was shot on location in the hot desert, and "I spent almost every night sleeping under the stars. It was great." The film almost ended tragically, though; at a party given by Joe Levine, executive producer, to celebrate the completion of filming, fire broke out on the set. Flames raced swiftly through the sets at two Hollywood studios, Paramount and Desilu, driving 1,500 guests, including Steve, Elke Sommer, and Martha Hyer from the tables where an outdoor banquet had been laid.

It was two more years before Steve appeared on the screen again, this time in a film that confirmed him as a superstar and made him America's biggest box-office attraction. As worried producers sought frantically for a formula that would attract cinema audiences away from television, one listed the kind of film he thought would succeed and then added "and anything with Steve McQueen." Steve became one of that triumvirate of stars which shared top popularity over the next five years—the other two being John Wayne and Paul Newman. He now entered upon a run of films during which it seemed impossible for him to do wrong—ending abruptly in the disaster of *Le Mans*. The first was *The Thomas Crown Affair*, for which he was paid $700,000, one of those films that is both maddening and attractive, memorable both for stunning sequences and, at the same time, sheer crassness. Blame lies with Norman Jewison, who appears to have sought to adapt the literary device used by Walter Lord in *Night to Remember*, the

166   STEVE MCQUEEN

story of the Titanic. What could have been a neat crime story, packed
with action and tension, was destroyed by berserk film tricks and
mannerisms, including the use of a multiple screen technique that
would have been useful for design purposes in a musical but had no
part in a film that sought to tell a taut tale of a bank robbery. The
story itself was simple, if idiotic.

Crown, a bored young millionaire, decides to mastermind an ingenious
bank robbery, controlling the movements of his gang (who are strangers
to each other) by telephone from his office across the street from
the bank he intends to rob. He gets away with $2,500,000. Jewison
uses the multiple screen to show Steve, the dominant image, at his
telephone, directing operations and assembling his gang for the attack,
while in smaller images one sees members of the gang simultaneously
getting out of taxis, arriving at airports, and waiting in telephone
booths. The effect, meant to show Steve as a spider in his web, is
merely confusing and fails to grip the audience, which is constantly
made aware that it is simply watching a film, not participating in
what appears to be a real event. Yet there are memorable scenes—
Steve alone in a glider, looking like a bronzed Icarus, and the sexy chess
game played with Faye Dunaway. In the story, Faye plays an insurance
investigator who, working by intuition (easily the best way to solve
crimes), deduces that the stolen money has been deposited in a Swiss
bank and, working on photographs of various suspects gathered by the
police, picks out Crown. She then arranges a meeting with him
during which she discloses that she knows he is the mastermind.
Crown begins dating her—only to fall in love. Crown then reveals that he
has another robbery planned and invites her to join him in the escapade
and fly off to South America. She decides on a double-cross, however,
and arranges for the police to trap him after the robbery. To her
delight, however, Crown makes a last-minute switch and gets away;
then he sends her a telegram inviting her to follow with the money,
which has been hidden. On the whole, the film is highly amoral. Alive
to this criticism, Steve insisted that crooks nearly always got away
with it, and he wanted to tell the truth.

Off-screen, life was a matter of family, machines, friends, lectures,
speed, philosophizing, giving interviews, eating, and just putting in time.
Immediately after *The Thomas Crown Affair*, he was out in the desert

near Palm Springs scorching about in his dune-buggy. Much of his daily life in Los Angeles seemed bound up with driving in and out of garages, having car batteries checked, putting in a certain kind of oil, sitting in his immense Ferrari playing pop records on a cassette tape recorder under the dashboard, and declaring, "I don't know anything about music. You could throw a stone out the window and hit somebody who knows more about it than me." If his language was no longer hipster, it was terser than ever. It was so laconic in fact, that reporters often got the impression that he had simply nothing of significance to say or, as Tom Hutchinson put it, "He seems to me like a Sphinx without a secret." As an alternative, perhaps, to weighty conversation, he had developed a little repertoire of homilies: "I'm so tight I wouldn't pay a quarter to see an earthquake."

Some days he walked with that quick, exuberant, almost euphoric stride of his along the Strip, where he knows and is known by everybody. It was his little world, one in which he was king of the castle. Every now and then he might stop to say hello to somebody. At the Whiskey-a-Go-Go he would pick up his old buddy Elmer Valentine—"we go way back"—an ex-cop, then lunch on the terrace of The Old World, facing the street and safe from interference because there are no pedestrians, only motorists in L.A. His meal? Hamburger, mixed green salad, Belgian waffle with syrup, and iced tea. At close quarters, his face gives an impression of tremendous range, lacking the open-jawed look of passive stupidity that often characterizes it on screen.

He might get a call about Chad who had fallen off his bicycle and hurt himself. "He pushes too hard, that kid." It was during this period that he delivered a lecture to students of the University of Southern California and got stuck when somebody flung a word like "conceptual" at him. But he could explain carefully to the students how he chose his film subjects: "I do it by instinct. But I have to be careful because I'm a limited actor. I mean my range isn't very great. There's a whole lot of stuff I can't do, so I have to find characters and situations that feel right." He frequently drove down to Palm Springs where his house was a modest one, standing beside other houses looking exactly alike and at the end of an ordinary street and with a pool—a small pool—in the backyard. Here he might regale a visitor with a piece of marvellous mimickry—and he can be very funny.

Or he might be sitting in a lounge chair beside his pool, looking up at the mountains behind which the sun is setting, and explaining that he sometimes went up there hunting: "Just birds, pheasants and stuff," or remarking, "There's some moon people who live over there near the hills"—a moon cult. Talking abut some of the less delightful aspects of being a film star—meeting a guy on the street who recognizes him and then "goes temporarily crazy just from looking at me, and the thing is I know what's going on in his head. He's got to 'make his mark.' He's got to do something because there's a movie star right in front of him, and it may be his only chance in his whole life. After a while, they all turn into the same person. Like you're always meeting this same guy flipping out, trying to *get* you, trying to *eat* you, man." But he found most people "OK"; he had settled for the fact that people were going to look at him, and there was no point in fighting it. He had to find "some way to groove inside it." New people however, "bugged" him. "I mean it's hard to know sometimes. They come on so strong, some of them. You wouldn't believe it, man. Some guy starts up and brings his whole soul into it, like he really *bares his soul*, and you just gotta believe it because he's way out there, way, way out, telling you things he wouldn't tell his own mother. Then later it turns out the guy is a son of a bitch. It makes you feel terrible. You feel sick inside."

Or perhaps he is at his plastics factory, which makes parts for motorcycles, housewares, and so on. He might next be found racing at Ascot Park where he tells a reporter, "Think I'll go out now and bounce around a little." Strapping himself into the "buggy" and putting on his helmet with no fewer than *five* press agents clustered around him. Coming in second—in a race with three runners. Next morning, wearing his second hat, as president of Solar, he might be in a round-table discussion about his next movie. He has an executive suite ("Not bad for a kid outta reform school, huh?") with wall-to-wall carpeting, antiques, trophies, and four-pound glass ashtrays. Everybody is equipped with sharp, new orange pencils, staring at blank writing pads while Steve more or less harangues them. Talking on. And on. His eyes covered with dark glasses, he is making such remarks as: "Got a coupla things to bounce around here, if I may''; or ''Conceptionwise, in my estimation''; or whenever somebody else tries to speak, saying, ''Excuse me for interrupting, Bob,'' and then he interrupts. He would then explain wryly, ''I guess I kind of like to think of myself as the head honcho.''

It is an open secret that while he affects to disdain publicity, Neile kept a book of newspaper clippings about him—as he put it, ''so my children can see what a horse's ass their old man was when they grow up.'' In these, he could read the various ponderings of others on his personality and character: Frank Conroy of *Esquire*, for example, underlining his enjoyment of physical sensation and discounting the probability that he saw speed as a symbol of his power to destroy himself or of something that made him a pawn in the hands of fate; that he did not know why he was rich and famous and did not want to know because he might lose his innocence and thus part of his power as an actor; that he pretended to be less intelligent that he really was, simply to retain his privacy and because he regards superficial manifestations of intelligence as misleading; that he no longer drinks spirits because they give him bad hangovers.

He could read his costar in *The Thomas Crown Affair*, Faye Dunaway, explaining why, despite the fact that he has a contempt for drooling women, he has such magnetism for the opposite sex. ''He stimulates that cuddly feeling. He's the misunderstood bad boy you're sure you can cure with a little warmth and some home cooking.'' Or the late gossip columnist Hedda Hopper's comment, ''He excites. I took a look at that hardened face and knew he had a past.'' He could read that he wanted to be ''dug'' for his intelligence and ability rather than as a sex symbol.

But in fact, around this time, just after *Bullitt*, he announced, ''I'm a filmmaker. I want the respect of the industry. Actors have a bad handle in the world. I'll tell ya, in my own mind, I'm not sure acting is a thing for a grown man to be doing.''

He could afford to talk like this, perhaps, because he and his company had just made the glorious *Bullitt*, more of an achievement, perhaps, than he had ever dreamed possible, particularly as the script was slight and confusing. ''We had a crappy script, and we made somethin' out of it,'' he later declared with pride.

Bullitt, of course, was a landmark for him. In 1969, as a result of it, he found himself named "Star of the Year."

12.

BULLITT AND THE HEIGHTS

THERE was this bit where I was supposed to swing around fast into a small side street and clip a parked car. Pete [Peter Yates, the director] wanted it kept authentic, so we thought we really would swipe this parked car near the bend. It was nothing to do with us, but we planned to leave a note on the guy's windshield, saying he could have his damage made good just by ringing the studio. Anyway, when I finally took the corner, I overcooked it completely. I smashed right into the parked car, completely wrote it off and cannoned into another car parked next to it!''

By 1968, Steve was not only a man whom the belles of Memphis could vote ''the sexiest man in America'' (a nice public relations ploy) but an actor-business tycoon ready to expand the scope of his Solar Productions (formed in 1961). Steve was paid a straight salary by producers, who also paid a proportion of their profits to Solar, whose sole shareholder and beneficiary was Steve. The effect of this arrangement was to increase Steve's real income well beyond his reported salary and allow him to accumulate capital.

Though Solar, in fact, was given credit as coproducer of *Soldiers in the Rain*, *Nevada Smith*, and *The Sand Pebbles*, it amounted to no more than a financial arrangement. In 1968, however, Bob Relyea, a chum of Steve's since they worked together on *The Great Escape*, joined Solar as executive producer; and Steve was ready to launch out as a full-fledged tycoon and *actually produce his own pictures*—the impulse being, as he had said, the desire to obtain the respect of the industry because he felt that actors "had a bad handle in the world." He probably could see himself at the center of a complex web of businesses, including his plastics factory, earning that "dignity" and "respect" that Americans feel only a real businessman deserves. The first "property" acquired by the new partnership was a run-of-the-mill crime thriller called *Mute Witness* by Robert L. Pike. The policy of the new company was to make realistic adventure stories, avoiding anything depressing, downbeat, or sordid.

Mute Witness had nothing very striking or original about it. It has been argued that the only thing that matters in a film is the story; star, direction, and quality of photography are mere trimmings. Certainly what attracts an audience is the story. And a star only becomes a star because he appears in good films. Even the most charismatic personality cannot survive more than two bad stories. Years ago, for instance, Clark Gable was almost destroyed because he appeared in an absurd adaptation of the story of Charles Stewart Parnell, the great Irish statesman. Today, new stars such as Clint Eastwood consider the story the first and most urgent priority; get that right and the rest follows. *Bullitt*, however, turned out to be an exception proving the rule. Many people, in fact, came away from the film totally confused as to the story line, not quite sure what had been going on or who was after whom or what, but nevertheless vastly entertained. The budget was $4,500,000 and quickly showed a return of five dollars for every one dollar invested (with more to come). It was among the top five box-office hits throughout the world in 1969. What lifted the film out of the rut was the most hair-raising car chase in film history—twelve searing minutes when Steve, as Lieutenant Bill Bullitt of the San Francisco police department, chases a criminal up and down the inclines of the San Francisco hillsides and where the big, soggy-springed American cars came

---

thumping down onto the flat of the intersecting avenues before rising in the air like ski jumpers to touch down on a lower level. The only comment Steve himself made after this thrilling chase was "Spooky, man, real spooky." A popeyed crewman who witnessed the scenes from a sane distance commented, "He must be a nut. He's got a death wish or something."

Bullitt was the first of six films Solar was supposed to make for Warner Brothers-Seven Arts, a backing company that initially saw it as little more than a fairly routine flick. Briefly, the story concerns Johnny Ross, a member of the underworld who is persuaded to give evidence at a Senate hearing, and who is hidden away in a seedy hotel for his own safety. Bullitt is assigned to protect him. Through no fault of his, Ross is shot down by gunmen whom he admits to his room. He is rushed to a hospital while a furious D.A. bears down on Bullitt and threatens to ruin his career if Ross dies. Ross does die; but Bullitt, by persuading the hospital staff to cooperate by not revealing the death, gives himself a short time to further investigate the affair. Then he discovers that the dead man is a decoy who has been deliberately planted on the police while the real Johnny Ross gets out of the country. After the spectacular car chase, Bullitt corners the real Ross at a San Francisco airport, and the film ends on yet another high note as Bullitt chases the villain across the runway where planes are taking off and shoots him in the departure lounge in front of crowds of panic-stricken onlookers.

The inspired decision was to make the film in San Francisco, considered by many to be America's most beautiful city. Oddly enough, Los Angeles, home of the film industry, is generally sparing in allowing facilities for filming. But Mayor Joseph L. Alioto, as mentioned earlier, had opened up the whole of San Francisco to Solar. Steve afterwards insisted that much of the credit for the film should go to other members of his team—he deserved no more than was due to him as an actor: "If I were to take credit as producer, it would mean very little to me." He said he wanted "more thinking heads" involved in his company. Not that he seemed short on energies or abilities. Production Manager Jack Reddish and producer Phil D'Antoni share the credit for personally approaching the mayor and getting his assistance. As a result, Steve had at his disposal a full-time police team consisting of a sergeant and two patrolmen. They kept "traffic control, security" and "leap-frogged ahead" to such sites as the "coffee house," where shooting was due next. It was largely the brilliant and unmannered use of San Francisco's streets that gave the film much of its distinction—leaving aside the great chase scenes, which were enhanced by the authenticity of the backgrounds.

Warner Brothers-Seven Arts was aware that a chase was built into the script but wanted it shot in the back lot at a savings of $40,000 plus insurance, plus saving of life and limb by some undercranking. Peter Yates, the plump, late-thirtyish English director who had been hired to make his first Hollywood film on the strength of a competently staged car chase in a British film, knew what Steve had in mind, however, and firmly rejected the demand that the back lot should be mocked up to look like San Francisco with sharp corners and other protruding objects coated in foam rubber. Steve insisted, "I wanted to make a film worth looking at. I felt very strongly about this, and I knew their way would never work. Anyway, we fell out. You know what Warners' did? They moved my parking spot into the corner so that no one would have to see me, and they banned my partner from the studio. The result was, I made the film my way."

Together Steve and Yates worked out the idea of using the steep San Francisco hillsides, and Steve talked his old friend and former racing motorcyclist Bill Hickman into playing the crook and driving the car which Steve chased. One of the better scenes in the film is when Hickman, looking like a typical middle-aged family motorist, suddenly clips on his seat belt as traffic lights change and scorches away in a cloud of smoking tires. Steve did all his own stunt driving, of course. Crew assistants literally laid their bodies in front of cross-intersection traffic so that he and Bill Hickman could thunder over the crossings safely. Their speeds were such that as the cars bounced on the flat crossings and then hit the inclines below, they rose six feet in the air, wheels waggling futilely, tires smoking, and hubcaps flying. "Every time I hit an intersection, my sump would ground heavily on the deck. I'd hear this 'twack-bang' noise exploding inside the car. Once or twice I got to the bottom of the hill and the sump was cracked open and the oil all gone. We just bolted on another sump, poured in more oil, and kept on filming. Toward the end, one of the Mustangs (four were used in the film, of which two were write-offs and the other had to be rebuilt) had everything from the doors to the engine mountings rattling. As I climbed out, the door came off in my hand. It was so funny—the door falling off, then a wheel crumbling, then a headlamp, and so on. We all fell down laughing—like a scene from the old Keystone Cops.''

It was anything but funny at the time, however. After the hillside scenes, there is a final sequence with the chase taking place along a freeway, ending spectacularly when the crook's car crashes and bursts into flames. This sequence called for Steve and Bill Hickman to ride almost alongside each other at very high speeds; and they were really going fast, for Steve was determined that there would be nothing phony about it—that there should be no camera undercranking (a technique whereby speeded-up effects are achieved when the film is projected at normal speed). These scenes are perhaps among the best in the entire film, for occasionally the two cars smack into each other with sickening effect as they try to knock each other off the road. The freeway, of course, was closed by the police during filming, and the oncoming cars and other traffic one sees in the film were driven by highly paid, pretty scared stuntmen. It was at this stage that Steve's car began to fall apart around him while an amazed Bill Hickman, careening alongside, watched open-mouthed. At one point, Hickman smashed into Steve's car and swiped a remote-control camera that had been mounted on it. "If there had been a crew behind that lens they would have been wiped out," says Steve.

The sequences were sufficiently hairy (the searing exhaust noises were dubbed in later) to cause the studio cameraman to think twice of shooting the most dangerous sequences. Yates realized he could not order the man to risk his neck, so he took over the camera himself and climbed into the back of Steve's car. "Pete's quite a guy," Steve said. "At one stage we were closing at nearly 110 miles per hour and there was Pete in the back seat, shouting out for more speed. Or for me to clout Bill's car harder." The scenes were so hair-raising and so obviously authentic that few people in Hollywood were prepared to believe that Steve had not used a stuntman double—one reason why he insisted on driving in the Sebring twelve-hour endurance tests. A few also considered it a little incongruous that Steve, the self-confessed reform school boy, ex-bum, ex-hobo, and ex-toughie, should play the role of that personification of authority, a cop!

To Steve, there was nothing odd about this. He had "shaped up," hadn't he? He was still growing, still expanding his interests and experiences. For instance, he could have remained simply a star—and Howard Hawks had offered him a gigantic fifty percent of the profits to star in a film for him, saying: "The offer is not extravagant. It's a myth that superstars are now working for a fraction of their previous money. Pseudo-stars, yes—but not real superstars like McQueen and John Wayne, who still sell tickets, no! They're more than worth their weight in gold!" As far as Steve was concerned, the road ahead of him was still rising, he was anxious to do more—to get into the business of hiring writers, building up his production company, approaching studios who had capital and offering them the whole package: script, production unit, and himself as star. And he was no longer a rebel—although he would never forget his origins. He tried to put some of his feelings in words to a reporter: "We don't have enough reporters in the country to see what's happening (on the streets of America today). We should have. We have to get writers to write about what's happening on our streets. And I think the public's ready. The intelligence is at a higher level; people are more hep because of TV. Young people are in a position to call the shots. They are going to be predominant in our political and economic structures. They need leaders—constructive leaders able to deal with them academically and politically. And on the stage and screen they need to see it as it is. That's the bag I'm in right now."

This was the kind of thinking that allowed him to feel that it was right for him to play a policeman. All right, so he had been chased by cops as a kid, and therefore, at first he had worried that he might not be able to play the part honestly. Then as he reread the script, he realized that this was simply the story of a man who had a job to do and did it: an honest, if unscrupulous, cop fighting a lone battle for truth and justice against impossible odds and obstructive superiors—a theme close enough to his own heart. The plot may have lacked great originality; the dialogue may not have been exceptional; but

Steve and Robert Vaughn in the immensely successful *Bullitt* (1968).

Jacqueline Bisset adds the necessary romantic dimension to *Bullitt*.

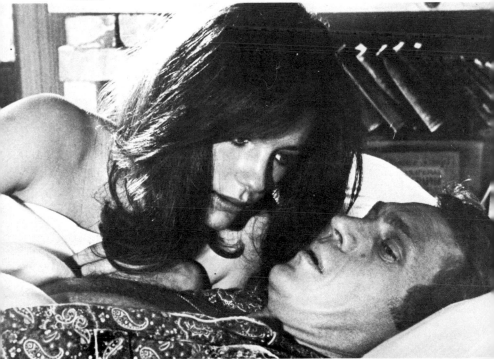

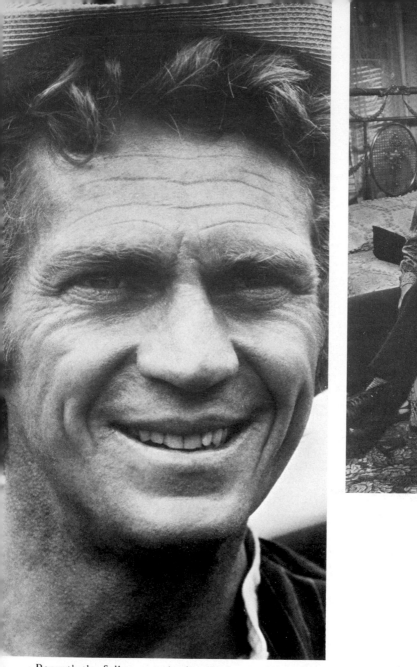

Beneath the folksy exterior lies the heart of the reiver.

(Left, above) Sharon Farrell with everyone's favorite reiver, Steve McQueen.

(Right, above) Steve, Rupert Crosse, and twelve-year-old Mitch Vogel in the 1905 Winton Flyer as they set off on their journey to Memphis in *The Reivers* (1969). The replica of this vintage automobile was presented to Steve after the filming.

Stills from *The Getaway* (1972), in which Steve and Ali MacGraw star as a husband and wife team who rob a bank and get away with it.

it was a true enough story of "today." To get the "feel" exactly right, he had actually gone up to San Francisco and driven around with the cops, seeing what they saw, watching what was going on in the streets, convincing himself that *Bullitt* could be something more than just a crime movie.

It was Steve's first venture as a producer in his own right, and although he insisted, as mentioned earlier, on taking credit only as an actor, nonetheless he had to face the problems involved in wearing his new "hat." So, at three o'clock one morning, in between shooting night scenes at the San Francisco airport, which form the climax of *Bullitt,* he delivered two important pronouncements on the state of the film industry, which were given wide publicity in the more serious columns of the press. His theme was the need to allow the trade unions a share in film profits and the need for federal subsidies to help the ailing industry. "Exhaling fire and determination" and "talking like a machine gun" (so much for his alleged inarticulateness), Steve declared: "This industry got me off the streets, and I feel a great responsibility and commitment to it. I have two kids, a wife, and a nice home. I don't like to leave home to make films, work here six days a week, get up at 4:00 A.M.—if 4 A.M. isn't, in fact, the middle of our working day. But optically the advantages are here, the feeling of the city is right, extras even look different."

He was, first of all, hitting out at the Hollywood unions who, he believed, were making life unnecessarily difficult, and unproductive, for producers. Steve's company, in fact, had hired 350 San Francisco teenagers as extras, kids who were not members of the powerful Screen Extras Guild; they had decided, however, that there should be no undercutting and had paid the union rate. The Guild had not resisted this innovation, which happily gave *Bullitt* that extra dimension of authenticity. "You only get your way if you have power," observed Peter Yates, "and McQueen has power." Steve declared, "I'm getting my education as we go along, using my power as an actor." He enlarged on his attitude: "I feel presumptuous in saying all this, but so much of Hollywood filmmaking is involved with the fear of losing your job. Fear has made blocks of wood out of everybody. Deep down, there's a part of Hollywood that doesn't want us to succeed up here because we're proving a point—locations, the theater of the streets, is where it's at in film." He added that whether he shot on location or in studios, the overheads remained basically the same. For example, more than one million dollars of his budget had already been swallowed up in overheads: "But that's the name of the game." What he spoke against were the built-in attitudes of the unions. "History has cartwheeled. Proprietors are not the heavies anymore. The unions are. Here's one example: I do my thinking behind the wheel of a car. I like to drive myself to the location, but the Producers Association has signed a contract with the Teamsters (union) saying that film workers, the stars, director, everybody, has to be driven to the set. So, if I'm filming in Malibu, I have to get up an hour-and-a-half earlier in Brentwood, drive to Warners, then get driven all the way west again to Malibu and the location. It's ridiculous. It's one area that can be negotiated. So much must be re-negotiated." And his remedy? "Give the unions a slice of the action. Unions must find a compromise and stop keeping out people; but in turn, the unions should be offered a percentage of the profit of a picture. Let's get more and more workers back to work by such re-negotiation and answering with a piece of the action. Profit-sharing is not exactly new to other American industries. Unions should forget about forcing people to do things. Pictures are not always runaways—they're push-aways. Somewhere there lies a percentage value for unions, a percentage of the film and negative cost." As for federal subsidies: "Films are the greatest public relations machine in the world, and the government should step in and help. If this industry is going to survive, let's have federal subsidies. I know this is dynamite, but if it's going to be a federal subsidy, let's do it."

One of the things that probably got under Steve's skin and could have led directly to this outburst was a decision by the local Screen Extras Guild to fine Solar for using four genuine nurses from the San Francisco General Hospital in one or two sequences instead of employing Guild extras.

The scene again is the San Francisco airport and the time is 3:30 in the morning; only the day is different and the temperature lower—thirty-seven degrees. Steve is jogging up and down, keeping warm, lithe, and graceful like an Olympic athlete, but wearing a certain look of apprehension. Out there on the runway, a big 707 jet is warming up and there is real tension in the air. Once again— as though he had not already run enough risks during the car sequences— Steve was going to do his own stunt. He intended to run in front of that big jet as it got ready to roll down the runway—not for the hell of it or to impress onlookers—but to ensure greater realism. Few producers would allow their greatest asset to run such a risk, but Steve was his own producer and could call the shots.

Peter Yates, the director, walked across and had a brief word with Steve to make sure he was ready. Nearby, cameraman William Fraker, who already had thousands of feet of magnificently photographed scenes of San Francisco in the can, was all set with a light Arrieflex camera. Yates nodded, everybody moved into position, and Yates gave the order, "OK, roll 'em!" The plane began to move, gradually picking up speed. At the appropriate moment, Steve, followed by the camera truck, started running directly towards the oncoming aircraft—allegedly in pursuit of the criminal. As man and plane converged, a collision seemed inevitable—was meant to seem inevitable. Then, at the very last moment, Steve dived to the ground as the enormous aircraft swept by, its jet pods blasting out 240 degrees of heat. The camera truck itself moved in to within a few feet of the passing wing—a hairy moment for star, director, and crew alike. Particularly, of course, for Steve, who was directly under the wing. As the plane passed and Steve picked himself up, members of the crew rushed to see if he were all right. "I'm OK, OK," Steve kept saying as the crew fussed over him. "It blew me around a little, but I'm OK." It had been dangerous all right—almost as dangerous as it looks in the film—but Steve shrugged it off. "The vibration tweaked my neck a little, that's all," he insisted. "You have to keep your mouth open and sort of hold your ears."

"Couldn't they have used a dummy?" demanded an onlooker, appalled at the risk. Steve grinned, "They did."

Relaxing over a cup of coffee, Steve explained why he took such risks—honesty. He wanted to cut out phoniness. And why shouldn't a star do a stunt himself? What was so special about a film star? "I don't much go with the emotional luxury of being a star. I have a tendency to go the other way, to search and make sure nothing happens. Then

I don't get too big for my britches.'' He was happy to talk a little about his private life. He had "settled down" in his community and hoped "to pass the house on to my children.'' He felt a great responsibility as a citizen and believed you could "use your juice as a successful actor towards constructive goals.'' Money did not matter that much to him. If he cared about it, it was because of his wife and kids. "When I was a kid I had nothing but bad luck, so it's natural I should dream of a bright future for my family.'' Making money was simply a part "of the struggle for life I have imposed on myself.'' He guessed it was "important to be successful,'' and he liked it. "But there's a compromise there somewhere I don't like. Because I don't want to be so successful that I can't do the things I want to do. I'm that selfish about it.''

There was only one thing wrong with the dream. Despite protestations by both parties, Steve's marriage was beginning to crack. He might still wear the gold Saint Christopher's medal Neile had given him inscribed "To part is to die a little,'' but the strain under which she was living had begun to tell. That time that someone "blew the whistle" on Steve's performing his own stunts, and she flew up to San Francisco and bawled him out in front of the whole crew—well, that was when the cracks were beginning to show in public.

Steve was now at the height of his success, the most successful and popular star in the world, particularly with women. Cinema Center Corporation offered to back him in *The Reivers* and even to supply him with his own executive jet, staffed by a bevy of beautiful hostesses, to fly him about the country—from Hollywood to the various locations. His marriage, despite Neile's public bawling-out, still seemed "very tight" to his friends, and although she hated traveling by plane, Neile was as ready as ever to ride in one if it meant keeping Steve happy.

For the making of *The Reivers* she flew to Carrollton, Mississippi, which still looks much as it did at the turn of the century. Most of the shooting was done in the countryside around Carrollton, but Steve and most of the company and crew holed up in a hotel in Greenwood. "Holed up is the right word,'' insists Neile. "I got there a week after Steve, and here is this two-story motel with its balconies all boarded up and with four policemen along the rails. I took one look at all that boarding and felt as if I were walking into a concentration camp. They finally took the boards from the railings up to the roof so we could at least look out the window. Sunday morning I peeked out to see what kind of a day it was and there, at eight in the morning, were thousands of people stacked up, waiting patiently to see Steve. It's such a small town, you'd wonder where they came from."

If filming—particularly on location with its inevitable discomforts and hazards—can be boring for the actors because of the long stretches when there is nothing to do, it is doubly so for the star's wife. Probably the last word one could apply to such proceedings is "glamor." Neile found herself totally at a loose end—the kids, of course, had to remain behind in Brentwood. Steve went to bed early each evening and she stayed up until midnight watching TV, at which time it closed down in Greenwood. Afterwards she read until 1:00 or 2:00 A.M. and slept till noon the next day. Then she bathed, had breakfast, and telephoned home. After a week of this, she told Steve that she was leaving.

There was nothing very new in such a decision; it was a familiar routine. Always, after about a week, wherever they were, she inevitably made the same announcement, and inevitably Steve would pat her cheek and repeat, "You stay and earn your bread, baby." And always she stayed—women, perhaps, will understand. Understand, too, that although she did not consider herself a sentimental person, she still kept in her wallet, folded up and dog-eared, the letter Steve had written her when she was in Las Vegas and she had wrecked their first car. It was, perhaps, her most sentimental treasure. "Twelve years," she remarked to a friend, "would you believe it, twelve years?"

In *The Reivers*, Steve broke with type—and admitted later that he regretted it, although many critics consider it his best film. He always has a knotty problem choosing scripts, of course; all actors have; but when a star is at the pinnacle, as Steve is, the choice of a subject is a matter for long, nail-biting sessions. "I go out of my way to do what is not expected of me as a talent," explains Steve. "When it comes off, it's tremendous; when it doesn't, it's regrettable, and you must expect the lambasting you get. An actor's life is all chance. So I've gambled on stories and lost. Several times. Somehow the pictures didn't gel. It's no one's fault. Most of the scripts

I get are of the safe and sane variety. I have to find what I want tucked away in cubbyholes.''

The Reivers brought both Steve and Neile together again with an old friend—none other than Mark Rydell, the man she was dating the night that Steve first met her in Downey's restaurant in New York. Mark, too, had come a long way since those days; he had won considerable critical acclaim for his direction of the controversial *The Fox* and was now ready to go to work on what by any standards promised to be a major film—the film version of Nobel Prize-winner William Faulkner's Pulitzer Prize-winning novel. The script was by that accomplished pair, Irving and Harriet Ravetch, who had already written two successful screenplays based on Faulkner's work, *The Long Hot Summer* and *The Sound and the Fury*. They had also won an Oscar for writing the screenplay of *Hud*, the successful Paul Newman film. All in all, the elements seemed drawn together to create another success. A big star, a big story, clever writers, a good director—and the setting, well, the setting was turn-of-the-century America, that golden nostalgic era that now seems to every citizen a lost paradise.

In outline, *The Reivers* is the tale of the adventures and the hilarious journey of a twelve-year-old boy (Mitch Vogel) who emerges into manhood on a spirited jaunt from Mississippi to Memphis, accompanying Steve and the Negro actor Rupert Cross. Following hard on the screaming excitements of *Bullitt* and *The Thomas Crown Affair*, the film was seen as an opportunity to give Steve a real change of pace. Steve actually had his own idea of who was going to be the star of the film—a specially rebuilt version of a vintage U.S. automobile, a 1905 Winton Flyer, with a top speed of only 20 miles per hour. Steve grinned from sheer pleasure when this classic replica was presented to him at the end of filming.

In the film he plays Boon Hogganbeck, the chief reiver—a word meaning rascal, scoundrel, louse, thief, gambler, cheat, delinquent. Prerelease advertising copy trumpeted, "You'll love him [meaning Boon]. McQueen kind of reminds you of Boon, doesn't he?" As an acid-tongued reporter pointed out: "If that were said about most of us, we'd be waving writs." Steve didn't mind though: "I act only in films where I'm satisfied I can work without hypocrisy. Everything I do is really a little piece of me." Whatever way one looked at it, indeed, the film seemed bound to succeed. It even starred a race-horse that would run properly only when fed sardines! Despite this and the top marks given the film by the critics, it could hardly hope to match *Bullitt* at the box office.

Back again in Los Angeles after filming had been completed, Steve and Neile threw a party at The Candy Store, a Hollywood discotheque, to celebrate their twelfth wedding anniversary, taking over the entire place one Saturday night and inviting eighty guests. Photographs taken that night show them dancing together and looking more like newlyweds than old-marrieds. Steve's hair was still all fluffed and curled the way he wore it in *The Reivers*, and he was clad in white pants and white turtleneck sweater. Neile wore a mod "gypsy" dress, then very fashionable. They appeared to be very happy. During the course of the evening, Neile revealed that when they first got married Steve had said: "We're going to have happiness. That's how it's going to be. We're going to do a lot of great things together, always. Extract from life that which makes you happy. Don't plan ahead. Let it happen" — and that's the way it had been. That evening, too, he had told her, "I'm still crazy about you."

Yet those twelve years had wrought astonishing changes in Steve. His whole outlook and behavior had changed. As a tycoon, he spent money on wardrobe and grooming; when somebody remarked on his multi-hued petit-point cuffs, he replied, "Yeah, they're great, aren't they? I have them made for me in Palm Springs. I've got three pairs." Twelve years before, he had only two suits; now he had twenty-two.

It was in the last year, however, that other remarkable changes had occurred. If he insisted on breaking the rules and driving fast cars and bikes and doing his own stunts, then Neile demanded a *quid pro quo*. The terms? A little expansion of their social life; a little more getting about and seeing people other than his racing buddies. So they had begun to give a few parties, go out a bit more. One gossip column noted that they had even "earned a bit of a reputation for throwing the swingingest parties in Hollywood, with the food invariably catered," and added the interesting detail that at one party Steve had hired two bands to play alternately—a party which had lasted until 5:00 A.M. This was really a new Steve.

Yet the crunch was coming. Life seemed great, perhaps too great. Everything was going too well. Something in the very nature of things had to give. And now it was about to give.

13.

Le Mans
and Other Disappointments

London, 1969. Steve is holding court in the river room of a famous London hotel. Guests: reporters, cameramen, film executives, publicity people, and all sorts of hangers-on. One or two celebrities, including the Duke and Duchess of Bedford, who had, apparently, invited Steve to spend a night or two at their stately home, Woburn Abbey. Steve's hair is blond, thick, and curling, his eyes are a marvelous blue, his figure as lithe as whipcord. His face is lined, rugged, questing. There is something polite about the way he listens, answers, questions, tries to be helpful. His eyes straying, as men's will do, over the nearest leggy blond. A concentrated frown appears on his forehead as he attempts to deal with several questions at once—trying to overcome the handicap of his growing deafness and yet do his job.

Steve the businessman. Up all night in a smoke-filled room with Bob Relyea and Bob Reddish. Air soggy with all-night smoke. Steve goes to open a window. "Let's get some air in here," he says.

"But don't get a cold," warns Bob Relyea.

So where was Steve heading? ''I've got a feeling I'm leaving stardom behind, you know. I'm gradually becoming more of a filmmaker,
acquiring a different kind of dignity from that which you achieve in
acting. After all, I'm no matinee idol, and I'm getting older. I don't
think I can be doing my kind of thing in the seventies; I want to be
more on the creative side of the business.''

Still very much a man of the times in tight, thigh-hugging jeans and a
screamingly colored shirt. Speaking with quiet precision as though
he were practicing his voice-school speaking. A man oddly lacking
in humor (or anxious not to show it), concerned almost wholly
with ''dignity''—his own and his craft's. Honesty and integrity
had been the keynotes of his words and work throughout the
previous decade; the new word was dignity. Behind the facade, though,
there is still a kind of slight suspicion amounting, not to wariness,
but a kind of *shyness*—a state, seemingly, of being afraid that he
might be asked questions that would expose his real or imagined
limitations. His gaze had the authority of a man who had fought
his way up and now *knows* he is some form of an elite person. He
looks you straight in the eye—said to be a sign that the man doing the
looking has something to hide.

Relyea and Reddish, both self-effacing and deliberately colorless
in the presence of Steve, to such a degree that it is hard to
distinguish which is which, perhaps could offer the phrase, ''We're
educating each other in this business.'' Steve might then carry the
conversational ball, not quite waiting for it to be passed to him. ''A
star has to become a business to survive. I have built a strong machine. A strong, legal machine that will work for me and that hopefully will make me money as well as release the creative thing I've
got going for me. All I can do is my thing as I see it. People say I
have this sexy thing for the girls. I'm not aware of it. I let it fall
as it will. . . .'' Business, not glamor or his alleged sex-appeal, was
what he was interested in. ''You know if you've become famous and
you're good and you demand a certain kind of respect and billing
and have a say over what material you are in, then you should have
a certain dignity. But in Hollywood, an actor or actress can be nailed,
and their security can be threatened, just by being rude to the wrong
person. It's the wrong people who control the industry—the distributors

and exhibitors, not the people who make films. It's like driving, I guess. You have to be in the driver's seat yourself to see what it's like."

He was fairly non-smiling and impassive, careful not to show any emotions—as though the deadliest of all sins was to "lose your cool." He admitted at one stage that he kept his "looseness" going to such an extent that he has sometimes forgotten his lines during a film. He showed concern for the young and with what they were being asked to shape up to. "What do the young have to shape to—the politicians are drowning in their own spit." He did not mind talking about speed: "It's a kind of happy infinity for me. That's the time when God and I have our little talks. Speed works for me. So I like speed. But, like I said, I've grown up a bit. . . ."

The year 1970 was, however one looks at it, some kind of landmark in Steve's life. There were the good things. In March, for example, he gained his greatest racing success by placing second to Mario Andretti in the Sebring twelve-hour endurance test. Almost simultaneously, Cinema Center Corporation agreed to back the film on Le Mans, upon which Steve had long set his heart. His subject was a majestic conception—the Twenty-four Hours of Le Mans, the most gruelling test for cars in the world. Lastly, this was the year that he "went public"; i.e., Solar Productions was floated off to the investing public. Before the year was out, however, the sweet smell of success had soured a bit. First, both Cinema Center and then the insurance companies refused to allow him to actually race at Le Mans itself, a bitter disappointment. Then, when finally realized, the film laid an egg. Lastly—and most seriously, perhaps—in July it was announced that he and Neile had separated, although no divorce was as yet contemplated. All in all, Steve would look back on 1970 as his bitter-sweet year.

He was in a state of high euphoria in March after his success at Sebring. Plans were soon announced—although many racing drivers thought the whole thing a bit of publicity—for Steve to actually be Jack Stewart's partner in that year's Le Mans: He had come a long, long way, indeed. On top of everything else, now partner to a world champion! It is possible to turn up old quotes alleged to have been made by Steve insisting that nobody was going to "put brakes on him"; that whatever insurance companies said or thought, he would risk his neck when he wanted to. Yet when it came to the crunch, Steve found that his status was such that he had to conform. Rebellion was no longer a practical proposition, even for him—particularly for him—and like the rest of us, he had to bow to reality. Although outwardly he gave every sign of being resigned and, indeed, quite philosophical when told he could not race, inwardly he must have raged for days because he refused to speak to anyone. This led some critics to inquire why, if he were so keen on racing, didn't he quit acting, and take up racing as a career? It was a criticism, however, which ignored the fact that, basically, he was an actor and had made that his career. His immense popularity, status, and earning power could not be tossed away as simply as that. Anyhow, forty was a bit late to begin a serious racing career. On the whole, therefore, the decision to stop him from taking part in the race was the only sensible one. Jackie Stewart himself was on record as saying, ''I don't like Le Mans. It scares me because there are too many amateurs driving powerful cars at speeds they are not capable of managing.'' And Steve, whatever his experience, was still an ''amateur'' in terms of competing with the likes of Jackie Stewart. Asked for his comment on the announcement of the partnership, the then world champion Graham Hill said he was puzzled. ''I can't imagine it as a serious attempt on the Le Mans race. I can only think they may be using it for a film or something. No doubt both Le Mans and Porsche will be delighted with the publicity.''

Le Mans, Steve intimated, was to be dedicated to the dignity of the racing driver. ''Some of these men are dealing with the unknown. That gives a man greatness. I'm making it so that my grandmother in Montana (he had no grandmother in Montana—he meant the average person) who knows nothing about cars will understand.'' He intended to have spectacular stunts but not to show death.

There is no doubt, however, that this time Steve had allowed his emotions to overrule his judgement. First, Cinema Center, the backers, were less than satisfied with the script—they wanted ''a drama'' super-imposed on what amounted to hardly more than a documentary. Steve argued that the racing itself was the drama. At no stage does he seem to have been capable of appreciating that the average moviegoer does not share his enthusiasm for fast machinery and that women fans might find the spectacle boring. He insisted, however, that he could make an exciting film, one that would still give "his grandmother in Montana" the message that lay behind auto racing. Second, the insurance companies put their foot down firmly, and April headlines read: "McQueen barred from Le Mans race," thus shattering the fondest of all his illusions—taking part. Original plans had to be hastily scrapped, and a compromise reached with the backers and the insurance companies. In June, Steve and a film crew went across to France to film the actual race, *minus* Steve. Shots were taken of him in helmet and racing uniform standing in the pits or moving among the crowds. In all, nineteen cameras were set up at different points along the eight-and-one-half-mile circuit, filming constantly, and a Porsche, similar to the one he was supposed to have driven in the race was used to shoot some competitor's-eye footage. In all, over 30,000 feet of the actual race, with its crowds, its color, and shots of the Porsche rocketing around the course were put in the can. They were then to be matched with sequences made later in the summer when Solar took over a closed circuit for twelve weeks, and the whole race would be simulated, this time *with* Steve.

Steve himself admitted beforehand that there were enormous techni-cal difficulties involved. "Le Mans really puts it down there. Movie industry people think we're out of our minds to attempt filming such a great race. They're afraid to tackle it, and I can understand why. You only get one chance at it. But am I excited! The emotional momentum of Le Mans is unbelievable." He insisted that he wanted it done with "feeling and understanding of the human drama involved in the excitement of the race itself." Certainly Steve, with his knowledge of racing and his sensitivity to the emotions involved, seemed the only man capable of getting away with it. He first put his writer, Harry Kleiner, alongside a man intimately involved in the Le Mans race and had Kleiner interview the eventual winner, Jackie Ickx. He then suggested a new method of putting such a film together: shooting film of the real event and using it as a basic bible. "Like if we have two drivers talking, we can have our script man watch the film and then try and recapture the simplicity of the scene, because the problem with actors is that they are actors and not emotionally fired drivers." Steve and Kleiner together carefully watched the scene after Ickx had won, for instance. They saw Ickx's pit crew, just below them, "blow their minds on victory."

Steve said: "The mob just went wild, it was fantastic, pouring champagne all over each other, smothering their car with their happy bodies, just letting go. But like I say, I watched by feeling, by trying to predict what I'd feel under such conditions and projecting that into this scene. Then I saw what I doubt anyone else saw. Ickx's crew chief—the man behind the entire victory, the man who commanded the program—had been under tons of pressure for months non-stop, especially over the past twenty-four hours. Well, he just picked up his champagne bottle, walked silently away to a nearby building, leaned up against it, and started sipping his champagne all alone. I mean, that was his own private moment. He had won, and this is how he wanted to taste his victory. It meant more to him than the glory, and that's the way it is with me. I love this sport so much I can't be satisfied until I try to do the impossible—to make the greatest film on it myself. Man, that's where life starts having its meaning—at a 160 miles per hour average around Le Mans—just balancing there on the boundary of death. There's nothing like it. Well, everybody starting telling me I'm nuts to try something like this. They say it can't be done cinematically like I want."

If the insurance companies had had the last word in banning him from the actual race, there was nothing much they could do to prevent him taking part in the simulation later in the summer in which twenty-five expensive cars (his own Porsche 917 cost $45,000 alone) and a handful of top-class drivers such as Mike Parkes, Derek Bell, Vic Elford, John Miles, Richard Attwood, Masten Gregory, Jonathan Wild, and David Piper all took part. This was the second stage of the filming—the stage at which Steve was laying not only life and limb on the line but also his whole bankroll. If he hurt himself or was in any other way prevented from completing the picture, he stood to be skinned alive. "My insurance company? Man, I hear it," he said. "You can imagine how they feel because once we get rolling, everybody's on salary, and if I go out there and bust myself up, we just don't stop paying the crew and tell them to come back when I'm well. Nope, we're talking about $25,000 to $50,000 a day—every day. If something happens, those insurance companies will automatically sue me for that money. For instance, if I can't finish the picture, they'll come right to me for the cost of the entire thing—and we're talking five or six million dollars. It's not so bad when you think all that can happen is that you get knocked off or lose your picture and a hell of an investment. However, when they can come and take away your house and your personal possessions and practically your entire non-professional life, it gets pretty spooky. But everywhere you turn, there's somebody telling you what not to do and what you must do, and the more success you get, the worse it gets. So I've made up my mind—to hell with it! The insurance thing? I'm just forgetting about it. When they start telling you what you must not enjoy in life, that's going too far. So I've decided just to do what I must do. When you're slipping around out there at a couple of hundred miles an hour surrounded by the sights, the smell, and the sound of speed, you somehow know this is what it's all about. It's just too bad you can get nailed for doing it."

Throughout filming of the simulation, as during some scenes shot during the actual Le Mans race, Steve sat around wearing a flame-proof driving suit over flameproof underwear. Grime, scraped knuckles, and sweat (actually water) were applied to him to make him look as authentic a racing driver as possible. Even dressed like this, he remained very much the overall boss—constantly around the set even when not working, talking over problems and chatting about them with directors and producers, suggesting camera angles, and making a point of indicating items of interest to auto racing enthusiasts. "I really wear three hats. I'm a driver, an actor, and a filmmaker. In fact, I'm living in a constant state of confusion. I've walked around and bumped into myself a couple of times, you know." He kept repeating that *Le Mans* wasn't just another film for him. "We'd like to leave some scratch marks on the history of filmmaking. We could fail, but as long as you fail with your ass hanging out, that's OK. But to fail when you're driving down the middle of the road, that's no good."

For all his so-called toughness and petulance, he probably could not prevent himself from sometimes showing that kind, thoughtful, and generous streak that is equally a part of his nature. Nobody at the Le Mans simulation impressed him more—and this went for racing

drivers and everybody else—than Sister Bridget, the Irish nun who was
the nurse in charge of first aid. "With all the rough and tough people you
get around here, it's wonderful to see Sister Bridget just sitting talking
quietly to one of the men in the crew. That's a good person." He
showed deep and genuine concern, apart from money or trouble for
the picture, when Derek Bell's Ferrari 512 suddenly caught fire (the
car was reduced to ashes) and Derek just managed to leap out with
minor injuries, including burns on his face. Steve made little or no
parade of wealth and made no special demands due to his status, although at no time did he yield his position as boss or give the impression that he was not The Man. He slept in his caravan, which he
used for production meetings during the day. It was fairly fancy;
but as though to excuse this little luxury, he ate all his meals with
the rest of the crew in the dining hall.

The twenty-five cars used in the mock-up of the race (the experts
also included a man who could create the effect of spattered flies or
bugs on windshields) created a fearful noise, particularly on the
Mulsanne straight. "Driving the 917 is actually easier than the 908,"
said Steve. "It puts so much meat on the ground that it doesn't skate
so much. But it's very quick, and you can get into trouble if you're
not careful. I'd never been quite so fast before, and I can tell you that
the first time I went through the Mulsanne kink at 215 miles per
hour, I really felt the hair on the back of my neck standing on end.
We do that straight—exactly what we would do in the race."

How good, exactly, was Steve as a driver? Masten Gregory, the
American driver who had competed alongside Steve at Sebring and
had followed him home, said: "I was third at Sebring in an Alfa
Romeo. I had an opportunity to do some dicing with Steve, and I
thought he was driving bloody well. He's a competitor, and that's
very important. He's got the professional attitude." Basing his judgement on what he saw at the *Le Mans* filming, Mike Parkes said, "It's
difficult to judge. I wouldn't say he's a 'natural,' but he's certainly very
high up." Attwood thought, "Yes, he's very good and could be a lot better.
I think he just needs practice, and he could be as good as any of us."
Andy Ferguson, the former Lotus team manager who was in charge
at the simulation, said: "The drivers rate Steve very highly. As team
manager, I thought we were going to have some problems. At first

everyone seemed to think they would be going down the straights at 40 miles per hour. Then when it became apparent that it was going to be full chat stuff, I thought they'd start getting apprehensive, but they weren't. He's a bright lad.'' Steve said, ''It's a marvelous opportunity for me, driving with all these professionals whose sole aim is to get that car through a corner as fast as they possibly can. And there's me being sucked right along with them.'' Parkes explained, ''So far as the driving is concerned, it's very near to actual race conditions. Steve is an extremely good driver, but not what you'd call 'Ferrari Works' driver standard, and therefore one has to be careful to look after him and not lead him into trouble. But going down the Mulsanne straight, we're doing exactly what we would do in the race.''

Yet with all the money, expertise, and dedication, the Twenty-four Hours of Le Mans came unstuck as a film. As it worked out, it had many shriek-making moments. In particular, one crash sequence done in slow motion, and then with an action replay, certainly tops anything, real or fictional, ever seen before—there wasn't an alien nut, bolt, or miscast character. The direction was meticulous. On a purely technical level, it was impossible to fault the film. That is, if one ignores the biggest technicality of all—the script. If a script does not stand up, ninety-nine times out of a hundred, a film will bomb. In *Le Mans* the story was simple and the dialogue sparse—to the point of non-happening. Love interest, fortunately enough, was confined to an exchange of looks, delivered in slow motion. The viewer had to be satisfied with the drama of cars charging about at merciless speeds— the kind of film that might appeal to raceway drivers. For all the noise, which was deafening enough, the film was a lifeless business involving robots. The story, for what it is worth, goes as follows: Michael Delaney (Steve) is part of a team assembled at Le Mans for the Twenty-four Hours. Lisa Belgetti (Elga Anderson) is the widow of a driver killed at Le Mans the year before; she is sullen and withdrawn and exchanges a few words with Steve before the race. The other two principals are Johann Ritter (Fred Haltiner), Steve's teammate, and Eric Stahler (Siegfrid Rauch), allegedly the top driver for Ferrari. The race soon settles into a contest between these two until, momentarily distracted by the crash of another car, Delaney crashes himself— though he escapes injury. At the hospital, he finds the widow waiting outside the door of the badly hurt driver of the crashed Ferrari and escorts her away. When she asks why he races, he says he needs to spend his life doing *something* the best he can. With the race going to Ferrari, the team manager substitutes Steve for the exhausted Ritter. Although unable to win, Steve thwarts Stahler and allows a teammate to get first prize. In the tumult to toast the winner, both Delaney and Stahler are, ironically, overlooked by the crowd.

Critics agreed that the film made a sincere attempt to capture the spirit of the sport and particularly the motives and attitudes of its devotees. They saw its quiet, almost downbeat attention to detail and its detached contemplation of inarticulate purpose and devotion as important, but negative, virtues. What the film lacked was inner conflict between the characters—and the presence of Lisa Belgetti was likened to a Shakespearean character symbolizing death who had strayed into the film by mistake. Everyone agreed that the ironies of the sport were well placed and that, visually, director Lee H. Katzin had done a remarkable job—but there praise ended. Despite the flow of criticism, Steve stuck to his guns: "Truth is what it is all about. *Le Mans* was the toughest film I ever made in my life. But it was worth it. Some sports events are being turned into carnivals with every goddamn hustler around trying to get a piece of the action. Not car racing, though. This is a sport for specialists. It's also the greatest 'high' of all time. But unlike acid or pot, you get 'high' with dignity. If you get killed, then that's a shame."

The sentiments do him justice. Yet not only did most critics fault it and audiences find it boring, but it scarcely met with universal acceptance among racing drivers themselves. Stirling Moss told me: "I thought it a ghastly film—although I consider Steve himself great. To me, it was a great letdown. I'm surprised it ever got past him. Absolutely abortive. It had neither passion nor emotion—utterly unrealistic. A very bad film in my opinion. One takes part in the sport because of the passion and the humor. Racing drivers are a special lot—great fun. But none of this comes over in the film at all." The film, therefore, and despite Steve's immense dedication and purpose, has to be judged a disaster, at least by conventional standards.

It was a disaster in more than one way. To friends of Steve and

Neile, it was the film that wrecked their marriage. Soon after shooting began, pictures of the Porsche 917 began appearing in the newspapers (once with the caption, "The car that smashed Steve McQueen's marriage"). The press was full of stories that, at long last, Steve's obsession with speed had placed too great a strain on Neile. There were other rumors, too—of an emotional entanglement. Whatever the real truth, a statement was issued by Solar Productions in July announcing that Steve and Neile had "separated a few days ago." It added that no divorce was contemplated. As the gossip on location went, Neile had offered him the choice, "Either that car goes, or I go." Steve himself refused to comment and just went on making the film. Then, before the finish of the film, another announcement was made— this time to the effect that they had been reconciled. With the danger over and Neile freed from worry—plus the good behind-the-scenes work of their friends—the cracks had been papered over, if only for the time being. In fact, the marriage was doomed. Steve was not only obstinately determined to risk life, limb, and neck if need be, but he had now reached the dangerous age emotionally. He was forty. Yet if middle-age were upon him, he had never appeared more sexy. His long, curling blond hair and lithe frame gave him the appearance of a Renaissance youth Michelangelo might have been happy to sculpt.

14.

THE MATURE STAR

A few weeks after his fortieth birthday, it was announced in Hollywood that Steve was "going public"—that is, he planned to sell 303,240 common stock shares at nine dollars each in his own 100 percent owned Solar Productions. Under a prospectus submitted to the U.S. Securities and Exchange Commission, Steve laid bare much of his financial situation.

Under the deal, for instance, he was personally to receive just short of $1,500,000 while Solar itself would scoop in just over one million. Of the Company's share, some $650,000 was to be devoted to financing a new program of relatively low-budget films, while $250,000 was to be set aside to procure new stories and subjects.

The idea of a star running his own production company was hardly new. Most big stars had formed personal companies as a way of reducing income taxes. But unlike other stars, Steve now proved, in the words of one writer, "as gutsy in his biz dealings as in his film roles," by throwing open his books to public scrutiny. The prospectus revealed that initially Steve had been collecting 25 percent

of the net profits of every picture he had appeared in since the forma-
tion of Solar back in 1961; by 1970, this had risen to 50 percent,
plus a percentage of the gross profit. Now, under a new contract, he
was to collect a $500,000 a year salary from Solar and to have a new
$5,000,000 insurance policy, placed through his own brokerage com-
pany (of which he owned 50 percent). The prospectus made it clear
that this huge sum was necessary because of Steve's "potentially
hazardous recreational activities such as motorcycling and sports
car racing."

The new board was to consist of: Steve as chairman-president;
Robert J. Schiller and Robert S. Colbert, two of his brokerage
partners; Matthew L. Bergen, an investment manager; Edward Ru-
bin, a lawyer; and, of course, Bob Relyea as vice-president. Relyea
not only had an employment contract with Solar but also participated
in profits. Solar, it was revealed, had an authorized total of 2,000,000
shares of which only 653,700 had been issued, all owned by Steve. He
intended to sell 178,940 of these, and to them would be added 124,300
new shares, making a total of 303,240 shares on offer to the public.
A quick calculation shows that Steve, with 474,760 shares, would still
own 61 percent of the stock.

How, however, had Solar been doing? Gross earnings for the previous year had been $3,341,270, which eventually came down to a net
of $475,848. The bulk of this (over $2,000,000) had come from Solar's
share of films made by Steve, while just over another $1,000,000
had come from production fees paid to the company. Steve's plastics
firm contributed $150,366. It had not been a roaring success, and its
activities had been curtailed because of losses over the previous
two years. Solar, it seemed clear, was Steve, and lived or died
with him.

Steve's attacks on exhibitors and distributors became understandable when figures for the seven features prior to *The Reivers*, in
which Solar had a participant interest, were made available. Only
two of these films had reached a profit level, according to distribu-
tor accounting. Most of the company's profits, in fact, derived from
the sensationally successful *Bullitt*. World rentals up to December,
1969, were $23,100,000, of which Solar, with a 42 1-2 percent
profit participation, collected $2,670,000. There would be further

earnings, of course, from re-releases and from sales to TV, which were delayed for five years. The only other profitable film, in fact, was the lightly regarded *Nevada Smith*, which had gone into the black following a million-dollar TV sale. The film cost $4,450,000 to make and picked up gross sums, including the TV leasing, of $11,007,196. But when all the deductions endemic in film production had been met, Solar's 25 percent of net profits amounted to a mere $202,862. Out of all profits, Solar still had to pay 10 percent to Steve's agents, the William Morris Agency, and a further, if smaller percentage, to Guild Management Corporation, which furnished management and administrative services to both Steve and Solar. (Soon afterwards, Steve negotiated his agent's take to 5 percent.) Other McQueen pictures that had not then yielded Solar a profit included *Soldier in the Rain, Baby, the Rain Must Fall, The Cincinnati Kid, The Sand Pebbles*, and *The Thomas Crown Affair. Crown*, however, was almost into the black. It had picked up $9,163,000 in world rentals and would go into the black when released to TV. Steve, it became clear, formerly had been paid his salary directly by the financing company; but since November, 1967, the production fee paid to Solar (which was a separate item from its profit participation) had included his salary. Under the new contract, his take would be $500,000 a year for the next seven years. He had to play in a minimum of four pictures during this period and his salary—$250,000 paid each January with the rest spread over forty weeks at $6,250 a week—was to be a nonreturnable advance against his salary for those four films. It was figured to amount to 80 percent of his final wages listed on production sheets. He was not to get more than $500,000 before making any of the four pictures; if, for example, he refused, or could not, appear in any of the four films, his salary would stop at $500,000.

Bob Relyea was to get $1,500 a week salary. This was to be deducted from any money paid to him for doing specific jobs on any of the films in which Solar was engaged. For instance, if he produced one of the films, he would get $50,000, and if he acted as executive producer, $25,000. If he actually directed any of Steve's films, he picked up between $75,000 and $125,000, or, at least, the balance after his salary of $1,500 weekly had been deducted. In addition, he was to get 25 percent of Solar's profits, unless it was a film starring Steve—then his take would drop to 15 percent. Reddish's figures were slightly lower. Since the foundation of Solar, the William Morris Agency and Guild Management had together collected $448,856, while Relyea had collected $298,921.

It seemed an auspicious time to launch the company, as the preceding year's gross profit (mostly from *Bullitt*) had amounted to almost $1,000,000. This figure was reduced to a final net profit of $103,914, however, because of losses on the plastics factory, which had managed to chalk up sales of almost $100,000, but had spent $305,997. The plastics company had been ordered to curtail its activities "since there is no assurance that it will ever be profitable." Solar's total assets were $1,962,773.

Steve's alleged prickliness, of course, had meant the end of his contract with Warner Brothers-Seven Arts, and so he had gone to Cinema Center Corporation for new financial backing. When Solar went public, however, they were locked in argument over production costs for *The Reivers*. It was shortly after this that Steve commented: "You know, twenty or twenty-five years ago they'd have nailed me up on a cross for doing what I'm doing today in the film industry. But it's time someone broke the stranglehold the big distributors have got over the film business. I am fighting them all the time—even now. It is up to the young people to get control now. I am not young any more, but I'll make a few dents here and there. I am just starting to fulfill one of my ambitions right now."

He had time and money enough now to stop a little and reflect on both himself and the world around him. What Steve McQueen has to say about life in general is neither particularly original nor profound. But he is, perhaps, worth listening to if only because he came out of that enormous mass of young, assertive, doubting, no-values, chip-on-shoulder, bewildered generation that seemed either anxious to protest and pull down the whole social fabric or to have no part of it. Steve was—and still is to some extent—one of them.

Two things pull at him. The first is filmmaking; the second, the attempt to live his own life. Yet the two things keep slipping over into each other, and Steve cannot quite reconcile himself to being pulled apart in this fashion. Nonetheless, he insists that   he has it all figured out. "It's pretty good, all of it. If you work, you get the goodies. It doesn't surprise me much. I didn't wake up one morning and find it there. It was years of hard work, OK? Nobody gave it to me. I feel grateful sometimes, but I'm not sure who to feel grateful to."

What about the kids coming up behind him? Well, he thought it necessary to escape "from our cities of cement. We are trying to move too fast, and we should try to return to the less frantic life which the world was enjoying around the turn of the century." Like other people, he was personally "struggling for answers to life's questions and the solutions to some of our problems. We must pay more attention to the conservation of our trees and other scenic beauties. And above all, we must prevent the further pollution of our rivers and streams. I think if everyone would try to get away from the hurly-burly for an hour or two each day (the country boy talking), there would be no need for psychiatrists and therapists who have to treat people for a host of nervous conditions, which have been brought on by the whirlwind kind of world we have created for ourselves."

He had led, by his own lifestyle, a sort of campaign to encourage people to assert themselves and not to be afraid to express opinions honestly held. The young—even the hippies—had a champion in him. "There's a lot of negative talk these days about hippies, yippies, or whatever current name you choose to give these groups. But what is incredible about these people is that they're not afraid to get nailed for what they believe in. And when you get nailed is when you find out where God is—sometimes he's within yourself." This last reflects a part of his philosophy: "The world is as good as you are. You've got to learn to like yourself first."

As to his childhood and the bitterness it brought him—well, "everybody's childhood is difficult. It's all hard. But what makes it difficult as an adult is overindulgence. Overindulgence is hard to straighten out because either you make your orbit very small or you start looking around at life and you find that the life you had is not what's going on out there. And the one out there will give you a lot of bumps. I think that all overindulgence is a bunch of nonsense. You go through life worrying about yourself all the time—which is a bad kick to keep, you know, toying with yourself and indulging yourself and patronizing yourself."

He had discovered what some Americans would call "patriotism,"
or what others might describe as a less jaundiced view of Western
society as it presently exists. "Soon about 70 percent of the popula-
tion will be under thirty. Then youth will take over. I can't wait for
it. Everything will be beautiful. The hippies ask me to lecture them
and I say, 'Don't waste your time protesting. Get out there and *compete*.
Sitting around there all day smelling the flowers is going to destroy
the country. I would like to see some of you cut your long hair and
become cops.' Why not? Already Haight-Ashbury (the San Francisco
hippie district) is dying. Murder Inc. and the professional dope pushers
have moved in. The kids who got out in time have become artists,
going into films and journalism, but it's tragic to see those who
didn't make it, to see them in the line at the clinics—kids on acid
who went on a trip and never came back, kids whose brains are
permanently scrambled. The survivors will take over the country.
Like those kids, I have been running all my life. I used to be running
away, now I'm running towards something—roots. And man, am I
happy." Well, he wasn't the first rebel to join the Establishment.
Nor was he the first to see that discontent primarily arises from
the fact that we all can't have the brass ring. Money, wealth, and
fame, in short, will cure most things.

But how did he become successful? He apparently didn't know—
at least he didn't know the reason for his own success. "I've thought
about it, and I just don't know what to put it down to. I really don't
know what the formula for my success is. I identify for young people,
I think, mainly because of the interpretation of the men I play in a
picture. However, I can't claim anything for myself here—it is purely
the work of the producer and the director" (once again he ignores
the real creator, the writer). Yet if the young identified with him,
he didn't necessarily identify with them—at least not all of them.
"Although I really dig young people, there are many things going
on today which I cannot regard as a healthy sign. For example, I'd
never support drug taking, and I'm very unhappy that so many
youngsters think it's the thing to do."

As to his own future—it seemed somewhat clouded and confused.
To one person, he would confide one thing; to another, another. He

admitted he wanted to keep his career as an actor going. "Some of the best parts for male actors come when they're over forty. I don't want to miss the good ones." Yet on another occasion, he could return to the subject of "dignity" and an actor's lack of it. "I like my work. But acting doesn't have any dignity. The real creative men of filmmaking are behind the cameras [and sometimes behind the men behind the cameras], and that's where I aim to finish up." Then he remarked: "I was talking to my wife the other day about retiring. If I had enough money never to work again, would I still work? I like my industry. I believe in it and feel a responsibility for it. I would go behind the cameras. But I'll never be able to walk away from them."

Yet apart from his age—and at forty-two a British newspaper could truthfully claim that he looked sexier at forty-two than thirty-two— his increasing deafness was imposing a severe handicap. Yet he insisted, "I ain't gonna wear a deaf aid for anyone." The risk was that as his hearing grew worse, backing companies might refuse to put up finance. "What if he misses an important cue during one of those tricky scenes? It could mean disaster for him and the entire film. Increasingly, nobody's going to take a chance on Steve—even with his enormous box-office power. One accident and you can find yourself faced with the loss of several million dollars. A Steve McQueen movie isn't any good if he isn't around to finish it," said one executive. He admits his deafness is increasing towards totality. "Of course, it's very upsetting for me, but I won't wear a hearing aid. I guess I'm just stubborn." Without doubt, movie making has become more difficult for him. He is not the first actor, of course, to be so afflicted, and others have overcome the handicap, but only after great patience and concentration. One well-known television actor said, "I guess you have to become a sort of lip reader." Steve is lucky, of course, that in most films he can always order a retake—and provided he sticks to the script, he should normally be able to overcome his handicap. The likelihood is that he will just have to work that little bit harder.

If his pronouncements do lack originality or depth, he is at least sincere in what he says. He has often talked of wanting to retire to a farm, and that is where he will probably end up—more or less where he began. Yet when he talks about conservation, he is not simply leaping on a popular bandwagon. As far back as 1964, long before the conservation issue had become popular, Steve led a campaign in Brentwood to save a local mountain from speculative builders, demanding that the area should be designated a national park: "It would help juvenile delinquency."

So he was pretty happy—or so he said. He had had his lumps. And no doubt, he felt that having had his share, things would run pretty smoothly from there on. However, whether he anticipated it or not, life had another apparent uppercut ready for him, another lump to hand out. When it happened, it shattered his existence, happy or otherwise, as he had known it for almost fifteen years. The question is why? Was it, perhaps, simply that his restlessness, his continuing fight against enveloping ennui, was to chalk up yet another victory over him?

Outwardly, all seemed sweet and calm. He spent his forty-first birthday quietly at home in Palm Springs with Neile and the kids. How was he going to celebrate the day, someone asked? How but as usual—at a auto race. That was, "if there's anything on within a 100-mile radius. I may even race myself if I feel like it."

Although still officially supposed to be recuperating from the hard work of *Le Mans,* he was soon busy again. Hard on the heels of *Le Mans,* cashing in on his enormous popularity, came *Junior Bonner,* filmed on location at Prescott, Arizona. It was the story of a former rodeo champion, a man out of his time in an age of jets and space travel. Steve himself insists he hates Westerns, mainly because of the horses: "They cannot be trusted. You never know what they'll do. I don't understand them, and I don't like them." And it was hardly surprising that it had been five years since he had made *Nevada Smith. Junior Bonner,* however, was intended to be different from the usual Western—an attempt to do for rodeos what *Le Mans* had done for car racing. This time, however, many of the mistakes made with the earlier venture were not to be repeated. In particular, a strong story was developed.

His dislike of horses—and one suspects he has his tongue partly in cheek—was fully justified in *Junior Bonner.* In this film, he not only had to deal with horses, which act like ejection seats equipped with sadistic minds of their own, but he also had to stay aboard bulls and even milk a wild cow. After the first week's shooting, he had suffered injuries as bad as any he had experienced in fifteen years of messing around with racing cars and motorcycles. He had a sprained finger, a gashed nose, and a suspected fracture of the left wrist. At the end of filming, he expressed pleasure with the film, but he was no fonder of horses—nor bulls or wild cows. When asked if he would consider making a documentary on rodeos, he snarled: "That I'll leave to John Wayne. The great thing about bikes and cars, however dangerous they may be, is that they don't kick and they never bite."

On the face of it, *Junior Bonner* ought to have been a great success. It had, first of all, Steve. But it also had Robert Preston, an old pro, who like Edward G. Robinson in *The Cincinnati Kid*, simply stole the picture right from under Steve's nose. It had a haunting and lyrical story by Jeb Rosebrook about the plight of a modern rodeo cowboy, plying his anachronistic trade. It was directed by that talented, if controversial director, Sam Peckinpah—controversial because he appears to inject gratuitous violence into his films, like *Straw Dogs*.

Junior Bonner (Steve) realizes that he is slipping from his role as champion into that of an also-ran in a game that is an also-ran against creeping urbanisation. Steve plays the part in a very downbeat way—not as a real old-fashioned cowboy yearning for the wide open spaces, but as a man who has realized that the world is becoming much too complicated for an individualist. He just moves from town to town, rodeo to rodeo, pulling his horse in a trailer behind him—and he is resigned, seemingly, to eventual defeat and the ash heap. As a last place to go, to find something, he decides to make for his home town— to go home. He arrives only to find that he has run out of places to go, that he is at the end of the line, at least as far as hope or optimism are concerned. The family farm is under the bulldozers when he gets there, part of a plan by his brother who has made himself a millionaire by building and selling mobile homes. His father, the celebrated "Ace" Bonner, once champion himself, is in the hospital following a drunken escapade. He refuses to take money from this son, Curley, who has, in fact, swindled him out of the family farm in order to pursue his money-making schemes. Junior's mother, now living in a caravan, is immersed in her memories and wants to have nothing more to do with her disappointing menfolk, all of whom have let her down.

Upon his arrival, Junior is offered a job by his brother, Curley, who dangles a vision of fat profits before him. But Junior cannot stomach the idea—particularly when he learns what Curley has done to their father. Eventually he finds his father—drunken, feckless, but still full of vigor and energy (a prodigious performance by Robert Preston)—talking about a new life in Australia, and yet clearly at the end of his rope. At first Junior is forced to turn down his father's request for money for an air ticket to Australia where he intends to prospect for gold or farm sheep, explaining that he, too, is broke. In a sudden resurgence of pride, energy, and determination, Junior decides to show his home town what a marvellous fellow he really is and what a success he has made of his life. He has the draw at a local rodeo fixed in such a way that he will be forced to tackle a wild bull nobody else has ever ridden, the same bull which had bested him on a previous visit home. This he sees as a last great throw that will restore his battered pride; it will revive him if only for a while, will chase the dark shadows away if only for a moment—and will help his father. In fact, he wins. After sending a first-class plane ticket to Australia to his father with his winnings, he shakes the dust of his home town from him forever, setting off on the never-ending rodeo circuit, towards the inevitable end, foreshadowed in his father's fate, disaster and despair.

The film cannot help but be sad and downbeat, although relieved from total gloom by the robust playing of Robert Preston and his ebullient spirits in the face of impending doom. It is a film that captures the feeling of how suburbia and its different values are steadily overwhelming the old times and the old freedoms—particularly in one scene where father and son slip away on horseback from the joyous hurly-burly of a Fourth of July parade, only to find themselves mixed up in washing lines and backyards before ending up sitting glumly in a deserted, disused railway station, the father dreaming of Australia and its wide open spaces and freedom. The theme of returning to find the family split apart is brilliantly handled, and much of the actual filmmaking is magnificently done—particularly the shots of Junior arriving to find his old home about to be bulldozed; the sense of *déja-vu* about the rodeo circuits; and the scene in the saloon where the Fourth of July is celebrated in a press of laughing, shouting, fighting, dancing bodies. One critic, indeed, was tempted to see a vague link with Eugene O'Neill's great *A Long Day's Journey into Night*. Steve gives a luminous performance, and there is only one moment when he fails to put himself over convincingly— when he captures Charmagne (Barbara Leigh) during the saloon party. The lack of dialogue here would, in real life, have left him wide open to a fast-talker who could have charmed the girl away. Yet, in the end, for all its haunting qualities, the film has long stretches of tedium, relying too often on Steve's personal charms, and interspersed as it is with rodeo scenes that match anything in *Le Mans* for boredom. The odds seemed stacked against *Junior Bonner* anywhere but in the American heartland where rodeos, presumably, are still an attraction.

In October that year, it was announced that, despite reports that Steve and Neile were happily living together again following the *Le Mans* blow-up, the marriage had, in fact, ended. This time, it was made clear, the breakup meant not "a separation" but divorce.

Oddly enough, only a week after their divorce papers had been filed, the two turned up at a party together, hand in hand as if they had made it up again. Nobody quite knew what to make of it—except that this was Steve once again at his most unpredictable. As unpredictable as his comment about the breakup (under California law Neile stood to get 50 percent of everything Steve owned): "She deserves every penny of it—for without my old lady, there wouldn't have been any in the first place."

15.

Looking Ahead

A ND so to El Paso in May, 1972. Two months before, on March 15 to be precise, Steve's fifteen-year-old marriage to Neile was finally dissolved at Santa Monica. The reason given—"irreconcilable differences." Neile, who had filed divorce papers the previous October, had already resumed her own career, working as the deaf-mute in the film *Fuzz*, starring Burt Reynolds. The property settlement, it was announced, was worth one million dollars, and Judge Goscoe Farley also awarded her an alimony settlement spread over ten years starting at $7,000 a month for the first year and scaling down eventually to $2,000 a month by 1982. She, of course, retained custody of Terri and Chad.

Steve had not met Ali MacGraw, aged thirty-three and with a two-year-old son, Joshua, from her marriage to film boss Robert Evans, production head of Paramount Studios, until they met on the set as costars of *The Getaway*. He was already footloose, and she was fed up with being married to Evans, who had thrown all his energies into making *The Godfather*. As she explained to Roderick Mann, the London newspaperman: "I loathe studio politics and all that. Bob worked so hard we didn't see too much of each other. That sort of life has nothing to do with where my head is. I am much more interested in living and being a mother. I am not wildly ambitious or very social. I am really quite private. Right now, with Steve, I've virtually gone into hiding."

Ali was first noticed in *Goodbye Columbus* (a film based on Philip Roth's novelette) but had not really made much of an impression until she turned up as the girl in that most extraordinary of films, *Love Story*, a piece of rubbish that predictably became a huge box-office success.

Once she and Steve went into the clinches, everyone on the set saw true love blossoming right under their eyes. "They certainly struck sparks off each other," said a member of the unit. Before filming had finished, she had filed divorce papers and was openly dating Steve. Soon Steve, symbol of rebellion and menacing masculinity, was docilely shopping with her, and they spent most of their time together on the beaches of Malibu, in California, where Ali had rented a beach house. Ali explained to all and sundry that Bob Evans had brought it upon himself. He had made her a "movie widow." As for Steve, he announced that all he wanted to do, after the divorce arrangements had gone through, was to take off to a mountain cabin somewhere for about a year and "do nothing but think." He rapidly changed his mind, however, and committed himself to *Papillon*, based on a best-selling novel about an escape from Devil's Island, insisting he could not afford not to work. He explained about owing the government some taxes, and of course, there was Neile's huge settlement to be taken into consideration.

In fairness to Steve, he was wifeless, childless, and seeking to start a new life. No wonder he was attracted by the slim, intelligent, well-educated ex-model with whom at least in the beginning, he appeared to have so little in common. Many who knew Ali and Steve thought them entirely wrong for each other; her background was slick and sophisticated, and she was not averse, whatever her protestations, to the social round. Yet when one looks back into Steve's past, one remembers that he had mixed with people like Ali before and had found the experience one of the most enjoyable in his life (when he ran around with the rich kids at Myrtle Beach). One thing seemed certain: she was likely to change his pattern of living, probably dramatically.

The girl herself had a lot going for her. If hardly an outstanding beauty, she had personality and verve and, seemingly, a fund of common sense. She was, surprisingly for the Hollywood *milieu*, engagingly modest. When *The Getaway* was released, most of the critics attacked her performance, claiming that she was wooden. "As a talent, she is embarrassing," announced *Time* magazine. Ali herself, however, explained: "I don't in all sincerity think I'm the most marvellous actress on earth. Right now, to be honest, I don't give a damn about my career. I have no idea when I'll do another picture. All I want is to be with Joshua (her son) and Steve. So far as I'm concerned, acting is just an interesting way of making a living. If I had an enormous talent, I'm sure I'd have different priorities." Although her private life was "complicated," things were working out. "They probably wouldn't if I were involved with anybody less pulled together than Steve. But he's marvellous. To get turned on, I don't need a drink or a great part. All I need is to dance with that man."

She was certainly thrilled by all that was happening around her, by Sam Peckinpah, by the exciting scene they were filming—and above all else, by Steve. "I just adore him. He's impossible—absolutely flat out 100 percent impossible—and terrific." They clashed consistently, yet understood each other. "I'm a fairly opinionated lady, which is not generally the kind Steve likes or is too thrilled to be around. He has very strong male attitudes, and I don't buy them all. If Steve and I ever lock horns, it's because I've said 'no' when he wants me automatically to say 'yes'. I find it funny. He doesn't like the women in his family to have balls. Neither do I, really. I approve of all his attitudes until they affect me personally. I'm too old and set in my ways and that's where we clash the most."

She admitted she had lost fifteen pounds making the movie and had changed a lot. "It's nerve-wracking, fraught with strong personalities." After *Love Story* she had decided to be a housewife, not a film star— had really *tried*. "But I got moody. I had talked myself into thinking how great it was not to be constructive, but I didn't realize how much I missed working. I like cutting flowers, making sure the table is set right, and all that stuff. But I can take just so much of it." She had laughed a lot when, during one of the film's big scenes, she and Steve were tipped out of the municipal garbage truck onto the local rubbish dump, and she found a fan magazine among the trash. And there on its cover was a picture of her, holding a big splash of daffodils in her hands and almost nine months pregnant—and the headline screamed, "What's wrong with Ali MacGraw?" She thought it "hysterical" to come across that in such a situation.

If Ali had "changed a lot," so it seemed had Steve. Popping two bits of gum into his mouth he explained: "I'm only into bikes now. No more cars. No racing. Just dirt-tracking in the desert, where I and my kids go every Sunday when I'm not working [part of the divorce arrangements]. I like the desert. I hate mob scenes. After my kids, my privacy is the most important thing in my life." This made shopping with Ali a hell of a problem for him, for they were unable to go anywhere without crowds peering and watching.

How would Ali stand up as a stepmother? Crew members and other friends noted that there was a lot of affection between Steve's children and Ali. When Ali made an appearance, both kids at once flew into her arms—she was obviously popular with them. What had Steve to say about his prospective bride? Predictably, it had to do with machinery. "This tall, skinny, long-legged Eastern intellectual didn't even know how to drive a car when she got here." Ali, it turned out, had to be sent to a driving school to learn to drive because her role in the film demanded that she drive the getaway car. "Let me tell you, she scared me. We'd be going down the road, cameras loaded and all, and man—she had to drive through people walking. Well, she'd be skiddin' on the left, then on the right . . . once she even got airborne. In fact, more'n once. She's driven one hopped-up car up a tree, and suddenly she's drivin' a car in a Peckinpah movie. That's pretty scary." As part of the fun, Steve insisted that he was a big coward when somebody else was driving. "They taped our dialogue in the car. It's funny, man, but unprintable."

Ali's view of Steve? "Mostly he's a big surprise. I guess Steve is one of the two or three movie actors in the world I think are always fabulous to watch. He's the greatest at what he does. I don't know what I expected. People told me he was difficult, and movie-starrish, which is something I can't stand. People who are prima-donnas are, excuse me, a big pain in the ass. I don't know why, but I thought it would be different.'' Different? Yes, because this was the first time she had ''ever worked with a legend.'' Steve, sitting nearby and busy eating, almost choked at this. ''You wanna know what a legend is, look at Duke Wayne,'' he mumbled.

He slouches on the seat of his Cortez caravan, which in passing, he points out has paid for itself six times over—part of his studied frugality. In front of him, hard-boiled eggs, chewing gum, butterscotch candies, and an unopened can of beer the tab of which he expertly pulls off in a street-smart way. He talks a little about having been angry once—having spent one-third of his life angry and never having known quite why. He says he thinks coming from the streets may have made him feel subservient and therefore angry enough to come on hostile. When he won success, he was able to take things a little easier and was no longer the big bastard so many people once thought he was. He didn't get ''moonsick'' over acting. ''Sometimes I get that buzz going, and I know I'm doing good work by my standards. Sometimes I fail. But I take life more seriously than I do my work. I want to learn from people and them from me. I don't want to dismiss anybody. I don't want to get to the point where I think because I am where I am, there is nothing more to learn. I don't really enjoy going to the movies but I do go—it's like doing my homework. I feel a responsibility not only to those who plunk down their two bucks to see me but also to the fellows who back me. If I mess up bad, no one's going to come and see my movies anymore. So, until I quit for good, I'm going to do the best I can.''

Later, he is sitting on the tailgate of a huge trailer truck, legs dangling, wearing a straw cowboy hat. Nearby, Ali knits while her son Joshua and Steve's children, Terri and Chad, play. Steve mentions idly, gazing at his rough hands: ''All my life I've wanted a manicure. I've always had calloused hands. Terrible, aren't they?'' He was glad that he had gotten Chad into motorcycles and that his son was ''very enthusiastic.'' Terri, still wearing braces on her teeth, smiles at Ali who in turn flashes back a wide, chic, toothy smile. Ali announces: ''I love the kids. They're great. They're real people and super intelligent. Steve is just great with them. So straight. But he's like that, really, with everyone close to him. He deals on a very straight level. He says exactly what he means to whoever he feels like talking to and ignores people he doesn't like. I think that attitude is often misinterpreted as rudeness or callousness, but at some point in our lives, that's where we find it's really at. One must learn to deal only with the people who mean something to you, and not go on bullshitting the rest of them by being such a charmer and all. . . ." She couldn't really say whether "his divorce [from Neile] is the best or worst thing that has happened to him. I think he's just beginning to find himself."

Later that evening, Steve was seen walking alone. The brash aggressiveness, the hostile masculinity had slipped away, and he seemed more like the man he probably really is—more gentle, introverted, and tender than anybody supposes him to be. Even the hip swagger had vanished. Even the chewing gum had been parked away.

The Getaway, Steve's penultimate film to date, is in the *Bullitt* genre—full of the action-thriller ingredients that are the staple of Hollywood film successes these days. The lengthy semi-documentaries on auto racing and rodeos that had proved so tedious to audiences were probably a thing of the past. Solar, putting out *Le Mans* just at a moment when the film industry was experiencing yet another of its numerous crises, had given the company its "lumps." Out the window, at any rate, had gone the swell executive suite, the bevy of secretaries— and out, too, Steve's idea of a personal empire. What was badly needed now was a straightforward thriller that would pack 'em in—just like *Bullitt*. Not that there could ever be another *Bullitt*.

In *The Getaway* Steve plays the part of a criminal called Doc McCoy who is released from prison through the machinations of a corrupt businessman, Jack Benyon (Ben Johnson). McCoy is expected to take charge of a bank robbery that Benyon has set up in a small Texas town. What Doc doesn't know is that his wife Carol (Ali MacGraw) has engineered his release by giving herself to Benyon, who wanted him out anyway. He is also unaware that once the robbery is committed, she and Benyon will double-cross him. Or so Benyon thinks. Doc is assigned two of Benyon's men to help him in the robbery, although he insists he doesn't want them. During the robbery, one of these men panics and shoots a guard while the McCoys make their getaway. The other assistant then guns down his friend and takes off after the McCoys to steal the money for himself. When he catches up with Doc, the latter manages to shoot and, as he thinks, kill the man, Rudy Butler—but the latter is saved by a bulletproof vest and lives to create trouble later. Doc turns up at the rendezvous with Benyon and then learns about the big double-cross. The impasse is resolved when Carol walks into Benyon's room and, instead of shooting her husband, guns down Benyon. Doc and his wife, believing they are on their own now, decide to make for Mexico via El Paso to enjoy the loot. What they do not know is that Benyon's men and the still-alive Butler are on their track. At one stage, a small-time thief switches suitcases and gets away with the money. There is a good comedy scene when the petty crook opens the case and finds himself rich beyond his dreams— a dream that ends abruptly when Doc slips into the railway seat beside him. The thief later tells the police that Doc has robbed him of his case, and Doc's picture is circulated—so that he has Butler, Benyon's men, and the police all on this trail. At the climax, Doc and his wife, who have bickered constantly since Doc learned of her unfaithfulness, finally reach a small hotel on the border where they imagine they are safe. Their enemies have traced them, however; and in the ensuing gun battle, Doc blasts his way out, killing Butler and most of Benyon's men. Then Doc and his wife manage to get a lift from an old cowboy in a rackety pickup truck and promise him a small fortune if he will take them into Mexico. This he does and the pair go off, still nattering at each other because of Carol's infidelity, but off to live happily ever after—or at least to enjoy their ill-gotten gains beyond the law's reach.

The film was savagely attacked by most critics, not merely because it had the usual quota of violence that marks Peckinpah movies, but because once again, the crooks are seen to get away with it. The film's moral appears to be that as everybody seems to be corrupt, it is OK to be corrupt also, even to the extent of violent criminality. The only thing you must do is make certain you win. There is no other justification for Doc's behavior than that he has suffered imprisonment, and has thus "paid his dues," and is entitled to the rewards freedom and money can give.

Although it is hardly the first time that a film has shown the crooks getting away with it, it seems a dubious message to put across in this day of increasing violence, greed, and obsession with money. There are some marvelous individual scenes, of course—the bank shootout, the scene where the couple hide in the garbage truck and are dumped on the rubbish heap, and finally, the gun-slinging showdown in El Paso. It is all good, old-fashioned crime stuff, the kind of film familiar to audiences since talkies began. And it can be argued, of course, that it is only a movie, after all—which, of course, is to duck the issue. For both TV and the movies, by their immediacy and increasing sense of realism, are educating the growing numbers of psychopaths within our great industrialized societies into seeing how easy it is to become rich through violence. In many ways, one feels that Steve ought to stop and think before allowing the baddies to win ever again.

On Friday, July 13, 1973, Justice of the Peace Arthur Garfield was playing golf in Cheyenne, Wyoming, when he received an emergency summons to the effect that his secretary was on the telephone and that his services were urgently required to perform a marriage ceremony for Steve McQueen. Mr. Garfield thought it a joke and continued playing. He had scarcely struck the ball more than a couple of times, however, when the summons was repeated. This time he decided to investigate. Steve, fresh back from Spain and Jamaica, where he had been filming *Papillon*, was at the other end of the telephone. Would Mr. Garfield marry him and Ali? Steve added that he had been in Cheyenne several times, particularly back in his hobo days, and he thought it was a wonderful town—so wonderful, indeed, that he had chosen Cheyenne in which to be married. That's how much he thought of the town and how much he hoped the town thought of him, and would Mr. Garfield do it?

Mr. Garfield, having, as he told reporters, "recognized" Steve's voice, decided it was no hoax and said he would be "delighted."

That morning, then, with Terri, Chad—and Joshua—as witnesses, Steve McQueen and Ali MacGraw, with a ten year difference in age between them, became man and wife.

With anything but a Steve McQueen scenario, that should be an automatic signal for a happy ending. And so it may well be. Except that he has not yet given up playing offbeat roles and still remains one of the moodiest and most unpredictable of men so that one is left wondering, exactly what happens next?

Filmography

SOMEBODY UP THERE LIKES ME (1956)

MGM: screenplay by Ernest Lehman based on the autobiography of Rocky Graziano written with Rowland Barber; directed by Robert Wise. (110 mins.)

Rocky	Paul Newman
Norma	Pier Angeli

Steve McQueen appeared as a nineteen-dollar-a-day extra

NEVER LOVE A STRANGER (1957)

Harold Robbins-Allied Artists: screenplay by Harold Robbins and Richard Day from a novel by Harold Robbins; directed by Robert Stevens. (91 mins.)

Frankie Kane	John Drew Barrymore
Julie	Lita Milan
Fennelli	Robert Bray
Martin Cabell	Steven McQueen
Moishe Moscowitz	Salem Ludwig
Flix	R.G. Armstrong

Brother Bernard	Douglas Fletcher Rodgers
Bert	Felice Orlandi
Mrs. Cazzolina	Augusta Merighi
"Fats" Crown	Abe Simon
Frances Kane	Dolores Vitina
Keough	Walter Burke

GREAT ST. LOUIS BANK ROBBERY (1958)

Charles Guggenheim & Associates, Inc.: screenplay by Richard Heffron; directed by Charles Guggenheim and John Stix. (86 mins.)

George Fowler	Steve McQueen
Gino	George Clarke
John Egan	Grahan Denton
Ann	Molly McCarthy
Willie	John Dukas

THE BLOB (1958)

Tonylyn: screenplay by Theodore Simonson and Kate Phillips from an original idea by Irvin H. Millgate; directed by Irvin S. Yeaworth. (83 mins.)

Steve	Steven McQueen
Jane	Aneta Corseaut
Police Lieutenant	Earl Rowe
Old Man	Olin Howlin

NEVER SO FEW (1959)

Canterbury: screenplay by Millard Kaufman from the novel by Tom Chamales; directed by John Sturges. (124 mins.)

Captain Reynolds	Frank Sinatra
Caria Vesari	Gina Lollobrigida
Captain Travis	Peter Lawford
Bill Ringo	Steve McQueen
Captain de Mortimer	Richard Johnson
Nikko Regas	Paul Henreid
General Sloan	Brian Donlevy
Sergeant Jim Norby	Dean Jones
Sergeant John Danforth	Charles Bronson

216

Nautaung	Philip Ahn
Colonel Parkson	Robert Bray
Margaret Fitch	Kipp Hamilton
Colonel Reed	John Hoyt
Captain Alofson	Whit Bissell
Mike Island	Richard Lupino
Billingsly	Aki Aleong

THE MAGNIFICENT SEVEN (1960)

Mirisch-Alpha: screenplay by William Roberts based on Akira Kurosawa's film *The Seven Samurai*; directed by John Sturges. (128 mins.)

Chris	Yul Brynner
Chico	Horst Bucholz
Vin	Steve McQueen
Calvera	Eli Wallach
Britt	James Coburn
O'Reilly	Charles Bronson
Lee	Robert Vaughn
Harry Luck	Brad Dexter
Old Man	Vladimir Sokoloff
Petra	Rosenda Monteros
Hilario	Jorge Martinez de Hoyes
Chamlee	Whit Bissell
Henry	Val Avery
Robert	Bing Russell
Sotero	Rico Alaniz
Wallace	Robert Wilke

THE HONEYMOON MACHINE (1961)

Avon: screenplay by George Wells based on the play *The Golden Fleecing* by Lorenzo Semple, directed by Richard Thorpe. (87 mins.)

Lieutenant Howard	Steve McQueen
Julie Fitch	Brigid Bazlen
Jason Eldridge	James Hutton
Pam Dunstan	Paula Prentiss
Admiral Fitch	Dean Jagger
Signalman Taylor	Jack Weston

Ensign Gilliam	Jack Mullaney
Inspector	Marcel Hillaire
Russian Consul	Ben Astar
Tommy Dane	William Lanteau
Captain Angle	Ken Lynch
Captain Adam	Simon Scott

HELL IS FOR HEROES (1961)

Paramount: screenplay by Robert Pirosh and Richard Carr from an original story by Pirosh; directed by Don Siegel. (90 mins.)

Reese	Steve McQueen
Corby	Bobby Darin
Sergeant Pike	Fess Parker
Homer	Nick Adams
Driscoll	Bob Newhart
Sergeant Larkin	Harry Guardino
Henshaw	James Coburn
Kolinski	Mike Kellin
Captain Loomis	Joseph Hoover
Cumberly	Bill Mullikin
Sergeant Frazer	L.Q. Jones
Monique	Michele Montau

THE WAR LOVER (1962)

Arthur Hornblow: screenplay by Howard Koch based on the novel by John Hersey; directed by Philip Leacock. (105 mins.)

Buzz Rickson	Steve McQueen
Ed Bolland	Robert Wagner
Daphne	Shirley Anne Field
Lynch	Gary Cockrell
Junior Sailen	Michael Crawford
Brindt	Bill Edwards
Lamb	Chuck Julian
Handown	Robert Easton
Prien	Al Waxman
Farr	Tom Busby
Bragliani	George Sperdakos
Haverstraw	Bob Kanter

218

Emmet	Jerry Stovin
Vogt	Edward Bishop
Murika	Richard Leech
Randall	Bernard Braden
Woodman	Sean Kelly
Sully	Neil McCallum
Braddock	Charles de Temple

THE GREAT ESCAPE (1962)

Mirisch-Alpha: screenplay by James Clavell and W. R. Burnett based on the book by Paul Brickhill; directed by John Sturges. (173 mins.)

Hilts	Steve McQueen
Hendley	James Garner
Bartlett	Richard Attenborough
Ramsey	James Donald
Danny Velinski	Charles Bronson
Blythe	Donald Pleasance
Sedgwick	James Coburn
Willie	John Leyton
MacDonald	Gordon Jackson
Ashley-Pitt	David McCallum
Cavendish	Nigel Stock
Sorren	William Russell
Ives	Angus Lennie
Nimmo	Tom Adams
Griffith	Robert Desmond
Haynes	Lawrence Montaigne
Goff	Jud Taylor
Von Luger	Hannes Messemer
Werner	Robert Graf
Strachwitz	Harry Riebauer
Posen	Robert Freytag
Kramer	Heinz Weiss
Frick	Til Kiwe
Kuhn	Hans Reisser
Dietrich	George Mikell
Preissen	Ulrich Beiger
Steinbach	Karl Otto Alberty

LOVE WITH THE PROPER STRANGER (1963)

Paramount/ Boardwalk/ Pakula-Mulligan: screenplay by Arnold Schulman;
directed by Robert Mulligan. (102 mins.)

Angie Rossini	Natalie Wood
Rocky	Steve McQueen
Barbie	Edie Adams
Dominick	Herschel Bernardi
Columbo	Tom Bosley
Julio	Harvey Lembeck
Guido	Nick Alexander
Mama Rossini	Penny Santon
Elio Papasano	Mario Badolati
Mrs. Papasano	Augusta Ciolli
Anna	Virginia Vincent
Beetie	Anne Hegira
Mrs. Columbo	Nina Varela
Gina	Marilyn Chris
Priest	Wolfe Barzell
The Woman	Elena Karam
Coloured Boy	Keith Worthey

SOLDIER IN THE RAIN (1963)

Allied Artists/ Cedar/ Solar: screenplay by Maurice Richlin and Blake
Edwards based on the novel by William Goldman; directed by Ralph Nelson.
(87 mins.)

Master-Sergeant Maxwell Slaughter	Jackie Gleason
Supply-Sergeant Eustis Clay	Steve McQueen
Bobby Jo Pepperdine	Tuesday Weld
Private Jerry Meltzer	Tony Bill
Lieutenant Magee	Tom Poston
MP Sergeant Priest	Ed Nelson
MP Sergeant Lenahan	Lew Gallo
Chief of Police	Paul Hartman
Frances McCoy	Chris Noel
Sergeant Tozzi	Lewis Charles
Sergeant William Booth	Rockne Tarkington
Battalion Major	John Hubbard
Old Man	Sam Flint
Captain Blekeley	Adam West

BABY, THE RAIN MUST FALL (1964)

Pakula-Mulligan: screenplay by Horton Foote based on his own play, *The Travelling Lady*; directed by Robert Mulligan. (93 mins.)

Georgette Thomas	Lee Remick
Henry Thomas	Steve McQueen
Slim	Don Murray
Judge Ewing	Paul Fix
Mrs. Ewing	Josephine Hutchinson
Miss Clara	Ruth White
Mr. Tillman	Charles Watts
Mrs. Tillman	Carol Veazie
Catherine	Estelle Hemsley
Margaret Rose	Kimberley Block
Mrs. T. V. Smith	Zamah Cunningham
Miss Kate	Georgia Simmons
Counterman	George Dunn

THE CINCINNATI KID (1965)

Filmways: screenplay by Ring Lardner, Jr., and Terry Southern, based on the novel by Richard Jessup; directed by Norman Jewison. (102 mins.)

The Cincinnati Kid	Steve McQueen
Lancey Howard	Edward G. Robinson
Shooter	Karl Malden
Christian	Tuesday Weld
Melba	Ann-Margret
Lady Fingers	Joan Blondell
Slade	Rip Torn
Pig	Jack Weston
Yeller	Cab Calloway
Hoban	Jeff Corey

THE SAND PEBBLES (1966)

Argyle/Solar: screenplay by Robert Anderson based on the novel by Richard McKenna; directed by Robert Wise. (193 mins.)

Holman	Steve McQueen
Frenchy	Richard Attenborough
Collins	Richard Crenna
Shirley Eckert	Candice Bergen

Maily	Marayat Andriane
Po-Han	Mako
Jameson	Larry Gates
Ensign Bordelles	Charles Robinson
Stawski	Simon Oakland
Harris	Ford Rainey
Bronson	Joe Turkel
Crosley	Gavin MacLeod
Shanahan	Joseph di Reda
Major Lin	Richard Loo
Franks	Barney Philips
Restorff	Gus Trikonis
Perna	Shepherd Sanders
Farren	James Jeter
Jennings	Tom Middleton
Cho-Jen	Paul Chinpae
Chien	Tommy Lee
Haythorn	Stephen Jahn
Wilsey	Jay Allan Hopkins
Lamb	Steve Ferry
Wellbeck	Ted Fish
Coleman	Loren Janes
Waldron	Glenn Wilder
Mama Chunk	Beulah Quo
Victor Shu	James Hong

NEVADA SMITH (1966)

Solar: screenplay by John Michael Hayes based on a character in *The Carpetbaggers* by Harold Robbins; directed by Henry Hathaway. (131 mins.)

Nevada Smith	Steve McQueen
Tom Fitch	Karl Malden
Jonas Cord	Brian Keith
Pilar	Suzanne Pleshette
Bill Bowdre	Arthur Kennedy
Neesa	Janet Margolin
Warden	Howard Da Silva
Father Zaccardi	Raf Vallone
Big Foot	Pat Hingle

Jesse Coe	Martin Landau
Sheriff Bonnell	Paul Fix
Sam Sand	Gene Evans
Elvira McCanles	Josephine Hutchinson
Ben McCanles	John Doucette
Buck Mason	Val Avery
Sheriff	Sheldon Allman
Jack Rudabaugh	Lyle Bettger
Quince	Bert Freed
Romero	David McClean
Buckshot	Steve Mitchell
Pilot	Merritt Bohn
Clerk	Sandy Kenyon
Cipriano	Ric Roman
Hogg	John Lawrence
Storekeeper	Stanley Adams
Paymaster	George Mitchell
Doctor	John Litel
Bartender	Ted de Corsia

THE THOMAS CROWN AFFAIR (1968)

Mirisch/ Simkoe/ Solar: screenplay by Alan R. Trustman; directed by Norman Jewison. (102 mins.)

Thomas Crown	Steve McQueen
Vicky Anderson	Faye Dunaway
Eddy Malone	Paul Burke
Erwin Weaver	Jack Weston
Carl	Yaphet Kotto
Benjy	Todd Martin
Dave	Sam Melville
Abe	Addison Powell
Arnie	Sidney Armus
Curley	Jon Shank
Don	Allen Emerson
Ernie	Harry Cooper
Bert	John Silver
Sandy	Biff McGuire
Miss Sullivan	Carol Corbett

223

John	John Orchard
Jamie MacDonald	Gordon Pinsent
Danny	Patrick Horgan
Honey Weaver	Peggy Shirley
Jimmy Weaver	Leonard Caron
Gwen	Astrid Heeren
Bank Guard	Richard Bull
Cashier	Judy Pace
Guards	Paul Rhone and
	Victor Creatore
Elevator Operators	Paul Verdier,
	James Rawley, and
	Charles Lampkin

BULLITT (1968)

Solar: screenplay by Alan R. Trustman and Harry Kleiner based on the novel *Mute Witness* by Robert L. Pike; directed by Peter Yates. (114 mins.)

Frank Bullitt	Steve McQueen
Walter Chambers	Robert Vaughn
Cathy	Jacqueline Bisset
Delgetti	Don Gordon
Weissberg	Robert Duvall
Captain Bennet	Simon Oakland
Captain Baker	Norman Fell
Stanton	Carl Reindel
Remick	Felice Orlandi
Johnny Ross	Pat Renella
Doctor Willard	George S. Brown
Eddy	Justin Tarr
Pete Ross	Victor Tayback
The Hired Killer	Paul Genge
Wescott	Ed Peck
First Aide	Robert Lipton

THE REIVERS (1969)

Cinema Center: screenplay by Irving Ravetch & Harriet Frank, Jr., based on the novel by William Faulkner, directed by Mark Rydell. (132 mins.)

Boon Hogganbeck	Steve McQueen

224

Corrie	Sharon Farrell
Boss McCaslin	Michael Constantine
Mr. Binford	Michael Constantine
Ned McCaslin	Rupert Crosse
Lucius McCaslin	Mitch Vogel
Maury McCaslin	Lonny Chapman
Uncle Possum	Juano Hernandez
Butch Lovemaiden	Clifton James
Miss Reba	Ruth White
Doctor Peabody	Dub Taylor
Alison McCaslin	Allyn Ann McLerie
Hannah	Diane Shalet
Phoebe	Diane Ladd
Sally	Ellen Geer
May Ellen	Pat Randall
Edmonds	Charles Tyner
Aunt Callie	Vinette Carroll
Minnie	Gloria Calomee
Sarah	Sara Taft
Otis	Lindy Taft
Uncle Ike	Raymond Guth
Cousin Zack	Shug Fisher
Walter Clapp	Logan Ramsey
Joe Poleymus	Jon Shank
Mrs. Possum	Ella Mae Brown
Mary Possum	Florence St. Peter
Van Tosch	John McLiam
Doyle	Lou Frizzell
Ed	Roy Barcroft

LE MANS (1971)

Solar/Cinema Center: screenplay by Harry Kleiner; directed by Lee H. Katzin. (108 mins.)

Michael Delaney	Steve McQueen
Erich Stahler	Siegfried Rauch
Lisa Belgetti	Elga Andersen
David Townsend	Ronald Leigh-Hunt
Johann Ritter	Fred Haltiner
Claude Aurac	Luc Merenda

Larry Wilson

Mrs. Anna Ritter

Lugo Abratte

Paul Jacques Dion

Vito Scalise

Loretto Fuselli

Paolo Scadenza

Bruno Frohm

Chris Barnet

Jonathan Burton

Peter Wiesen

Tony Elkins

Josef Hauser

Max Kummel

Christopher Waite

Louise Edlind

Angelo Infanti

Jean Claude Bercq

Michele Scalera

Gina Cassani

Carlo Cecci

Richard Rudiger

Hal Hamilton

Jonathan Williams

Peter Parten

Conrad Pringle

Erich Glavitza

Peter Huber

Featuring forty Grand Prix drivers including Derek Bell, Masten Gregory, Mike Hailwood, Jacky Ickx, Michael Parkes, and David Piper

JUNIOR BONNER (1972)

Joe Wizan-Booth Gardner/ Solar: screenplay by Jeb Rosebrook; directed by Sam Peckinpah. (103 mins.)

Junior Bonner

Ace Bonner

Elvira Bonner

Curly Bonner

Charmagne

Ruth Bonner

Buck Roan

Red Terwiliger

Nurse Arlis

Homer Rutledge

Barman

Burt

Tim Bonner

Nick Bonner

Flashie

Steve McQueen

Robert Preston

Ida Lupino

Joe Don Baker

Barbara Leigh

Mary Murphy

Ben Johnson

Bill McKinney

Sandra Deel

Donald Barry

Dub Taylor

Charles Gray

Matthew Peckinpah

Sundown Spencer

Rita Garrison

THE GETAWAY (1972)

Solar/First Artists: screenplay by Walter Hill based on the novel by Jim Thompson; directed by Sam Peckinpah. (122 mins.)

Doc McCoy	Steve McQueen
Carol McCoy	Ali MacGraw
Jack Benyon	Ben Johnson
Fran Clinton	Sally Struthers
Rudy Butler	Al Lettieri
Cowboy	Slim Pickens
Thief	Richard Bright
Harold Clinton	Jack Dodson
Laughlin	Dub Taylor
Frank Jackson	Bo Hopkins
Cully	Roy Jenson
Accountant	John Bryson
Swain	Thomas Runyon
Soldier	Whitney Jones
Train Boys	Raymond King, Ivan Thomas, and C. W. Shite
Boy's Mother	Brenda King
Parole Chairman	Dee Kutach
Commissioner	Brick Lowry
McCoy's Lawyer	Martin Colley
Field Captain	O. S. Savage
Store Owner	A. L. Camp
TV Shop Owner	Bob Veal
Salesman	Bruce Bissonette
Carhop	Maggie Gonzalez
Cannon	Jim Kannon
Max	Dud Dudley
Stacy	Stacy Newton
Cowboy's Helper	Tom Bush

PAPILLON (1973)

Allied Artists: screenplay by Dalton Trumbo and Lorenzo Semple Jr. based on the book by Henri Charriere; directed by Franklin J. Schaffner. (150 mins.)

Papillon	Steve McQueen
Dega	Dustin Hoffman
Indian Chief	Victor Jory
Julot	Don Gordon
Leper colony chief	Anthony Zerbe
Maturette	Robert Deman
Clusiot	Woodrow Parfrey
Lariot	Bill Mumy
Dr. Chatal	George Coulouris
Zoraima	Ratna Assan
Warden Barrot	William Smithers
Antonio	Gregory Sierra
Mother Superior	Barbara Morrison
Nun	Ellen Moss
Butterfly trader	Don Hanmer
Commandant	Dalton Trumbo

Index